P9-BJB-556

THE BASIC/NOT BORING MIDDLE GRADES SCIENCE BOOK

Grades 6–8+

Inventive Exercises to Sharpen
Skills and Raise Achievement

Series Concept & Development
by Imogene Forte & Marjorie Frank

Incentive Publications, Inc.
Nashville, Tennessee

Illustrated by Kathleen Bullock
Cover art by Mary Patricia Deprez, dba Tye Dye Mary®
Cover design by Marta Drayton and Joe Shibley
Edited by Jean K. Signor

ISBN 0-86530-565-X

Copyright ©2002 by Incentive Publications, Inc., Nashville, TN. All rights reserved. No part of this publication may be reproduced, stored in a retrieval system, or transmitted in any form or by any means (electronic, mechanical, photocopying, recording, or otherwise) without written permission from Incentive Publications, Inc., with the exception below.

Pages labeled with the statement ©2002 by Incentive Publications, Inc., Nashville, TN are intended for reproduction. Permission is hereby granted to the purchaser of one copy of **THE BASIC/NOT BORING MIDDLE GRADES SCIENCE BOOK** to reproduce these pages in sufficient quantities for meeting the purchaser's own classroom needs only.

1   2   3   4   5   6   7   8   9   10   07   06   05   04

PRINTED IN THE UNITED STATES OF AMERICA
www.incentivepublications.com

TABLE OF CONTENTS

General Science Investigations

Life Science Investigations

Earth & Space Science Investigations

Physical Science Investigations

INTRODUCTION

Do basic skills have to be boring? Absolutely not! Mastery of basic skills provides the foundation for exciting learning opportunities for students. Content relevant to their everyday life is fascinating stuff! Kids love learning about the wonders of the physical world (from the tiniest sub-atomic particles to the expanse of the cosmos). They're fascinated with the mysteries of the Earth's interior and exterior, the wonderful variety of living things, the complexities of the human body, and the magic of chemistry and physics. It is on such acquired knowledge bases that they build basic skills that enable them to ponder, process, grow, and achieve school success.

Acquiring, polishing, and using basic skills and content is a cause for celebration—not an exercise in drudgery. *The BASIC/Not Boring Middle Grades Science Book* invites you to celebrate with students as you help them sharpen their abilities in the essentials of science.

As you examine *The BASIC/Not Boring Middle Grades Science Book*, you will see that it is filled with attractive age-appropriate student exercises. These pages are no ordinary worksheets! *The BASIC/Not Boring Middle Grades Science Book* contains hundreds of inventive and inviting ready-to-use lessons based on captivating themes that invite the student to join an adventure, solve a dilemma, tackle a problem, or unravel a mystery. Additionally, each fittingly illustrated exercise provides diverse tools for reinforcement and extension of basic and higher-order thinking skills.

The BASIC/Not Boring Middle Grades Science Book contains the following components:

- **A clear, sequential list of skills for 6 different content areas**
  Checklists of skills begin each content section. These lists correlate with the exercises, identifying page numbers where specific skills can be practiced. Students can chart their progress by checking off each skill as it is mastered.

- **Over 200 pages of student exercises**
  Each exercise page:
     . . . addresses a specific basic skill or content area.
     . . . presents tasks that grab the attention and curiosity of students.
     . . . contains clear directions to the student.
     . . . asks students to use, remember, and practice a basic skill.
     . . . challenges students to think creatively and analytically.
     . . . requires students to apply the skill to real situations or content.
     . . . takes students on learning adventures in a variety of enticing settings!

- **A ready-to-use assessment tool**
  Six skills tests, one for each content area, follow each series of exercises. The tests are presented in parts corresponding to the skills lists. Designed to be used as pre- or post-tests, individual parts of these tests can be given to students at separate times, if needed.

- **Complete answer keys**
  Easy-to-find-and-use answer keys for all exercises and skills tests follow each section.

HOW TO USE THIS BOOK:

The exercises contained in *The BASIC/Not Boring Middle Grades Science Book* are to be used with adult assistance. The adult may serve as a guide to ensure the student understands the directions and questions.

The BASIC/Not Boring Middle Grades Science Book is designed to be used in many diverse ways. Its use will vary according to the needs of the students, the form of instruction, and the structure of the learning environment.

The skills checklists may be used as:
> . . . record-keeping tools to track individual skills mastery.
> . . . planning guides for the teacher's instruction.
> . . . progress reports to share with parents.
> . . . a place for students to proudly check off accomplishments.

Each exercise page may be used as:
> . . . a pre-test or check to see how well a student has mastered a skill or content area.
> . . . a tool around which the teacher may build a mini-skills based lesson.
> . . . one of many resources or exercises for teaching a lesson or unit.
> . . . a way to practice or polish a skill that has been taught.
> . . . a review of a skill taught earlier.
> . . . reinforcement of a single basic skill, skills cluster, or content base.
> . . . a preview to help the teacher identify instructional needs.
> . . . an assessment for a skill that a student has practiced.

The exercises are flexibly designed for presentation in many formats and settings. They are useful for individual instruction or independent work. They can also be used under the direction of the teacher with small groups or an entire class. Groups of exercises on related skills may make up the practice materials for a series of lessons or may be used as a unit enhancement.

The skills tests may be used as:
> . . . pre-tests to gauge instructional or placement needs.
> . . . information sources to help teachers adjust instruction.
> . . . post-tests to review student mastery of skills and content areas.

The BASIC/Not Boring Middle Grades Science Book is not intended to be a complete curriculum guide or textbook. It is a collection of inventive exercises to sharpen skills and to provide students and teachers with tools for reinforcing concepts and skills, and for identifying areas that need additional attention. This book offers a delightful assortment of tasks that give students just the practice they need—and to get that practice in a manner that will definitely be remembered as non-boring.

As your students take on the challenges of the enticing adventures in this book, they will increase their comfort level with the skills, facts, and understandings of science concepts, science processes, physical science, earth science, space science, life science, the human body and human health, and science investigations. Watching your students check off the skills they have sharpened will be cause for celebration!

SCIENCE
CONCEPTS & PROCESSES
Skills Exercises

SKILLS CHECKLIST FOR SCIENCE CONCEPTS & PROCESSES

✔	SKILL	PAGE(S)
	Show understanding of the nature of scientific research and discoveries	18, 19
	Show understanding of science as a human endeavor	18, 19
	Show understanding of the limitations of science	18, 19, 28, 29
	Distinguish among different branches of science; Identify the topics and areas associated with different branches of science	19–21
	Identify and recognize the significance of some important scientific discoveries and inventions	22, 23
	Identify some key events in the history of science	22–25
	Show recognition of the relationship between science and the personal and social realms; identify ways science impacts personal life	26, 27
	Identify some uses of science and technology	28, 29
	Show understandings of the relationship between science and technology	28, 29
	Show understanding of the benefits and consequences to society of science and technology	29
	Recognize some key scientific theories and laws	30, 31
	Show understanding of the nature and method of scientific inquiry	32, 33
	Recognize and distinguish between key concepts in science	34, 35
	Show understanding of the concept of systems	36
	Show understanding of the concepts of order and organization	37
	Show understanding of the concept of structure and function; explain how structure and function are related in specific instances	38, 39
	Show understanding of the concept of the energy-matter relationship	40
	Show understanding of the concept of cause and effect	41
	Show understanding of the concepts of change	42
	Show understanding of the concept of constancy	42
	Show understanding of the concept of equilibrium	43
	Show understanding of the concept of evolution	43
	Show understanding of the concept of cycle; identify stages in various kinds of cycles	44
	Relate the big ideas of science (the concepts) to life situations	45
	Understand and use the process of observation	46, 47
	Understand and use the process of classification	48, 49
	Understand and use the process of forming a hypothesis	50, 51
	Understand and use the processes of measurement and using numbers	52
	Understand and use the processes of interpreting data and predicting outcomes	53
	Understand and use the process of using models	54
	Understand and use the processes of communicating results	55
	Understand and use the process of designing an experiment (including identifying and controlling variables)	56, 57
	Recognize some safety procedures for science experimentation	58

SCIENCE STATEMENTS UNDER SCRUTINY

The brilliant physicist, Dr. R. R. Radon, knows plenty about science. So, his scientific statements are generally accurate. Scrutinize each group of statements. In each group, identify the statement or statements that he would make (assuming he's making true statements). Circle the correct letter or letters.

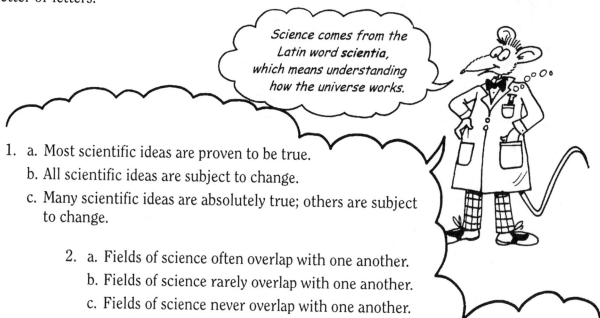

Science comes from the Latin word *scientia*, which means understanding how the universe works.

1. a. Most scientific ideas are proven to be true.
   b. All scientific ideas are subject to change.
   c. Many scientific ideas are absolutely true; others are subject to change.

2. a. Fields of science often overlap with one another.
   b. Fields of science rarely overlap with one another.
   c. Fields of science never overlap with one another.

3. a. Most scientists have the same set of skills and abilities.
   b. Scientists have a wide range of different interests, skills, and abilities.
   c. All scientists in one field of study share the same skills and abilities.

4. a. Science did not exist until after the Middle Ages.
   b. The first scientific discovery was the discovery that the Earth is round.
   c. Scientific discoveries began thousands of years ago, probably as early as human life began.

5. a. Important contributions to science have been made by men and women of many different cultures, countries, and ethnic backgrounds, over a long period of time.
   b. Most important scientific discoveries have been made by men in the Western Hemisphere.
   c. Most important scientific discoveries have been made in the last one hundred years.

6. a. When different scientists investigate the same problem, they keep working until they all agree on the results of their studies before they publish the results.
   b. Scientists researching the same problem often find and publish different results.
   c. Scientists researching the same problem usually publish similar results.

Use with page 19.

Name

7. a. Good scientific research requires the use of human qualities such as curiosity, creativity, honesty, and judgment.

   b. Good scientific research requires that scientists disregard personal beliefs and ethics.

   c. Good scientific research requires that scientists start with a brand new idea or question that has not been considered before.

8. a. Eventually, science will probably be able to solve all human problems.

   b. Eventually, science will probably be able to solve most human problems.

   c. There will continue to be human problems that science cannot solve.

9. a. Scientific explanations place heavy importance on evidence.

   b. Most scientific explanations or conclusions also raise more questions.

   c. Math is important to all aspects of scientific discovery.

10. a. Most scientists work alone.

    b. Most scientists work in teams.

    c. All scientists work in laboratories

Professor Radon's poster shows the main branches of science. Look at the fields of scientific study shown below. For each field, identify the branch to which it belongs.
(*Write L, E & S, P, M, or Soc for each field.*)

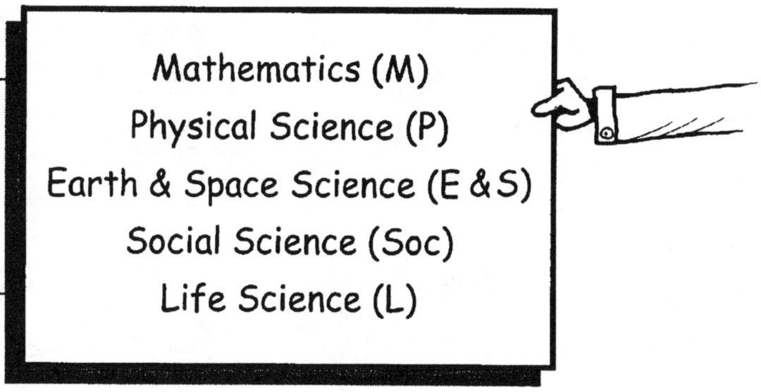

Mathematics (M)
Physical Science (P)
Earth & Space Science (E & S)
Social Science (Soc)
Life Science (L)

_____ 11. seismology

_____ 12. genetics

_____ 13. psychology

_____ 14. chemistry

_____ 15. aeronautics

_____ 16. biology

_____ 17. statistics

_____ 18. meteorology

_____ 19. zoology

_____ 20. anthropology

_____ 21. geometry

_____ 22. economics

_____ 23. astronomy

_____ 24. anatomy

Use with page 18.

Name _____

     Copyright ©2002 by Incentive Publications, Inc., Nashville, TN.

WHO STUDIES WHAT?

There are dozens of different kinds of scientists, all asking dozens of questions about the way the world works. If you follow a scientist around for a while, you would notice what kinds of things she or he studies. Here are just a few of the things scientists study. Which scientist from which field of study would study which topic? Choose the best answer for each area of study on this page and page 21.

Which scientist would study . . .

1. stars and planets?
   a. an anatomist
   b. an electrician
   c. an astronomer
   d. a physician

2. prehistoric forms of life?
   a. a paleontologist
   b. a mechanical engineer
   c. a hydrologist
   d. a political scientist

3. living organisms too small to be seen with the human eye?
   a. a microeconomist
   b. a psychologist
   c. a sociologist
   d. a microbiologist

4. birds?
   a. an entomologist
   b. a botanist
   c. an embryologist
   d. an ornithologist

5. rocks?
   a. an astronomer
   b. a petrologist
   c. a hematologist
   d. a rheumatologist

6. ways the body can be protected against disease?
   a. a metallurgist
   b. an immunologist
   c. an ophthalmologist
   d. an ecologist

Dr. R.R.Radon,
a. _____

Dr. Felicia Femur,
b. _____

Prof. Agnes Igneous,
c. _____

7. soil and crop-raising?
   a. a psychiatrist
   b. an aeronautic engineer
   c. an agronomist
   d. an anatomist

8. structure of matter?
   a. a statistician
   b. a political scientist
   c. a chemist
   d. a cytologist

9. behavior of human groups?
   a. a sociologist
   b. a civil engineer
   c. a physicist
   d. an organic chemist

10. development of language?
    a. an oncologist
    b. a morphologist
    c. a linguist
    d. a hematologist

11. tides and waves?
    a. an oceanographer
    b. a mineralogist
    c. a microeconomist
    d. a geologist

Use with page 21.

Name

12. financial systems?
    a. an economist
    b. an ecologist
    c. a taxonomist
    d. a cryogenist

Ozzie Moses,
d. _____

13. past cultures?
    a. an archaeologist
    b. an agronomist
    c. an histologist
    d. a radiologist

Lester Asteroid,
e. _____

14. human DNA?
    a. an oceanographer
    b. a geographer
    c. a geneticist
    d. an astrophysicist

15. fission and fusion of atoms?
    a. a neurologist
    b. a nuclear physicist
    c. a physiologist
    d. a cartographer

16. weather?
    a. an organic chemist
    b. a pathologist
    c. a biologist
    d. a meteorologist

17. energy and force?
    a. a dermatologist
    b. a bacteriologist
    c. a mathematician
    d. a physicist

18. insects?
    a. an entomologist
    b. an etymologist
    c. a paleontologist
    d. an histologist

19. human behavior?
    a. a physiologist
    b. a molecular biologist
    c. a psychologist
    d. a petrologist

20. pollution?
    a. a psychiatrist
    b. an ecologist
    c. an anthropologist
    d. an embryologist

21. matter at very low temperatures?
    a. an anatomist
    b. a linguist
    c. a cryogenist
    d. an orthodontist

22. human cultures?
    a. an anthropologist
    b. a biochemist
    c. a neurologist
    d. a bacteriologist

23. behavior and properties of cells?
    a. a geologist
    b. a meteorologist
    c. a taxonomist
    d. a cytologist

24. logic?
    a. a mathematician
    b. a biophysicist
    c. a climatologist
    d. a geneticist

25. plants?
    a. a zoologist
    b. a botanist
    c. an ornithologist
    d. a criminologist

26. human body systems?
    a. an ichthyologist
    b. a quantum mechanic
    c. a seismologist
    d. a physiologist

27. Look at the professors pictured on these two pages.
    Make a careful guess about what kind of scientist each
    one might be. Write your guess beside each one.

Use with page 20.

Name _____

DAZZLING DISCOVERIES & INGENIOUS INVENTIONS

Wow! Look at the ideas pouring out of the "Good Idea" Machine.

Match each description with a discovery or invention. Write the correct letter on each line.

(Use the descriptions and inventions on both pages—22 and 23.)

DING

A. anesthetics
B. antibiotics
C. antiseptics
D. atom
E. cathode ray tube
F. combustion
G. DVD
H. ECG
I. electric light bulb
J. electricity
K. electromagnetic power
L. fax machine

Thousands of inventions and discoveries fill the science books and journals. Here are a few of the most dazzling, awesome, life-changing, ingenious, or memorable.

___ 1. Dr. Alexander Fleming's 1920 discovery revolutionized medicine and treated millions of people with serious diseases.

___ 2. In 1910, a French chemist, George Claude, ran electricity through a tube of gas and produced a colored light that led to the "lighting up" of advertising signs.

___ 3. In 1777, French scientist Antoine Lavoisier made a discovery about the role of oxygen in the burning of matter.

___ 4. In 1803, English chemist John Dalton came up with the idea that matter consists of small, indivisible particles.

___ 5. An invention of the late 20th century gave TV and computer viewers ways to listen to richer sounds and watch cleaner pictures than were ever before available.

___ 6. In the mid-1400s, Johann Gutenberg invented a machine for publishing books quickly.

___ 7. Samuel Morse's 1838 invention sent long-distance messages over a wire using bursts of electricity to make sounds.

___ 8. In 1898, Marie and Pierre Curie discovered an element that made the development of atomic energy possible.

___ 9. In 1831, Michael Faraday discovered a new way to produce electricity, which made it possible to build electric generators.

___ 10. After German scientist Wilhelm Conrad Roentgen made this 1895 discovery by accident, doctors had a new look inside bodies.

___ 11. Roger Bacon's discoveries in the late 1200s led to better eyesight for centuries to follow.

___ 12. A 1543 Copernicus discovery led to greater understanding of the universe.

Use with page 23.

Name

___ 13. As early as 3000 B.C., the Egyptians used this system to make measurements they needed to build the pyramids.

___ 14. Vladimir Zworykin's work in the 1930s led to the invention that made the first televisions possible.

___ 15. A 1904 invention by German physicist Arthur Korn allowed someone to send writing and pictures across a telephone line.

___ 16. This 1901 invention by Dutch scientist Willem Einthoven allowed hospitals to check the heartbeats and look for signs of heart disease in patients.

___ 17. British surgeon Joseph Lister's discovery in the 1800s reduced the chances of infection developing in the wounds created by surgery.

___ 18. In the mid 1500s, Gerardus Mercator found a way to represent distances on the Earth's surface on pieces of paper.

___ 19. Galileo Galilei's invention allowed him to see the surface of the moon in the early 1600s.

___ 20. When Alexander Graham Bell invented the machine that allowed him to talk to someone far away in 1876, he probably never dreamed of e-mail or fax machines.

___ 21. Charles Goodyear found a way to make tires softer by putting air inside them.

M. geometry

N. gravity

O. helicopter

P. Heliocentric Theory

Q. inner tube

R. jet engine

S. genome project

T. lenses

U. logic

V. maps

W. X-rays

X. microscope

Y. neon lights

Z. printing press

AA. radium

BB. telegraph

CC. telephone

DD. telescope

___ 22. Benjamin Franklin discovered this while flying a kite in a thunderstorm in 1752.

___ 23. Robert Hooke's tube for viewing very tiny objects was invented in the 1600s.

___ 24. With this 1930 invention, Sir Frank Whittle increased the speed of air travel.

___ 25. This invention, created by Sir Joseph Swan and Thomas Edison in the 1870s, gave light to rooms without burning out quickly.

___ 26. At the beginning of the 21st century, scientists developed the first maps of human genes.

___ 27. During the 300s B.C., Aristotle developed a system of reasoning for reaching conclusions.

___ 28. Igor Sikorsky developed the first flying machine that was able to take off and land vertically.

___ 29. As the story goes, a falling apple led to this Isaac Newton discovery in 1687.

___ 30. Surgery was a terribly painful process until 1846, when William Morton, an American dentist, discovered a way to put patients to sleep to overcome the pain.

What a great list!

Use with page 22.

Name

Copyright ©2002 by Incentive Publications, Inc., Nashville, TN.

HISTORY MYSTERIES

Scientists spend a lot of time tracking down unanswered questions and mysterious events.
Do your own research to find out about some past happenings in science.

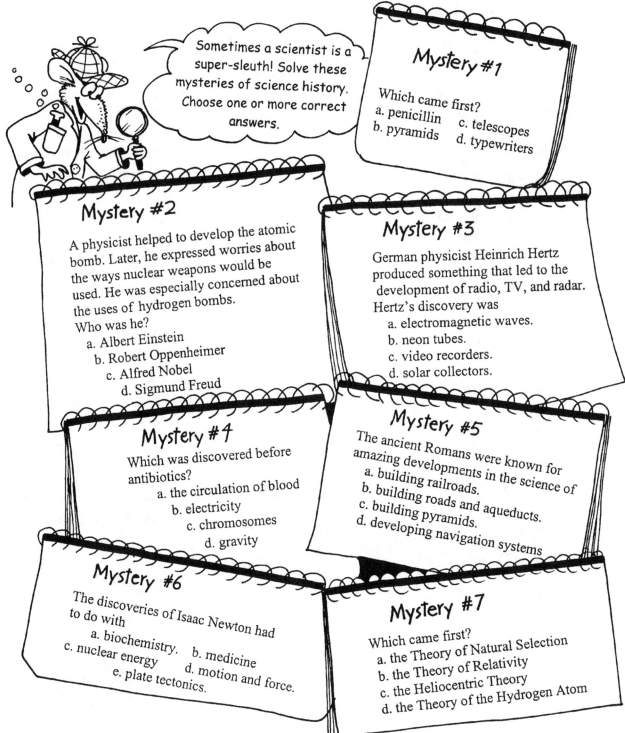

Sometimes a scientist is a super-sleuth! Solve these mysteries of science history. Choose one or more correct answers.

Mystery #1

Which came first?
a. penicillin   c. telescopes
b. pyramids   d. typewriters

Mystery #2

A physicist helped to develop the atomic bomb. Later, he expressed worries about the ways nuclear weapons would be used. He was especially concerned about the uses of hydrogen bombs. Who was he?
a. Albert Einstein
b. Robert Oppenheimer
c. Alfred Nobel
d. Sigmund Freud

Mystery #3

German physicist Heinrich Hertz produced something that led to the development of radio, TV, and radar. Hertz's discovery was
a. electromagnetic waves.
b. neon tubes.
c. video recorders.
d. solar collectors.

Mystery #4

Which was discovered before antibiotics?
a. the circulation of blood
b. electricity
c. chromosomes
d. gravity

Mystery #5

The ancient Romans were known for amazing developments in the science of
a. building railroads.
b. building roads and aqueducts.
c. building pyramids.
d. developing navigation systems

Mystery #6

The discoveries of Isaac Newton had to do with
a. biochemistry.   b. medicine
c. nuclear energy   d. motion and force.
e. plate tectonics.

Mystery #7

Which came first?
a. the Theory of Natural Selection
b. the Theory of Relativity
c. the Heliocentric Theory
d. the Theory of the Hydrogen Atom

Use with page 25.

Name

     Copyright ©2002 by Incentive Publications, Inc., Nashville, TN.

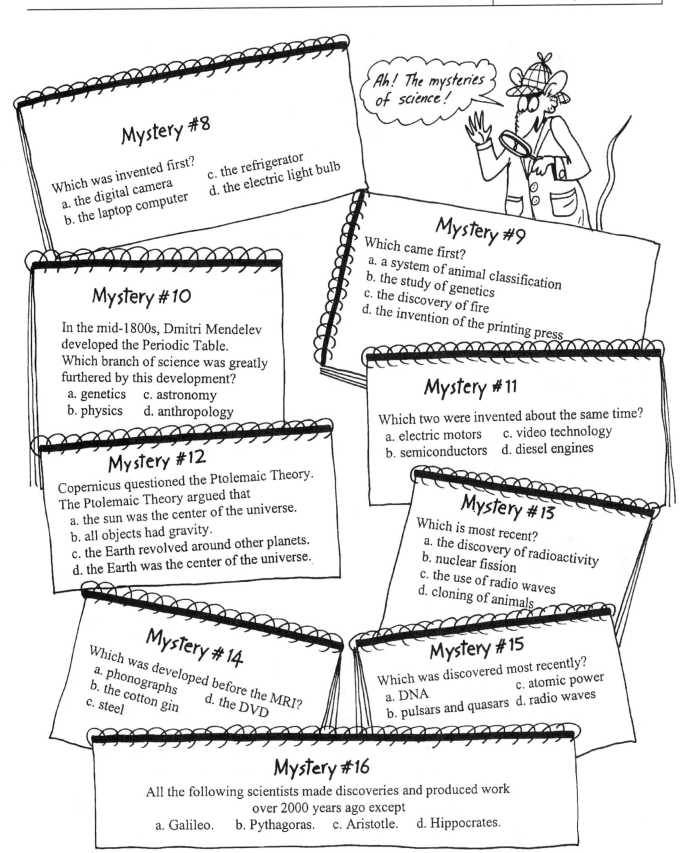

Ah! The mysteries of science!

Mystery #8

Which was invented first?
a. the digital camera
b. the laptop computer
c. the refrigerator
d. the electric light bulb

Mystery #9

Which came first?
a. a system of animal classification
b. the study of genetics
c. the discovery of fire
d. the invention of the printing press

Mystery #10

In the mid-1800s, Dmitri Mendelev developed the Periodic Table. Which branch of science was greatly furthered by this development?
a. genetics   c. astronomy
b. physics   d. anthropology

Mystery #11

Which two were invented about the same time?
a. electric motors   c. video technology
b. semiconductors   d. diesel engines

Mystery #12

Copernicus questioned the Ptolemaic Theory. The Ptolemaic Theory argued that
a. the sun was the center of the universe.
b. all objects had gravity.
c. the Earth revolved around other planets.
d. the Earth was the center of the universe.

Mystery #13

Which is most recent?
a. the discovery of radioactivity
b. nuclear fission
c. the use of radio waves
d. cloning of animals

Mystery #14

Which was developed before the MRI?
a. phonographs
b. the cotton gin
c. steel
d. the DVD

Mystery #15

Which was discovered most recently?
a. DNA
b. pulsars and quasars
c. atomic power
d. radio waves

Mystery #16

All the following scientists made discoveries and produced work over 2000 years ago except
a. Galileo.   b. Pythagoras.   c. Aristotle.   d. Hippocrates.

Use with page 24.

Name

SCIENCE GETS PERSONAL

Professor Ozzie Moses is getting ready for a discussion with his students. They will talk about how science affects their personal lives. Unfortunately, his typist made many errors in the notes for his class. Something is wrong in almost every or every item on his notes.

If you find a correct item, circle its number. For the other items, make changes to correct the wrong information.

1. Individual humans can have no effect on the ecological or health problems of a whole society.

2. Natural hazards, such as earthquakes and storms, can be eliminated with the help of science.

3. Technology has very few risks or negative consequences for human life and health.

4. There is no way to reduce the risks of harm from biological or chemical hazards.

5. With enough research, time, and money, science can meet all human needs.

6. Scientific research in a society is not affected by politics of the society.

7. There is no way to reduce the risks of damages from natural hazards.

8. Hazards in the natural world cannot be caused by human activities.

9. Prescription drugs only have healing effects on the human body.

10. Inventions of all kinds bring more benefits than hazards to humans.

11. Eventually science and technology will solve all human problems.

12. All natural substances are safe and healthy for the human body.

13. Regular exercise is the only element needed for good physical fitness

Choose one of the items above and give a full explanation of your answer. Relate it to your own life experience.

14. Science can protect people from all natural disasters.

15. Scientists can freely do research on human subjects.

16. Use of tobacco products has no connection to illness.

Name

     Copyright ©2002 by Incentive Publications, Inc., Nashville, TN.

SURROUNDED BY SCIENCE

It's everywhere! In today's world, scientific discoveries and inventions affect every corner of our lives.

Describe at least one way
that science is present
in each of these places.

1. in a backpack
_____
_____

2. a downhill ski race
_____
_____

3. a roller coaster
_____
_____
_____

4. a soccer game
_____
_____

5. a rock concert
_____
_____

6. ice cream shop
_____
_____

7. a city street
_____
_____

8. a school cafeteria
_____
_____

9. your bedroom
_____
_____

10. a subway
_____
_____

Name _____

The BASIC/Not Boring Middle Grades Science Book Copyright ©2002 by Incentive Publications, Inc., Nashville, TN.

A TIGHT RELATIONSHIP

What do noisy jet engines, dry desert, splitting atoms, and black holes have in common? They are all connected to the needs and curiosities of humans and the technologies that develop from their scientific activities. Human society, science, and technology have a close relationship.

Put your scientific mind to work and answer these questions about science and technology and the way they work together in human society.

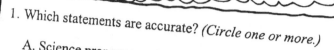

1. Which statements are accurate? *(Circle one or more.)*

   A. Science proposes answers for things happening in the natural world.
   B. Technology proposes solutions for human needs.
   C. Scientific study has consequences. The development of new technology does not.
   D. Science explores questions that require instruments or tools to answer.
   E. Scientists may identify problems that a technological tool can solve.
   F. New technology may cause problems that scientists must try to remedy.

Write another example for each of these.

2. Needs of society lead to the development of technology.

Example: The need for water to grow crops in dry land led to the development of irrigation systems.

Another Example: _____

3. Scientific discovery leads to technological developments.

Example: The discovery that the splitting of atoms gave off a tremendous amount of energy led to the development of nuclear power plants.

Another Example: _____

4. A technological tool can lead to scientific discovery.

Example: The invention of powerful telescopes made possible the discovery of black holes.

Another Example: _____

5. A technological development can create a societal need.

Example: The development of jet engines created issues of noise pollution and safety in cities.

Another Example: _____

Use with page 29.

Name

    Copyright ©2002 by Incentive Publications, Inc., Nashville, TN.

NO ESCAPE FROM CONSEQUENCES

Ingenious inventions and tricks of technology surround us. Every day, more awesome tools and toys are produced through scientific processes. We love the benefits of these tools and toys brought to us by the world's inventors, but every invention comes with costs or consequences of some kind.

DVD PLAYERS

Benefit_____
_____
Consequence _____
_____

AIRPORTS NEAR CITIES

Benefit_____
_____
Consequence _____
_____

ELECTRIC SCOOTERS

Benefit_____
_____
Consequence _____
_____

AUTOMATED FACTORIES

Benefit_____
_____
Consequence _____
_____

CREDIT CARDS

Benefit_____
_____
Consequence _____
_____

The INTERNET

Benefit_____
_____
Consequence _____
_____

Ponder each of these wonders of technology.
Then describe a benefit and a consequence or hazard of each.

Use with page 28.

Name

FANTASTIC EXPLANATIONS

Scientists come up with explanations for happenings they observe or discover. Those explanations often are stated in the form of theories or laws.

Someone has started a file of some scientific laws and theories. Finish the file by writing a brief statement or summary of the theory named on each card. (Continue with the laws on page 31.)

A **scientific theory** is an explanation based on many observations during repeated experiments.

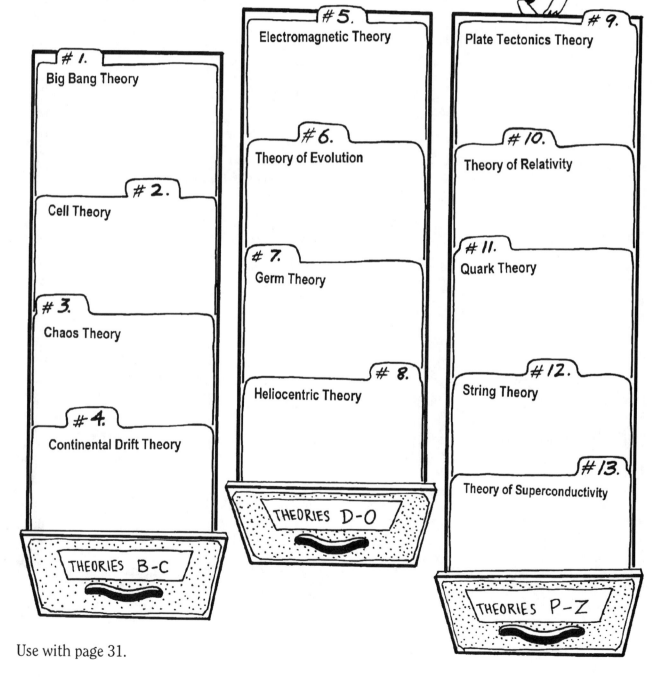

1.
Big Bang Theory

2.
Cell Theory

3.
Chaos Theory

4.
Continental Drift Theory

5.
Electromagnetic Theory

6.
Theory of Evolution

7.
Germ Theory

8.
Heliocentric Theory

THEORIES D-O

9.
Plate Tectonics Theory

10.
Theory of Relativity

11.
Quark Theory

12.
String Theory

13.
Theory of Superconductivity

THEORIES P-Z

THEORIES B-C

Use with page 31.

Name

On each card, write a brief statement or summary of the law named.

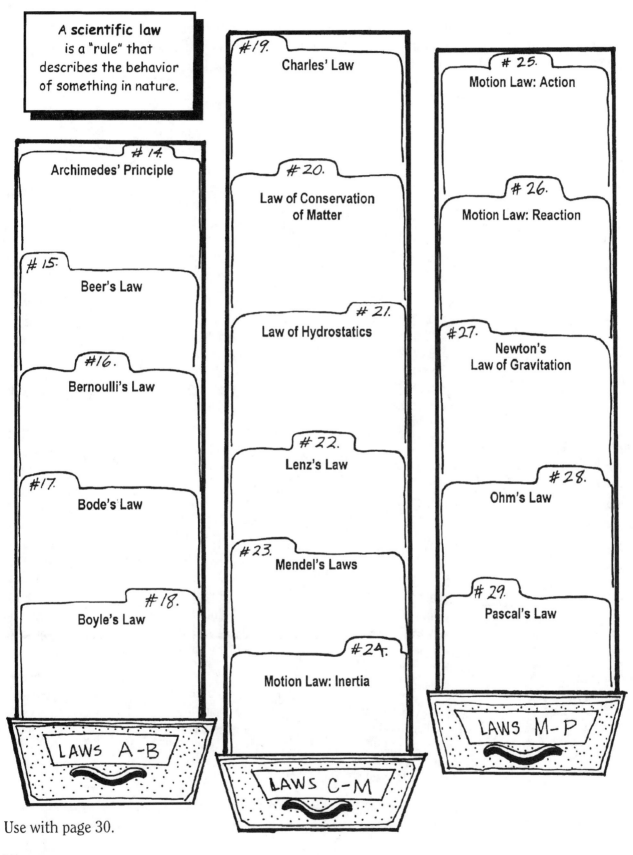

A **scientific law** is a "rule" that describes the behavior of something in nature.

14. Archimedes' Principle

#15. Beer's Law

#16. Bernoulli's Law

#17. Bode's Law

18. Boyle's Law

LAWS A-B

#19. Charles' Law

20. Law of Conservation of Matter

21. Law of Hydrostatics

22. Lenz's Law

#23. Mendel's Laws

#24. Motion Law: Inertia

LAWS C-M

25. Motion Law: Action

26. Motion Law: Reaction

#27. Newton's Law of Gravitation

28. Ohm's Law

29. Pascal's Law

LAWS M-P

Use with page 30.

Name

THE SEARCH IS ON

Scientists have inquiring minds. They are always searching for answers. Over time, science has developed a general way of doing investigations and looking for explanations about happenings in the universe. This is called the scientific method or steps to scientific inquiry.

THE DROPPED EGG INVESTIGATION

As Kiko and Thomas were carrying eggs into the house from the grocery store, a huge clap of thunder struck just outside their door. They were so shocked that they both dropped the eggs. Some eggs stayed in the containers, others dropped out. Some fell on the carpet, others landed on the wooden kitchen floor. They were surprised that all the eggs did not break. Many eggs still in their containers and eggs on the carpet were unbroken. This accident made them curious about what might cause some eggs to break when falling, while others did not break. They guessed that eggs falling on carpet or staying in their containers were less likely to break than eggs flying out of their containers onto a hard floor.

They decided to investigate. They realized that the height from which the eggs dropped and the force of the drop might affect the results. So they chose a precise distance for the drop and decided to let the eggs go gently, with no throwing force. They planned to drop eggs for four different kinds of landings. They thought they should drop enough eggs to avoid chance results. They also planned to do the investigation twice, in two trials, to see if results were similar. They gathered measuring tools, eggs, egg containers, and a sheet to protect the carpet. They planned to drop 12 eggs for each kind of landing. With two trials, there would be a total of 24 eggs dropped in each way. They measured a spot exactly 5 feet off the floor, and marked that spot on the wall. Then they made a table for tallying the results.

Finally they were ready. Kiko stood on a stool and held her arm out level with the mark. She dropped 12 eggs in a carton onto the carpet, and 12 eggs in a carton onto the wooden floor. Next, she dropped 12 eggs, one at a time, onto the carpet. Last, she dropped 12 eggs, one at a time, onto the floor. While she dropped eggs, Thomas kept a tally of the number of eggs broken in each of the four groups. When they finished this trial, they repeated the whole process. They showed their results by creating a summarizing table.

Kiko and Thomas cleaned up their mess and reviewed their results. They came to the conclusion that eggs dropped onto a soft surface in an egg container were the least likely to break. Eggs dropped in the container onto a wooden floor were more likely to break. Just about as likely as this, however, were eggs dropped out of the container onto carpet. The most likely of all to break were eggs dropped outside of a container onto the hard floor. They believed these results showed that the carpet and the containers gave enough protection to the eggs to keep them all from breaking.

After the investigation, they still wondered about breaking eggs. They wanted to know why some eggs didn't break at all, on the carpet, and even on the hard floor. They wondered if eggs in the center of the cartons were more protected than those on the ends. They wondered whether different materials of cartons would make a difference in the number of eggs broken. They got busy planning some more investigations.

Read this report on the *Dropped Egg Investigation.* Then answer the questions about the inquiry process on page 33.

Egg-Drop Method	Trial # 1 Number of Eggs Broken	Trial # 2 Number of Eggs Broken	% of Total Eggs Broken in 2 Trials
Eggs in Container, Dropped on Wood Floor	11	9	41.6%
Eggs in Container, Dropped on Carpet	1	2	6.2%
Eggs Dropped on Wood Floor Out of Container	22	24	95.8%
Eggs Dropped on Carpet Out of Container	13	11	50%

Read the investigation described on page 32. Then review the steps in scientific inquiry below. Use the questions to make a record of how these scientists used the process of scientific inquiry.

1. **OBSERVE:** *What observation led to an experiment?*

_____

2. **ASK QUESTIONS:** *What question(s) did they want to answer?*

_____

3. **HYPOTHESIZE:** *What was their hypothesis?* _____

4. **PLAN AND CARRY OUT AN INVESTIGATION:** *What plan did they follow?*

_____

5. **USE TOOLS TO GATHER AND ANALYZE DATA:** *How did they collect the data?*

What tools and supplies did they use? _____

_____

6. **ANALYZE AND INTERPRET DATA:** *What were the results?*

_____

7. **PURPOSE EXPLANATIONS:** *What explanation did they give for the results?*

_____

8. **COMMUNICATE RESULTS:** *How did they show or share the results?*

_____

9. **OFFER OTHER QUESTIONS OR IDEAS:** *What other questions or ideas did they offer?*

_____

10. **MATHEMATICS:** *How did they make use of math in their process?*

_____

Use with page 32.

Name _____

SORTING OUT BIG IDEAS

Professor Agnes Igneous teaches geology to a group of students. Her students also study many other kinds of science with other scientists. They keep running into some big ideas that stretch into all areas of science. Here are some of the events and facts they have studied. Each of them is related to one or more of the big concepts of science.

Find one or more facts, events, or theories that might be included in each of the 10 books shown. Write the letters on the matching books.
(An item might relate to more than one of the concepts!)

A. When Agnes jogs on her treadmill, she begins to sweat and the evaporating sweat causes her body to cool so it does not over-heat. The body responds to the falling temperature, and blood vessels in her skin contract to reduce the loss of heat.

B. The plants and animals that live in and around Lost Canyon Pond have complex and important relationships with one another. They depend upon each other for survival, and the welfare of each species affects the lives of the others.

C. A shoulder joint is actually a ball and socket. The upper arm bone has a rounded end that fits into a hollow space in the shoulder bone. This allows the shoulder to rotate in a circle.

D. Agnes left her motorcycle outside in the damp San Francisco weather all winter. By spring, the bike was terribly rusty.

E. There are thousands of species of animals—all of different levels of complexity. Fortunately, scientists have developed a classification system that organizes them all, from the simplest to the most complex.

Use with page 35.

F. The sum of total mass (of matter) plus the total energy in the universe always remains the same.

G. When Agnes waters her lawn, the water from her sprinkler does not quite reach to the edge of the lawn. The trees at the outer edge of its lawn get no water soaking into the ground near them. Eventually the trees start to lose their needles and look rather sickly.

H. During six months of research along the ocean, Agnes has watched the rise and fall of the tides. In particular, she has been fascinated by the patterns of the spring tides, neap tides, and tropic tides.

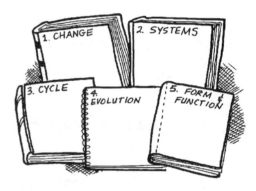

I. When Agnes stepped off the dock into her canoe, the boat took a quick move backward, even though she had stepped forward into the canoe. This quick motion of the boat made her lose her balance and topple into the water.

J. Most scientists believe that interactions among the Earth's land, water, atmosphere, and living organisms have caused a series of changes in the whole Earth system. Some changes, such as those produced by earthquakes, are sudden. But most of the changes, such as mountain-building, take place gradually, over a period of hundreds or thousands of years.

Name

K. The molecules in chocolate milk are not as close together as the molecules in a solid, such as a chocolate bar. With molecules far apart, the substance is more flexible, so the milk can be poured!

L. As the flame on the burner heats up the teakettle, the water molecules move faster and faster, knocking each other farther apart, until some of them actually change into a gas. These escape the kettle as steam.

M. The fluffy feathers that cover birds have thousands of spaces where air can become trapped and warmed by the bird's body. This ability to trap air in and around the feathers provides a great insulation system for keeping the bird warm as it soars through cold air.

N. A load of passengers climbed into the roller coaster while it was parked at the starting point. Then the coaster began gaining speed, slowly climbing that first big hill.

R. The Periodic Table of Elements arranges all the chemical elements in rows according to their atomic numbers and grouping in columns elements with similar properties.

S. A loaf of bread sat on the counter in its plastic bag. By the end of three weeks, the slices were covered with a lovely blue-green mold.

T. After Agnes has a nasty crash on her motorbike, her knees and elbows are badly scraped and covered with dirt and germs. Her body responds by sending an army of white blood cells to the areas to destroy the germs.

U. The Big Bang Theory is one explanation of the origin of the universe. According to this theory, the universe began with a major explosion billions of years ago. Since then, the matter from the explosion broke into clumps that became galaxies, which continue to expand and change.

O. Jupiter follows the same path around the sun, over and over. It takes Jupiter 11.86 Earth years to return to the place it started in its orbit.

P. After Agnes eats her favorite chicken taco, it takes many organs working together to digest the food and turn it into the energy she needs to maintain and use her body well.

Q. The charge of any electron in any element or other substance is always a negative charge.

V. Agnes was standing in a pool of water when she turned on her hairdryer. This was not good, because water is a very good conductor of electricity, and the situation was dangerous for her. Fortunately for Agnes, she was wearing shoes with rubber soles, so that the rubber came between her body and the water—and rubber is a very poor conductor of electricity.

W. The thermostat in Agnes's hot tub is set at 100°. When the water temperature falls below 100°, the thermostat sensors trigger the thermostat to turn the heater on until the water again reaches 100°.

Use with page 34.

Name

THE WHOLE THING

The natural and designed world is brimming with systems—from minute and simple to monumental and complex. Every system has components (parts), boundaries, and some sort of input and output. Take a close look at a few systems.

A SYSTEM is an organized group of related parts that form a whole, working together to perform one or more functions.

1. The Circuit

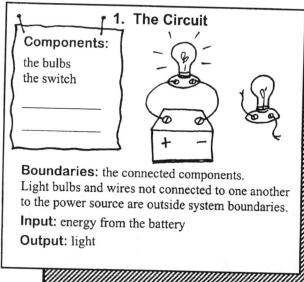

Components:
the bulbs
the switch
_____
_____

Boundaries: the connected components. Light bulbs and wires not connected to one another to the power source are outside system boundaries.

Input: energy from the battery

Output: light

2. Amoeba

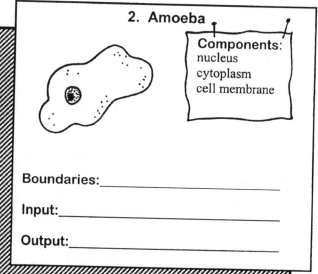

Components:
nucleus
cytoplasm
cell membrane

Boundaries:_____

Input:_____

Output:_____

3. a river

Components:

Boundaries:_____

Input:_____

Output:_____

4. respiratory system

Components:

Boundaries:_____

Input:_____

Output:_____

5. pulley

Components:

Boundaries:_____

Input:_____

Output:_____

6. Name 4 other systems:

_____ _____

_____ _____

Name _____

Copyright ©2002 by Incentive Publications, Inc., Nashville, TN.

LOOKING FOR ORDER

ORDER

is the predictable behavior of objects, units of matter, events, organisms, or systems. In the natural world, certain events follow others; certain behaviors of organisms and matter can be expected.

ORGANIZATION

is an arrangement of independent items, objects, organisms, units of matter, or systems, joined into a whole system or structure.

1. Lightning strikes a body of water. What will happen to the electric charge?

_____

2. An animal cell is fertilized. What behavior can you expect from the cell?

_____

3. What can you expect from seawater that has become colder and denser due to cold temperatures and evaporation?

_____

4. What behavior can you expect from molten material under high pressure that flows toward a crack in the Earth's crust?

_____

5. As winter comes to the Arctic, the Arctic tern travels 11,000 miles to its breeding ground in Antarctica. What behavior is likely to occur when the Antarctic weather begins to cool and summer comes to the Arctic?

_____

6. One example of organization in nature is the classification of animals. Number these components in order from simplest (1) to the most complex (7).

_____species   _____family

_____phylum   _____order

_____class   _____genus

_____kingdom

7. This is a list of components of living systems. Number them in order of complexity, from the simplest (1) to the most complex (6).

_____tissues   _____cells

_____organs   _____communities

_____populations   _____organisms

8. The Periodic Table arranges elements according to their properties. Which of the following elements would be in a nonmetal group on the Periodic Table? *(Circle them.)*

fluorine	chlorine	iodine
helium	radon	krypton
mercury	titanium	bromine
argon	neon	magnesium

Name _____

WHAT IS IT ABOUT THAT SHAPE?

FORM & FUNCTION
The shape (form) of an organism, object, or system is often related to the operation (function). Frequently the function of an organism, object, or system is very dependent on the shape.

A periscope has a long tube with reflecting mirrors at each end, arranged parallel to each other. The mirrors are at 45° angles to the axis of the tube. The shape and structure of the periscope make it useful to see around corners or to see from distances above or below the object being viewed.

X-rays have very short wave lengths and move very fast. This form gives them great kinetic energy—enough energy to penetrate through soft tissue. These rays can be used to help make pictures of the bones inside bodies.

Starfish have tube-like feet, which are perfect for attaching like suction cups. These structures allow the starfish to grab onto things and move, or to attach to shells while they pull them apart and eat the animals inside.

The form is described. You describe the function made possible by the form.

1. the webbed feet of a duck

   the function ⟶ _____

2. the long tubes of kelp, with anchoring ends and gas-filled bladders

   the function ⟶ _____

3. the extreme flexibility and stretchable form of copper

   the function ⟶ _____

4. the whip-like tail (flagellum) on a bacterium

   the function ⟶ _____

5. the layers in a space suit that allow for circulation of liquid

   the function ⟶ _____

Use with page 39.

Name

What function or operation is possible because of each form?
Describe the form and the function for each term listed below.

	The Form (or shape)	**The Function** (or operation)
6. planetary orbits →	_____	_____
7. a wedge →	_____	_____
8. any gas →	_____	_____
9. plant roots →	_____	_____
10. a bobsled →	_____	_____
11. cell membrane →	_____	_____
12. convex lens →	_____	_____
13. outer ear →	_____	_____
14. muscle cells →	_____	_____
15. compact disc →	_____	_____
16. plant cell wall →	_____	_____
17. dandelion seeds →	_____	_____
18. hypodermic needle →	_____	_____
19. intestine →	_____	_____
20. microscope →	_____	_____

Hmmm. Very interesting!

Use with page 38.

Name _____

OPERATION INTERACTION

ENERGY and MATTER
have an extremely close relationship.
They are constantly interacting with one another.
Matter can be changed into energy,
and energy can be transferred to matter.
The total amount of energy plus matter
in the world always stays the same.

The principles of energy and matter are the same in my galaxy, too.

Identify the energy and the matter in each example.
Then describe what will happen when they interact.

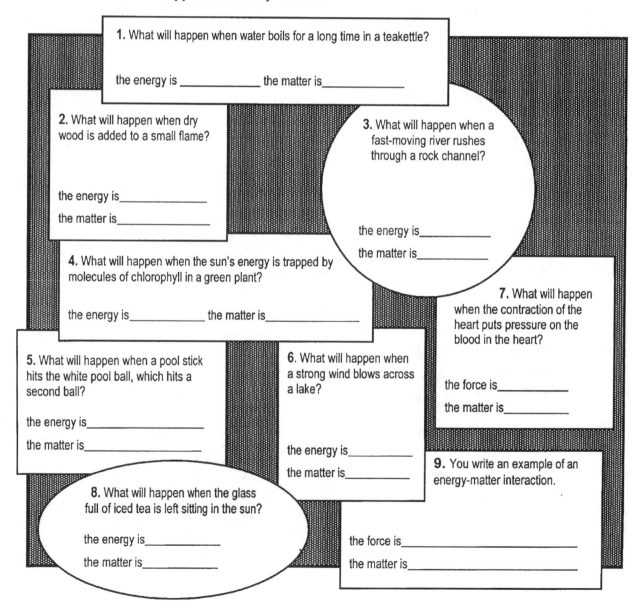

1. What will happen when water boils for a long time in a teakettle?

the energy is _____ the matter is _____

2. What will happen when dry wood is added to a small flame?

the energy is _____
the matter is _____

3. What will happen when a fast-moving river rushes through a rock channel?

the energy is _____
the matter is _____

4. What will happen when the sun's energy is trapped by molecules of chlorophyll in a green plant?

the energy is _____ the matter is _____

5. What will happen when a pool stick hits the white pool ball, which hits a second ball?

the energy is _____
the matter is _____

6. What will happen when a strong wind blows across a lake?

the energy is _____
the matter is _____

7. What will happen when the contraction of the heart puts pressure on the blood in the heart?

the force is _____
the matter is _____

8. What will happen when the glass full of iced tea is left sitting in the sun?

the energy is _____
the matter is _____

9. You write an example of an energy-matter interaction.

the force is _____
the matter is _____

Name

     Copyright ©2002 by Incentive Publications, Inc., Nashville, TN.

CONNECTION INSPECTION

Professor Radon is thinking of cause & effect relationships to use as examples for his students. Give a close inspection to the connection between the two statements in each pair below. For each pair of statements, identify the cause with a C. Identify the effect with an E.

CAUSE & EFFECT

A cause is anything that brings about a result. An effect is the result—the event or situation that follows from the cause. Everywhere you look in the physical world, you can spot cause-effect relationships.

1. _____A. Hot magma which has been trapped beneath Earth's surface begins to cool.
   _____B. The liquid magma solidifies to form intrusive igneous rock.

2. _____A. A drummer strikes a drum; the surface vibrates, producing compressional waves.
   _____B. Compressional waves carry the sound to the drummer's ears.

3. _____A. A highly productive fishing area is created.
   _____B. Upwellings of cold water bring high concentrations of nutrients to the ocean surface.

4. _____A. A mother bird flies around, squawking and madly flapping her wings.
   _____B. A stranger hikes through the territory where a mother bird has a nest of babies.

5. _____A. In its orbit around the Earth, the moon moves into a position that is in a straight line with the Earth and sun, on the opposite side of Earth from the sun.
   _____B. A lunar eclipse occurs, meaning that the moon is not visible from Earth.

6. _____A. Guard cells in the epidermis of a leaf swell and open the stoma.
   _____B. Guard cells in the epidermis of a leaf absorb water.

Briefly describe one cause-effect relationship for each area of science:

7. Life Science _____

8. Physical Science _____

9. Earth Science _____

10. Space Science _____

Name _____

TO CHANGE OR NOT TO CHANGE

Search with Dr. Ozzie Moses to find real examples of things that change or stay the same, evolve, or balance. Find examples in the physical world around you.

CONSTANCY
is the opposite of change—a state characterized by lack of variation.

CHANGE
is the process of becoming different.

Describe...

1. a **CHANGE** in physical properties of a material

_____

2. a **CHANGE** in chemical properties of a material

_____

3. a **CHANGE** in state or form of a material

_____

4. a **CHANGE** in position of matter

_____

5. a **CHANGE** in function of an object or organism

_____

6. a **TRANSFER** of energy

_____

Something is about to change....

Identify or describe TWO objects, processes, entities, or characteristics that **remain constant** in the physical world.

7._____

_____

8._____

_____

Use with page 43.

Name _____

          Copyright ©2002 by Incentive Publications, Inc., Nashville, TN.

EVOLUTION

is a series of changes that cause the
form or function of an object, organism,
or system to be what it currently is.
Some of the changes happen over
a long period of time;
others may happen suddenly.

EQUILIBRIUM

is the state
in which equal forces
occur in opposite directions
and offset (or balance) each other.

9. Describe or identify a system,
object, or organism that has taken the
form it currently has because it has
made a gradual series of changes.

_____

_____

_____

_____

_____

_____

_____

Describe or name 5 examples of
equilibrium in the physical (natural)
world or in the world of human-designed
objects or systems.

10._____

_____

11._____

_____

12._____

_____

13._____

_____

14._____

_____

Use with page 42.

Name

SCIENCE REPEATS ITSELF

Cycles are everywhere in science. They are so common in the natural world that many of them hardly get noticed. Write a few sentences to explain each of these cycles shown. Then name at least three other cycles in the natural world.

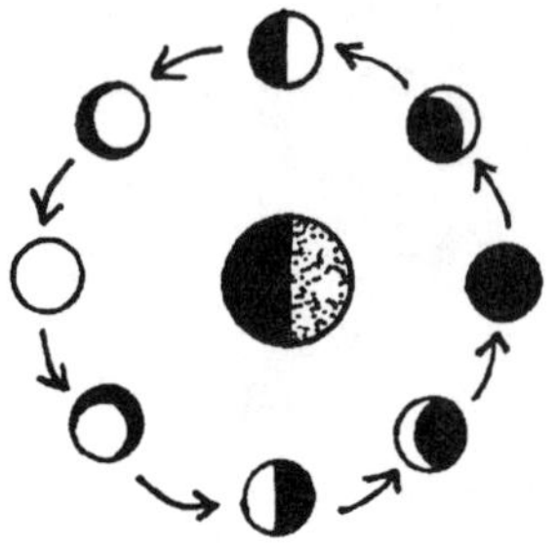

A CYCLE
is a series of events or operations that regularly occur and usually lead back to the starting point.

2. BUTTERFLY LIFE CYCLE

_____
_____
_____
_____
_____

1. MOON PHASES

_____
_____
_____
_____

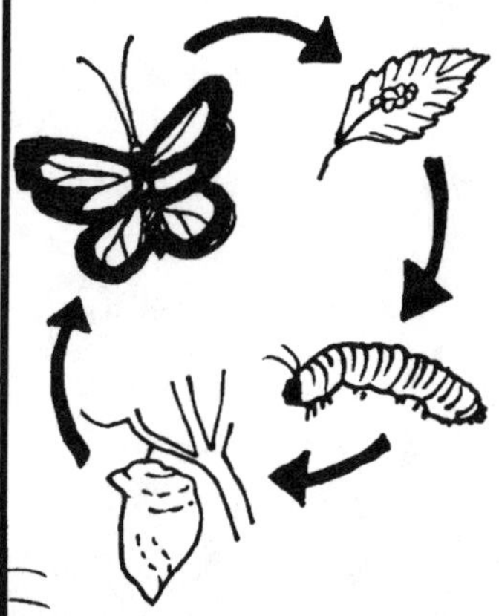

3. THE ROCK CYCLE

_____
_____
_____
_____
_____
_____

4. Name at least 3 other cycles:_____

Name
_____

 Copyright ©2002 by Incentive Publications, Inc., Nashville, TN.

CONCEPTS GET REAL

Are there cycles in your health?
Do energy-matter relationships affect any of your hobbies?
Do form and function relationships hang around your classroom?
Are there cause-effect relationships in your backyard?
Can you find any systems in your bathroom?
Is equilibrium at work in your kitchen?

Think about the ways these big ideas of science show up in your life.
Describe one way that ONE of these science concepts shows up in
each of the following areas of your life. Choose a different concept for each area.

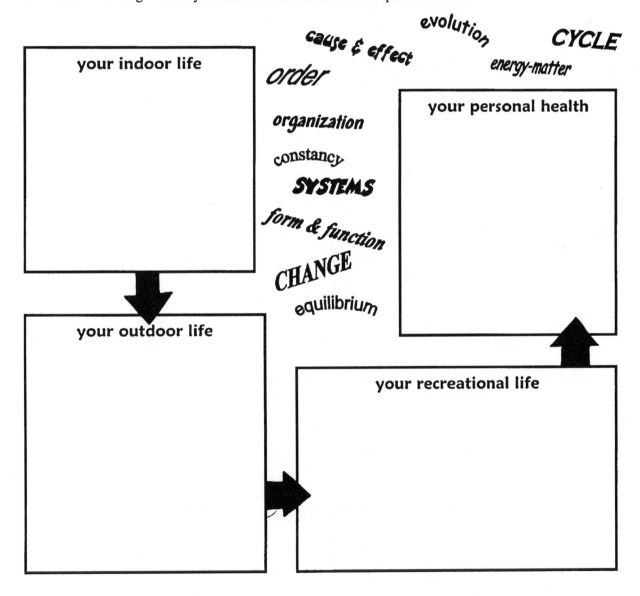

your indoor life

your outdoor life

your personal health

your recreational life

evolution   CYCLE
cause & effect   energy-matter
order
organization
constancy
SYSTEMS
form & function
CHANGE
equilibrium

Name

The BASIC/Not Boring Middle Grades Science Book   Copyright ©2002 by Incentive Publications, Inc., Nashville, TN.

PAY ATTENTION!

Pay close attention to each of the events on this page and on page 47.
Use all your senses. Keep a record of your observations.

Watch carefully!

To **OBSERVE**
is to recognize and note facts or occurrences,
or to watch carefully. In scientific inquiry,
observation uses ALL the senses.
Attend to events and facts with your senses
of sight, smell, touch, taste, and hearing.
(But do NOT taste any substances other than foods.)

1. Fill two identical bowls to the top with water, but do not let the water spill over the edge. Gently set a ping pong ball into the water of one bowl. Gently set a golf ball into the other bowl.

   What do you observe?_____

2. Spin a hardboiled egg (in the shell) on a hard surface.

   What do you observe?_____

3. Spin an uncooked egg on a hard surface.

   What do you observe?_____

4. Peel a green banana. Slice it into chunks. Eat a chunk.

   What do you observe?_____

5. Hold a fork by its handle, so the fork is hanging down. Bang it with a spoon.

   What do you observe?_____

6. Tie a string around a fork handle. Let the fork hang suspended by the string. Bang the fork with a spoon.

   What do you observe?_____

7. Pour some vinegar into a glass cup. Stir in a spoon full of baking soda.

   What do you observe?_____

8. Light a candle. Watch the wick carefully as the candle burns. Watch for 10 minutes.

   What do you observe?_____

Use with page 47.

Name

Pay close attention to each of the events on this page and on page 46.
Use all your senses. Keep a record of your observations.

9. Pour very hot water into a metal cup. Place your hands carefully near the cup—but do not touch the cup.

What do you observe?

10. Pour very hot water into a ceramic cup. Place your hands carefully near the cup—but do not touch the cup.

What do you observe?

11. Pour very hot water into a plastic cup. Place your hands carefully near the cup—but do not touch the cup.

What do you observe?

12. Blow up a balloon. Rub it against a wool sweater. Hold it above your hair.

What do you observe?

13. Cook an egg in boiling water for 10 minutes. Drop it into cold water. Peel the egg as soon as you can handle it. Smash the egg and egg white with a fork.

What do you observe?_____

14. Stand in a narrow doorway. Hold your arms out from your sides. Press the backs of your hands hard against the door jam. Keep pressing for 3 full minutes. Step away from the doorway, leaving your arms loosely at your sides.

What do you observe?_____

15. Put some red food coloring in the bottom of a glass jar. Fill the jar two-thirds full of water. Cut two tall stalks of celery. Remove the leaves from the top of one stalk. Leave them on the other. Place the celery stalks in the red water. Check on them in a few hours.

What do you observe?_____

16. Press your first two fingers gently against the right side of your neck just next to your Adam's apple.

What do you observe?_____

17. Cut a large square from a brown paper grocery bag. Rub a piece of cheddar cheese in a streak across the paper. Hold the paper up to the light.

What do you observe?_____

18. Fill 5 glasses of water ½ full with warm water. Mix a teaspoon full of each of these into one of the glasses: salt, pepper, flour, sugar, cinnamon.

What do you observe?_____

Use with page 46.

Name

47   Copyright ©2002 by Incentive Publications, Inc., Nashville, TN.

SCIENCE HAS CLASS

To CLASSIFY
is to assign objects or processes to a group
or category based on a common characteristic.

Dr. Femur thinks the study of science is a classy profession.
She's busy classifying different organisms, events, objects,
and processes.

Join her in this activity. All the items in each list belong to
at least one category. Write a label that could be used to name
the classification of those items.

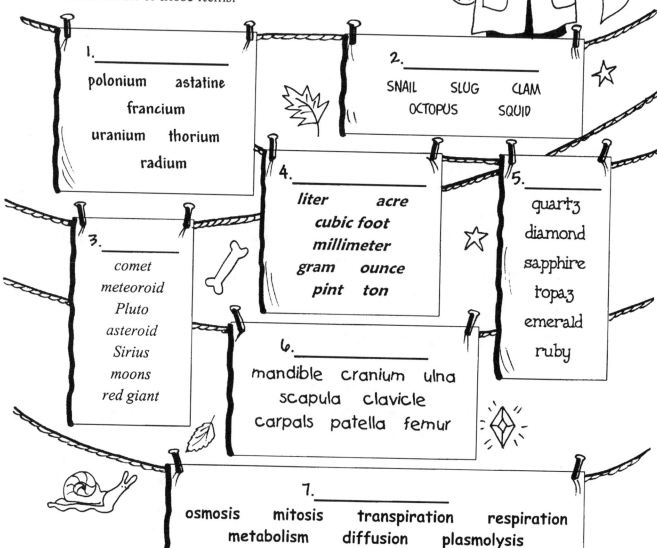

1. _____

polonium   astatine

francium

uranium   thorium

radium

2. _____

SNAIL   SLUG   CLAM

OCTOPUS   SQUID

3. _____

comet
meteoroid
Pluto
asteroid
Sirius
moons
red giant

4. _____

liter   acre

cubic foot

millimeter

gram   ounce

pint   ton

5. _____

quartz

diamond

sapphire

topaz

emerald

ruby

6. _____

mandible   cranium   ulna

scapula   clavicle

carpals   patella   femur

7. _____

osmosis   mitosis   transpiration   respiration

metabolism   diffusion   plasmolysis

Use with page 49.

Name _____

Copyright ©2002 by Incentive Publications, Inc., Nashville, TN.

8. Which of these should be in a group labeled **Good Conductors of Electricity?** *(Circle them.)*

water   wood   glass
rubber   copper   plastic
human body   zinc

9. Which of these should be in a group labeled **Organisms with Bilateral Symmetry?** *(Circle them.)*

ant   jellyfish   hydra   sponge
lobster   frog   gorilla   octopus
starfish   anemone

abyssal plane
barrier island
ocean ridge
beach
ocean trench
ooze
continental shelf
spit
seamount
tombolo

10. Which of the above would be classified as shore deposits?

_____
_____
_____

mite   **scorpion**   **lobster**
beetle   **crab**   **mosquito**
centipede
millipede   **ladybug**

Write three different labels under which these organisms could be classified (with ALL of them belonging to each group).

11. _____
12. _____
13. _____

water   nitrogen   lead   carbon dioxide
wood   iron   sodium chloride   propane

14. Which of the above substances would be classified as compounds? *(Write them.)*

_____

15. Which of the above substances would be classified as organic substances? *(Write them.)*

_____

Use with page 48.

Name

The BASIC/Not Boring Middle Grades Science Book Copyright ©2002 by Incentive Publications, Inc., Nashville, TN.

MORE THAN JUST A GUESS

To **HYPOTHESIZE**
is to make an assumption in order
to test an idea further.

Hypothesizing is more than just a guess. It is a smart guess that you arrive at after making some careful observations of facts or events.

Read each description of an event. Then make a smart guess (a hypothesis) about each one.

Make sure the hypothesis is something that could be tested through scientific inquiry.

Ozzie left his plate out on the counter after lunch. On the plate he left a piece of an egg sandwich, some apple slices, a strawberry, a piece of banana, and some chips. When he returned two hours later, the plate was full of fruit flies. He noticed that the flies were mostly settled on the apples, strawberry, and banana.

1. Write a hypothesis that could be tested.

_____

_____

_____

_____

Ozzie sets a paper clip on the surface of a glass of water. The paper clip does not sink. When he sets a thumbtack on the water, it does sink.

Ozzie notices that his pet rat is not interested in a round toy that is sitting in the middle of the floor. When he kicks the toy and it rolls around, the rat perks up and chases it.

2. Write a hypothesis that could be tested.

_____

_____

_____

3. Write a hypothesis that could be tested.

_____

_____

_____

Use with page 51.

Name

Ozzie slices some potatoes, because he intends to make potato chips. He lets them soak in very salty water. (He thinks this will make them into nice, salty chips when he fries them.) When he comes back several hours later to fry the chips, the slices are very limp.

When Ozzie is getting ready to wash dishes, he mistakenly bangs two pot lids together. He notices the sound. Then, while washing the lids, he bangs them together under water. He is surprised that the sound is louder and clearer than before.

4. Write a hypothesis that could be tested.

_____

_____

_____

_____

5. Write a hypothesis that could be tested.

_____

_____

_____

Ozzie watched a friend do a magic trick. The friend filled a cup of water almost to the top with cold water. Then she floated a big ice cube on the top. The friend laid a piece of wet string across the ice cube. Then she sprinkled salt over the string and waited three minutes. When she picked up the ends of the string, she also picked up the ice cube because it stuck to the string.

Ozzie had a liter bottle full of water. He wanted to empty the water. He turned the bottle upside down. It took a very long time to empty. The water just did not seem to want to come out, even though he was holding the bottle directly upside down.

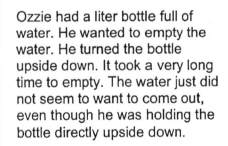

6. Write a hypothesis that could be tested.

_____

_____

_____

_____

7. Write a hypothesis that could be tested.

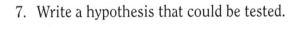

_____

_____

_____

Use with page 50.

Name _____

     Copyright ©2002 by Incentive Publications, Inc., Nashville, TN.

YOU DO THE MATH

To **MEASURE**	**USE NUMBERS**
is to compare an object to some standard quantity in order to find out an amount or an extent.	Numbers are used constantly in science. Numbers allow for measurements and they describe amounts.

What unit would you choose to measure . . .

1. the distance from your home to Paris, France?

   _____

2. the fuel in your gas tank? _____

3. the length of a fruit fly? _____

4. the water in a swimming pool? _____

5. the temperature of a milkshake? _____

6. the capacity of your school locker? _____

7. the length of the school day? _____

8. the length of a shoelace? _____

9. the length of your friend's tongue _____

10. the weight of an elephant? _____

Find each of these measurements:

11. the distance from your nose to your knee _____

12. the capacity of your backpack

   _____

13. the weight of all your school books

   _____

14. the circumference of your head

   _____

15. the temperature inside your refrigerator

   _____

Professor Radon did a tug-of-war experiment. He wanted to find out if the number of people pulling on one side was more a factor in winning than the weight of the people. He marked the center of the rope. Then he put six people on one side, and ten people on the other side. The total weight of the six was greater than the total weight of the ten.

16. Describe the ways that the professor used math in his experiment.

_____

_____

Name

Copyright ©2002 by Incentive Publications, Inc., Nashville, TN.

SO WHAT?

So, Professor Igneous has finished some investigations. She has some results. What will she do with those results? What do they mean? What has she learned? Two processes that follow the collection of data in an inquiry are inferring and predicting. Dr. Igneous can use the information she gathered to draw some conclusions and make some judgments about what else might happen.

Read her results.
Then make your own inferences and predictions.

> **To INFER**
> is to draw a conclusion based on facts or information gained from an inquiry.

> **To predict**
> is to foretell what is likely to happen based on an observation or experiment.

THE SINGING GLASSES

The Experiment: Testing sounds produced by banging a metal spoon against glasses filled with different amounts of water. The experiment used 5 glasses, each the same size and shape—8 inches tall. They were filled to the heights of 1, 2, 3, 4, and 5 inches.

Results: The glass filled to 1 inch produced the highest sound. Next highest was the 2-inch full glass; third highest was the 3-inch full glass. Next highest was the 4-inch full glass. The 5-inch full glass had the lowest sound.

1. What can you infer about the relationship of sounds to the amounts of water in the glasses?

2. What kind of a sound will probably result from a glass that is full to the brim?

A MAP OF THE TONGUE

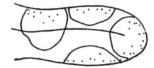

The Experiment: Tasting several food items by touching them (with cotton swabs) on each of four areas of the tongue: front, back, and sides.

Results: She tasted the honey, molasses, and sugar on the tip of her tongue. On the sides, she tasted the lemon juice and vinegar. On the back of her tongue, she tasted the bitter black tea.

3. What can you infer about the tongue from these results?

4. On which part of her tongue is Dr. Igneous likely to get the full taste of pickle juice?

Name

NOT THE REAL THING

To **USE MODELS**
is to use some sort of a structure
or scheme that visually represents
real objects or events.

Many models are three-dimensional.
Imagine that Professor Aster Oid's
representation of two atoms is
three-dimensional. Use information
from the model to fill in the blanks
in his explanation.

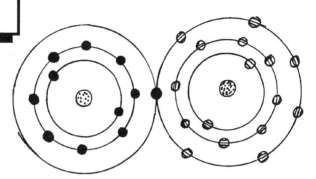

1. This model shows a chemical reaction between the elements _____ and _____.

2. _____ has only 1 electron in its outer ring, making it _____ (stable, unstable).

3. _____ has only 7 electrons in its outer ring, making it _____ (stable, unstable).

4. When the two chemicals combine, the element _____ takes the extra electron from

_____. This way, its last ring is filled. The other element, _____, has

lost one electron, but now its outer orbit (second ring) is full. Both elements are happy with the

combination!

5. Which formula is a model (representation)
of a chemical reaction between
magnesium and chlorine
to produce magnesium chloride?

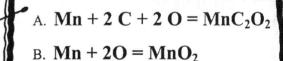

A. $Mn + 2\,C + 2\,O = MnC_2O_2$

B. $Mn + 2O = MnO_2$

C. $Mg + 2\,Cl = MgCl_2$

D. $3\,Md + Cl = Md_3\,Cl$

E. $Mg + Cl = MgCl$

Name _____

     Copyright ©2002 by Incentive Publications, Inc., Nashville, TN.

SO, WHY DOES THE EGG FLOAT?

Professor Radon has been trying to get an egg to float. He has succeeded, but no one can learn anything from his experiment if he does not share it and try to explain its meaning. Scientific discoveries, answers to questions, and results of inquiries do not do much good if they are kept secret.

To **INTERPRET**
is to explain or tell the meaning
of the results in an experiment.
To **COMMUNICATE**
is to tell or show others the
process and results of the experiment.

Read about Professor Radon's inquiry and the results. Then help with the explanation.

Ah ha!

Observation: A friend showed him an egg floating in water, but Reginald could not get an egg to float. Then, he remembered how easily he could float in the ocean.

Hypothesis: Objects will float more easily in salt water than in fresh water.

Experimental Process: He filled a glass two-thirds full with fresh water. He set an egg in the glass. Then he stirred in some salt. He kept adding salt and stirring.

Results: At first, the egg sank. As he added more salt, the egg floated higher and higher.

1. **INTERPRETATION:** Explain the meaning of Professor Radon's results.

   _____

   _____

2. **EVIDENCE:** An explanation or interpretation should be based on evidence. What evidence led you to the explanation you gave?

   _____

3. **FURTHER QUESTIONS:** A good inquiry usually raises new questions, even while it provides some answers. Write at least one question you have after reading Dr. Radon's results.

   _____

Name _____

IN PURSUIT OF ANSWERS

To DESIGN AN EXPERIMENT
is to make a plan to find an answer for a question or to test a hypothesis.
The plan includes all the steps to take and equipment to be used in the process.

Dr. Igneous wants to make frozen juice pops for her picnic. She is curious about how long it will take for the pops to freeze. She knows that juice is a solution—not a pure substance. So, she wonders how the freezing time will compare to the freezing time of water. She assumes that the juice (a solution) will take longer to freeze than water.

Agnes makes a plan to answer her question about the freezing time of juice pops. She gets five small paper cups and five wooden sticks for "handles" for her frozen pops. She finds a measuring cup and measuring spoons, and a bigger spoon for stirring. Then, she opens a bottle of grape juice. She also has a pitcher of water handy, and a pen for writing on the cups.

On one cup, she writes *water*, and fills the cup with water. On the next cup, she writes *pure juice*. She fills this with juice. On the third cup, she writes *one-half juice*. She fills the measuring cup to the ½ cup mark with juice, and adds water to the 1-cup mark. After mixing this, she pours some into the third cup to fill it. On the fourth cup, she writes *one-fourth juice*. After emptying the measuring cup, she fills it to the ¼ cup mark with juice, then to the 1-cup mark with water. She stirs this and pours some in to fill the cup. She writes *one-eighth juice* on the last cup. In the empty measuring cup, she measures two tablespoons of juice. She fills the cup to the 1-cup mark and stirs. Then, she pours this mixture into the last cup.

All the cups are placed in the freezer. Every 10 minutes, she will check the pops to see how the freezing is coming along. She will keep a record of what happens for each of the five cups.

1. What is her hypothesis? _____

2. What are the variables in the experiment? _____

3. What variable is controlled? _____

4. What measurement tools does she use? _____

5. How does her plan include the use of numbers? _____

Use with page 57.

Name _____

     Copyright ©2002 by Incentive Publications, Inc., Nashville, TN.

Professor Igneous hates ants-especially on her food! She remembers a picnic once where the ants attacked her sticky sugar-apple cake. She hopes ants do not come to tomorrow's picnic at all. But, just in case they are around, she wishes she could choose food that would NOT attract ants.

What foods do ants like best? What foods might they avoid?

Design an experiment that would help Professor Igneous answer this question.

Hmmm, kibble-burger!

QUESTION:_____

HYPOTHESIS:_____

TOOLS & SUPPLIES:_____

_____

STEPS FOR THE INVESTIGATION:

_____

_____

_____

_____

_____

_____

_____

_____

_____

HOW RESULTS WILL BE SHOWN:

_____

Use with page 56.

Name _____

PROCEED WITH CARE

Professor Moses is constantly reminding his students about proper lab procedures. He has asked some of them to make a poster about safe behaviors in the lab. This is the poster his students prepared. It has some flaws.

Circle the number of any rules that are correct. Fix the rules that are not correct by crossing out wrong information and writing it correctly.

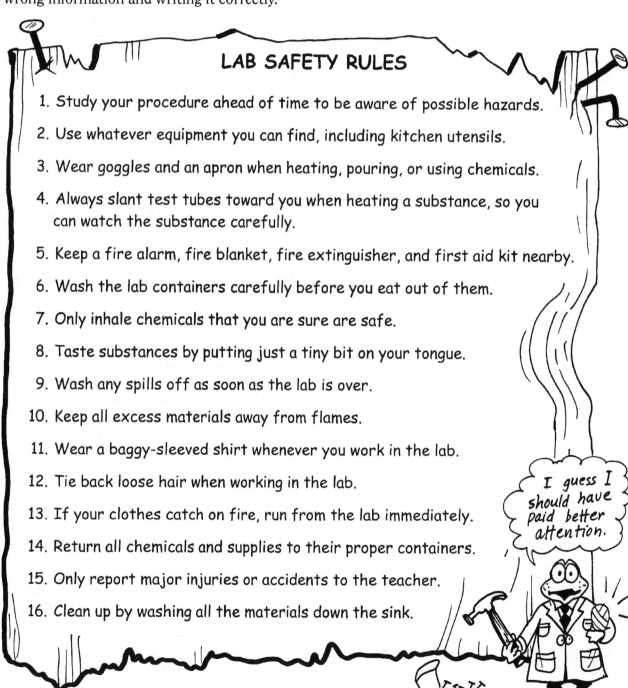

LAB SAFETY RULES

1. Study your procedure ahead of time to be aware of possible hazards.

2. Use whatever equipment you can find, including kitchen utensils.

3. Wear goggles and an apron when heating, pouring, or using chemicals.

4. Always slant test tubes toward you when heating a substance, so you can watch the substance carefully.

5. Keep a fire alarm, fire blanket, fire extinguisher, and first aid kit nearby.

6. Wash the lab containers carefully before you eat out of them.

7. Only inhale chemicals that you are sure are safe.

8. Taste substances by putting just a tiny bit on your tongue.

9. Wash any spills off as soon as the lab is over.

10. Keep all excess materials away from flames.

11. Wear a baggy-sleeved shirt whenever you work in the lab.

12. Tie back loose hair when working in the lab.

13. If your clothes catch on fire, run from the lab immediately.

14. Return all chemicals and supplies to their proper containers.

15. Only report major injuries or accidents to the teacher.

16. Clean up by washing all the materials down the sink.

I guess I should have paid better attention.

Name

SCIENCE CONCEPTS
& PROCESSES
ASSESSMENT AND ANSWER KEYS

SCIENCE CONCEPTS & PROCESSES
SKILLS TEST

Each correct answer is worth 1 point. Total possible points = 66

*1–16: Which field of science is related to each of the topics listed here?
Write a letter from the list.*

_____ 1. insects

_____ 2. blood

_____ 3. rocks

_____ 4. fish

_____ 5. heredity

_____ 6. diseases

_____ 7. plants

_____ 8. cells

_____ 9. soils and crops

_____ 10. the human mind

_____ 11. organisms and their environment

_____ 12. substances at very low temperatures

_____ 13. the structure of matter

_____ 14. the structure of organisms

_____ 15. prehistoric life

_____ 16. functions of living matter

A. paleontology
B. ornithology
C. histology
D. entomology
E. physiology
F. hematology
G. chemistry
H. anatomy
I. psychology
J. agronomy
K. cytology
L. physics
M. botany
N. petrology
O. geology
P. genetics
Q. pathology
R. ecology
S. cryogenics
T. ichthyology

*17–26: Decide which statements below are true.
Circle their numbers.*

17. Technology is the use of scientific discoveries.

18. Math is rarely a part of scientific investigations.

19. Most scientific ideas are absolute, and not subject to change.

20. Fields of scientific study rarely overlap with one another.

21. Scientists researching the same problem often find and publish different results.

22. A scientific law is an explanation based on many observations during repeated experiments.

23. Scientists disregard personal beliefs and ethics when they carry out scientific inquiry.

24. There is no right or wrong way to solve a scientific problem.

25. Scientists use models to represent actual objects, systems, or ideas.

26. A scientific theory becomes a law when it has been sufficiently tested and validated.

27. Which of the following is theory and not a law? *(Circle only one answer.)*

    A. A warm object placed in a cold place will cool, and objects around it will become warmer.

    B. Earth has an outer shell of rigid plates that move about on a layer of hot, flowing rock.

    C. An object at rest will remain at rest unless acted on by an outside force.

    D. Pressure applied to a fluid in a closed container exerts equal force throughout the container.

Name

Copyright ©2002 by Incentive Publications, Inc., Nashville, TN.

28–30: Write a rule for science lab safety related to each of the following behaviors or lab situations.

28. holding a test tube while heating _____

_____

29. what to do if your clothing catches fire _____

_____

30. tasting substances used in experiments _____

_____

31. Write a benefit and a consequence for the development of the jet engine.

Benefit: _____

_____

Consequence: _____

_____

32. Write a title to show one group in which all the substances listed could be classified.

helium   nitrogen
neon   krypton
radon   argon
oxygen

33–35: Circle one correct answer.

33. Dr. Fleming's 1920 discovery that enabled the cure of many diseases was the discovery of
    a. antiseptics.   b. antibiotics.   c. anesthetics.   d. DNA.

34. Which was invented most recently?
    a. telescopes   b. the fax machine   c. the microchip   d. the electric light bulb

35. Which was discovered first?
    a. gravity   b. electromagnetic waves   c. quarks   d. penicillin

36–44: Which page (below) describes each of these theories or laws? Write A, B, C, D, E, or N (for none).

_____ 36. Law of Motion (Inertia)
_____ 37. Law of Conservation of Matter
_____ 38. Law of Motion (Reaction)
_____ 39. Archimedes' Principle
_____ 40. Continental Drift Theory
_____ 41. Plate Tectonics Theory
_____ 42. Boyle's Law
_____ 43. Theory of Relativity
_____ 44. Heliocentric Theory

A. Earth's continents have been in different positions through geologic time.

B. A moving object or an object at rest resists change in velocity.

C. Mass is neither gained nor lost in a chemical reaction.

D. The sun is the center of the solar system, with planets revolving around it.

E. Decreasing the volume of a gas will increase the pressure it exerts.

Name _____

45–52. Which concept (from the chart) is shown by each of the examples below? Write the code letter or letters of one concept to match each example. (There may be more than one right answer for each.)

BIG IDEAS

systems (SYS)
order (ORD)
organization (ORG)
form & function (F&F)
energy-matter (E-M)
change (CH)
constancy (CON)
cycle (CY)
equilibrium (EQ)
evolution (EV)
cause & effect (C&E)

_____ 45. Summer follows spring.

_____ 46. A tidal wave results from an earthquake.

_____ 47. The heart, blood vessels, and blood work together to circulate nutrients around the body.

_____ 48. The charge of an electron is always negative.

_____ 49. When a candle is lit, the wick ignites and wax begins to melt and vaporize.

_____ 50. A beaver's large, sharp teeth are good for cutting tree branches.

_____ 51. A skater's foot pushes the skate blade backward, and the skater glides forward.

_____ 52. Rain and snow fall to the earth. The run-off collects in rivers, lakes, and oceans. Water evaporates from these bodies of water and returns to the atmosphere as water vapor.

53–58: Give an example for each of the following:

53. a cycle in life science _____

54. the function of an object is made possible by its form _____

_____

55. a cause-effect relationship in earth or space science _____

_____

56. a technological advance that led to a scientific discovery _____

_____

57. a technological invention that led to a problem for individuals or society _____

_____

58. a societal need that led to the development of a new technology _____

_____

Name _____

Agnes left her bike, scooter, and skates outdoors for months during the damp winter. In the spring, the scooter was very rusty. The bike had some rust, but not as much as the scooter. The skates had no rust at all.

59. Read the observation. Write a hypothesis that could be tested through scientific inquiry.

_____

_____

_____

_____

60–65: Read the experiment. Write your answer to each question.

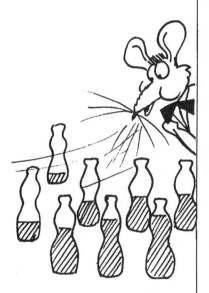

Reginald has just finished an experiment with sound. When he tapped a metal spoon against glasses of water, he discovered that the tapping produced a higher sound as the water got lower in the glasses. So he assumed that the same thing would be true if he blew across the tops of bottles filled to different levels.

He found 8 glass bottles of the exact same size, shape, and material. He filled them to varying levels with water. He labeled the bottles #1 - #8. *(The bottle with the least amount of water was #1.)* He measured the different heights of the water and kept a record of the measurements.

Then, he began blowing. He kept a record of the pitches of sound produced *(according to how they related to the other sounds).* He found that the sounds got higher and higher as the bottles got more full. The bottle with the least amount of water produced the lowest sound. The bottle with the highest level of water produced the highest sound.

60. What observation led to the investigation?_____

61. What was his hypothesis? _____

62. How did he use math in his experiment? _____

63. What results did Reginald get from his experiment? _____

_____

64. What variables were controlled in the experiment? _____

_____

65. What sound would result if one of the bottles was empty? _____

66. What explanation would you suggest for Reginald's results?_____

Name _____

     Copyright ©2002 by Incentive Publications, Inc., Nashville, TN.

SCIENCE CONCEPTS & PROCESSES
SKILLS TEST ANSWER KEY

1. D
2. F
3. O
4. T
5. P
6. Q
7. M
8. K
9. J
10. I
11. R
12. S
13. L
14. H
15. A
16. E

17–26: Circle the following numbers to indicate the true statements: 17, 21, 24, 25, 26

27. B

28–30: Answers may vary somewhat. The general idea of each answer is given here:

28. Hold the test tube pointing away from yourself or anyone else.

29. Do not run. Roll up in a safety blanket or heavy coat.

30. Never taste substances in the laboratory, except for food substances.

31. Answers will vary. Possibilities: Benefit: fast travel; Consequences: pollution, noise, safety problems with jet airplanes

32. elements or gases
33. b
34. c
35. a
36. B
37. C
38. N
39. N

40. A
41. N
42. E
43. N
44. D
45. ORD
46. C&E or E-M
47. SYS
48. CON
49. CH or E-M or C&E
50. F&F
51. EQ or C&E
52. CY or CH

53–58: Answers will vary. Check to see that student has given a reasonable and accurate example for each.

59–66: Answers will vary. Answers given here are possibilities.

59. Different substances rust at different rates. Or, different substances are more or less susceptible to rusting.

60. The previous experiment showed that higher-pitched sounds came from less water in the glasses.

61. A higher-pitched sound would result as water levels decreased.

62. He measured heights of water and counted bottles.

63. The pitch was higher as the water levels increased.

64. The size, material, shape of the bottles; the person doing the blowing

65. The pitch of the sound would be lower than any of the others.

66. Answers will vary—accept any thoughtful explanation, whether or not it is accurate scientifically.

ANSWERS

Pages 18–19

1. b	13. Soc
2. a	14. P
3. b	15. P or E & S
4. c	16. L
5. a	17. M
6. b	18. P or E & S
7. a	19. L
8. c	20. Soc
9. a, b, c	21. M
10. b	22. M or Soc
11. E & S	23. E & S
12. L	24. L

Pages 20–21

1. c	8. c	15. b	22. a
2. a	9. a	16. d	23. d
3. d	10. c	17. d	24. a
4. d	11. a	18. a	25. b
5. b	12. a	19. c	26. d
6. b	13. a	20. b	
7. c	14. c	21. c	

27. Answers will vary.
    Some possibilities are:
    a. chemist or physicist
    b. anatomist or biologist
       or archaeologist
    c. geologist or archaeologist
    d. botanist
    e. astronomer, rocket
       scientist

Pages 22–23

1. B	11. T	21. Q
2. Y	12. P	22. J
3. F	13. M	23. X
4. D	14. E	24. R
5. G	15. L	25. I
6. Z	16. H	26. S
7. BB	17. C	27. U
8. AA	18. V	28. O
9. K	19. DD	29. N
10. W	20. CC	30. A

Pages 24–25

1. b	9. c
2. b	10. a
3. a	11. b, c
4. a, b, d	12. d
5. b	13. d
6. d	14. a, b, c
7. c	15. b
8. d	16. a

Page 26

Answers will vary. Check to see
that student has changed or
corrected the statements with
reasonable changes.

The answers provided here are
possible changes:
1. Individuals CAN have an
   effect.
2. The effects of natural hazards
   cannot be eliminated, but can
   be alleviated by science.
3. Technology has some risks
   and negative consequences.
4. There are many ways to
   reduce risks.
5. Science still cannot meet all
   human needs.
6. Research IS affected by
   politics.
7. There ARE ways to reduce the
   risks.
8. Hazards CAN be caused by
   human activities.
9. Prescription drugs have
   healing effects, but some can
   have harmful effects too.
10. Some inventions bring more
    benefits that hazards.
11. Science and technology will
    never solve all human
    problems
12. Some natural substances are
    safe and healthy; some are
    not.
13. Regular exercise is ONE
    IMPORTANT thing needed.
14. Science can protect people
    from SOME natural disasters.
15. Scientists CANNOT freely do
    research on humans.
16. Use of tobacco products
    DOES have a connection to
    illness.

Page 27

Student answers will vary.
Examine the answers to see that
each describes accurately one way
science is present in each place.

Page 28

1. A, B, D, E, F
2–5. Answers will vary. Check
   to see that each answer
   gives a clear and accurate
   example of the statement.

Page 29

Student answers will vary.
Check to see that student has
given a thoughtful and reasonable
benefit and consequence for each
invention.

Pages 30–31

Student answers will vary. Make
sure student has the general idea
of the theory or law. It is accept-
able if the theories and laws are
stated in their simplest forms.

1. Big Bang Theory: the
   universe formed as the result
   of a giant, violent explosion
2. Cell Theory: the cell is the
   basic structural and
   functional unit of all animals
   and plants
3. Chaos Theory: systems behave
   unpredictably and randomly
   even though they clearly
   appear to be governed by
   well-understood laws of
   physics
4. Continental Drift Theory:
   continents were once all one
   land mass, but have moved
   from their original locations
5. Electromagnetic Theory:
   electric and magnetic fields
   act together to produce
   electromagnetic waves of
   radiant energy
6. Theory of Evolution: all
   species of plant and animal
   life developed gradually from
   a small number of common
   ancestors
7. Germ Theory: infectious
   diseases are caused by
   microorganisms
8. Heliocentric Theory: the
   earth and other planets
   revolve around the sun
9. Plate Tectonics Theory: the
   earth has an outer shell of
   rigid plates that move about
   on a layer of hot, flowing rock
10. Theory of Relativity:
    observations of time and
    space are not absolute, they
    are relative to the observer
11. Quark Theory: the nucleus of
    atoms (the protons and
    neutrons) are made up of
    subatomic particles
12. String Theory: the
    fundamental particles that
    make up objects (electrons
    and quarks) are tiny strings
    that vibrate in different
    patterns

13. Theory of Superconductivity:
    the electrical resistance of a
    substance disappears at very
    low temperatures
14. Archimedes' Principle: an
    object that is partly or fully
    immersed in a liquid is
    pushed upward by a force
    equal to the weight of the
    liquid that the object
    displaces
15. Beer's Law: no substance is
    perfectly transparent; some of
    the light passing through any
    substance is always absorbed
16. Bernoulli's Law: the pressure
    of a fluid increases as its
    velocity decreases, and
    decreases as its velocity
    increases
17. Bodes' Law: a way to calculate
    approximate distances of the
    planets from the sun
18. Boyle's Law: the pressure of a
    gas increases as the volume of
    gas decreases if there is no
    temperature change
19. Charles' Law: the ratio
    between the volume of a gas
    and its temperature remains
    constant if the pressure does
    not change OR a gas's volume
    expands by the same ratio of
    its original volume with each
    degree of rise in temperature
20. Law of Conservation of
    Matter: The mass of all
    substances in a chemical
    reaction is the same after the
    reaction as before the
    reaction. In a chemical
    reaction, matter is not gained
    or lost.
21. Law of Hydrostatics: the
    pressure caused by the weight
    of a column of fluid is
    determined by the height of
    the column
22. Lenz's Law: when electric
    current is created by a
    changing magnetic field, the
    current creates its own
    magnetic field in a direction
    that opposes the change in
    the original magnetic field.
23. Mendel's Laws: heredity
    characteristics are
    determined by units called
    genes which occur in pairs

24. Law of Motion: Inertia: an object at rest stays unless a force acts on it to move it; a moving object will continue moving at the same velocity and in the same direction unless a force acts to change it

25. Law of Motion: Action: the amount of force needed to change the speed of an object depends on the mass of the object and the acceleration required

26. Law of Motion: Reaction: for every action (or force) there is an equal and opposite action (or force)

27. Newton's Law of Gravitation: the gravitational force between two objects is proportional to the size of their masses

28. Ohm's Law: electromotive force equals the electric current multiplied by the resistance in a circuit

29. Pascal's Law: pressure that is applied to a fluid enclosed in a container is transmitted with equal force throughout the container

Pages 32–33

Answers will vary.
1. Eggs dropped by accident did not all break.
2. Why did some eggs break, while others did not?
3. Eggs dropped in a container or on a carpet will be less likely to break than eggs dropped on a hard floor.
4. They dropped 24 eggs in each of 4 different ways—all from the same height and with the same force.
5. They used eggs, egg containers, measuring tape. They collected data by counting and tallying broken eggs.
6. The eggs in containers and eggs dropped on the carpet broke in smaller numbers than eggs dropped on the hard floor.
7. The eggs were protected by the containers and the soft carpet.
8. a table
9. Why didn't all the eggs break? Did the position of the egg in the container make a difference? Would the material of the egg container make a difference?
10. Math was used to count eggs to be used, count eggs broken, and to measure the height of the drop. Math was used to calculate percentages of eggs broken.

Pages 34–35

Answers may vary. Make sure each letter A–W is assigned to one of these books, and that the choice of the placement makes sense or can be explained by the student.
1. D, L, N, S, A, G, J
2. B, P, E, T, C, H
3. H, O
4. J, U
5. C, K, M

6. F, Q
7. G, V, T, D
8. A, I, W
9. E, R
10. N, V, I, Q, L, P

Page 36

Answers may vary.
1. Other components: battery, wires
2. Boundaries: the cell membrane forms the boundary
   Input: food, water
   Output: energy, wastes
3. Components: any streams that flow into the river
   Boundaries: determined by water that flows into the river; other flowing water is out of boundary
   Input: water flowing from melting snow, streams, tributaries; silt and debris carried by river
   Output: energy created by flowing water, water vapor evaporating
4. Components: lungs, diaphragm, bronchial tubes, trachea, mouth, bronchioles, alveoli
   Boundaries: limited to these organs
   Input: air containing oxygen for cells
   Output: air containing wastes (carbon dioxide)
5. Components: wheels and rope or chain
   Boundaries: limited to the wheels and rope or chain
   Input: pulling energy exerted by an outside force
   Output: increased work or energy made possible by design of pulley
6. Answers will vary.

Page 37

Answers may vary somewhat on 1–5.
1. It will travel through water.
2. It will begin to divide.
3. It will sink.
4. It will erupt through the crack.
5. They will fly back to the Arctic.
6. 1–6–5–7–3–4–2
7. 2–3–5–1–6–4
8. fluorine, chlorine, iodine, helium, radon, krypton, bromine, argon, neon

Pages 38–39

Answers will vary. Allow any answers that give reasonable and accurate descriptions of form and function.
1. act as paddles to help duck swim and dive
2. anchors plant to bottom to keep it from washing away; floats near surface to get light
3. can be made into wires or shaped into objects
4. helps the organism move

5. keeps body temperatures normal
6. Form: elliptical; Function: changes in seasons and positions of planets
7. Form: narrow at one end, widening toward other end; Function: fits into small spaces and spreads something open
8. Form: molecules are far apart; Function: allows substance to spread to fit a container
9. Form: long, skinny, flexible: Function: reach into cracks and around obstacles to get water and food
10. Form: sleek, smooth, bullet-shaped; Function: shape with little wind resistance enhances its speed
11. Form: solid; Function: holds in cell material OR Form: very thin, permeable; Function: allows substances to pass through it
12. Form: thick in the middle; Function: refracts light rays toward each other and thus magnifies objects
13. Form: cup-shaped; Function: directs sound into inner ear
14. Form: long and skinny; Function: allows for stretching and movement
15. Form: flat, hard plastic; Function: laser can "write" on it, durable, long-lasting
16. Form: rigid, hard; Function: supports plant stem
17. Form: fluffy top; Function: floats through air to carry seeds where they can germinate
18. Form: long, skinny, hollow; Function: holds liquid, punctures skin and tissue
19. Form: long, skinny, flexible, muscular; Function: wraps around other organs, squeezes substances along
20. Form: constructed with magnifying lenses and lights; Function: allows tiny things to be seen

Page 40

1. Water turns to water vapor (evaporates).
   energy—heat;
   matter—water
2. Fire will grow bigger.
   energy—heat;
   matter—wood
3. Rock will wear away.
   energy—power of moving water;
   matter—rock
4. The plant will make food (photosynthesis).
   energy—sun;
   matter—plant cells or chlorophyll
5. The second ball will move and the white ball may stop or change direction.
   energy—human muscle power, transferred to stick, transferred to white ball;
   matter—pool balls and stick

6. Waves are created on the surface.
   energy—wind power;
   matter—water

7. Blood will flow out of the heart to the body.
   energy—heart pumping;
   matter—blood

8. The ice will melt and the tea will warm.
   energy—sun;
   matter—ice and tea

9. Answers will vary.

Page 41

1. A. C	3. A. E	5. A. C
B. E	B. C	B. E
2. A. C	4. A. E	6. A. E
B. E	B. C	B. C

7–10. Answers will vary. Check to see that student has adequately described four cause-effect relationships, one pertinent to each area listed.

Pages 42–43

Answers will vary. Check to see that student has described examples that accurately demonstrate the four concepts listed.

Page 44

1–3. Answers will vary. Answers should each give an accurate summary of the cycle shown.

1. Moon Phases: As the moon revolves around the earth, it changes position in relation to the earth and so looks different in different places. It moves from a full moon toward 3/4 visible, then 1/2 visible, then 1/4 visible, then to a new moon (none visible), then 1/4 visible, 1/2 visible, 3/4 visible, back to a full moon.

2. Butterfly Life Cycle: Adult butterfly lays eggs; eggs hatch into a worm-like caterpillar; caterpillar spins a cocoon; butterfly emerges from the cocoon.

3. Rock Cycle: Through cooling, compacting under pressure, weathering, and erosion, the three different rock forms can change to other forms of rock.

4. See that student has named three other cycles.

Page 45

Answers will vary. Check to see that student has addressed 4 different concepts and given a clear example related to each life area.

Pages 46–47

Answers will vary somewhat. These are general ideas about what will probably be observed.

1. Ping pong ball will float; golf ball will sink.

2. Spins smoothly and evenly.

3. Spins less smoothly—is wobbly.
4. Feels dry in mouth; "pinches" mouth.
5. Fork makes a dull sound.
6. Fork makes a ringing sound; fork swings.
7. Mixture bubbles and fizzes.
8. The wick curls; wax vaporizes; smoke rises; heat travels out from candle; candle wax turns liquid, etc.
9. The cup is very hot.
10. The cup is hot, but not as hot as the metal cup.
11. The cup does not get very hot.
12. Your hair stands up.
13. The egg is gooey; has a strong smell.
14. The arms seem to lift without effort.
15. The celery gets red stripes.
16. You feel a rhythmic beating in the neck.
17. A greasy streak is left.
18. The salt and sugar dissolve; the flour, cinnamon, and pepper float on the water and do not mix in well.

Pages 48–49

Answers may vary on 1–7, 11–13.
1. elements or radioactive elements
2. mollusks, animals, or invertebrates, or sea animals
3. space objects
4. units of measurement
5. elements or gemstones
6. bones
7. life processes or plant processes
8. water, copper, human body, zinc
9. ant, lobster, frog, gorilla
10. beach, barrier island, spit, tombolo
11–13. animals with segmented bodies, arthropods, animals, invertebrates, animals with many legs
14. water, carbon dioxide, wood, sodium chloride, propane
15. carbon dioxide, wood, propane

Pages 50–51

Answers will vary. Check to see that student has written a hypothesis for each example that makes sense, given the observation provided.

Page 52

1. miles or kilometers
2. gallons or liters or quarts
3. millimeters
4. gallons, liters, or cubic feet
5. degrees
6. cubic feet, cubic meters
7. hours or minutes
8. inches or centimeters
9. inches or centimeters
10. tons, pounds, or kilograms
11–15. Answers will vary.
16. He measured the weight of each person; measured to find the center of the rope; counted the people; calculated the total weights.

Page 53

Answers will vary.
1. Pitch of sound becomes lower as the glass becomes more full.
2. very low sound
3. The tongue senses different tastes on its different parts.
4. the sides

Page 54

1. sodium; chlorine
2. sodium; unstable
3. chlorine; stable
4. chlorine; sodium (or from the outer ring of sodium); sodium
5. C

Page 55

Answers will vary. Check to see that student has adequately provided explanations and answers for items 1–3.

Page 56

Answers will vary.
1. The juice will take longer to freeze than the water.
2. the concentration of the juice solutions
3. the amount of liquid in each solution (or the concentration of juice); the water is a controlled variable also.
4. cups, measuring spoons
5. measuring amounts of water and juice, timing the freezing, counting the cups

Page 57

Answers will vary. Check student plans to see that each section is adequately and sensibly completed.

Page 58

Answers will vary.
1. correct
2. Use only special lab equipment. Do not use kitchen utensils.
3. correct
4. Always slant tubes away to keep dangerous fumes away from you.
5. correct
6. Never eat from lab containers.
7. Never inhale any chemicals.
8. Do not taste any substances in the lab.
9. Wash any spills off immediately.
10. correct
11. Do not wear baggy sleeves or loose clothing.
12. correct
13. If your clothes catch on fire, do not run. OR If your clothes catch on fire, wrap yourself in a rug or safety blanket.
14. correct
15. Report ALL injuries or accidents
16. Do not dispose of chemicals and lab materials in the sink.

PHYSICAL SCIENCE

Skills Exercises

SKILLS CHECKLIST FOR PHYSICAL SCIENCE

✔	SKILL	PAGE(S)
	Define, describe, and draw the structure of atoms	70, 71
	Define and distinguish between elements and compounds	70–83
	List names and properties of common elements; compare elements	71–76
	Find information on a Periodic Table	71–76
	Identify composition and formulas for common elements	71–76
	Describe properties of different kinds (groups) of elements	73, 75
	Identify, define, and distinguish between 3 states of matter	77, 84–86
	Describe the behavior of particles in states of matter and changes in states	77, 78
	Explain physical changes: melting, boiling, freezing, condensation, evaporation	78
	Identify characteristics and properties of matter	78, 79, 82, 84–86
	Distinguish between physical and chemical changes in matter	79
	Identify common compounds and their formulas	80, 81
	Define, describe, and give examples of mixtures, suspensions, solutions, colloids	82, 84–86
	Define, identify, and give examples of organic and inorganic compounds	83–86
	Define and distinguish between acids, bases, and salts	83–86
	Define and explain concepts, terms, and laws related to motion	87–90
	Define and give examples of forces	87, 92, 93
	Define and explain energy; describe different forms of energy	89–93, 97, 100–103, 108
	Calculate speed, time, and distance	90
	Define and describe concepts and terms related to heat	91
	Identify and explain six types of machines	94, 95
	Describe features of radio waves, microwaves, X-rays and gamma rays	96, 97
	Define and describe waves, diagram and explain features of a transverse wave	96, 97
	Define sound and vibrations, and describe properties of sound	98, 99
	Explain how sound travels	98, 99
	Explain and give examples of static electricity	100, 101
	Define and describe electric current; distinguish between kinds of current	102
	Describe and diagram parallel and series circuits	102
	Define electric power and calculate it in watts	103
	Define light; explain reflection, refraction, transparent, translucent, opaque	104–106
	Show understanding of properties of light	104–106
	Explain how color is seen and why objects have color	105
	Explain how mirrors and lenses work	106
	Describe and define properties of magnets, including electromagnets	108
	Describe, define, and give examples of magnetic fields; explain how they work	108

ON THE INSIDE

A Greek philosopher called Democritus, who lived over 2000 years ago, taught people that all things were made of grains which could not be divided. He called these grains *atoms* because in Greek *atom* means *indivisible*. Today, *atom* is the common name for the tiny particles of matter that cannot be further divided (and still be the same substance). If you could look inside an atom, you'd find that it looks like a miniature solar system, with something in the center and other things orbiting around it.

I. Label the parts of this atom (nucleus, protons, electrons, neutrons).

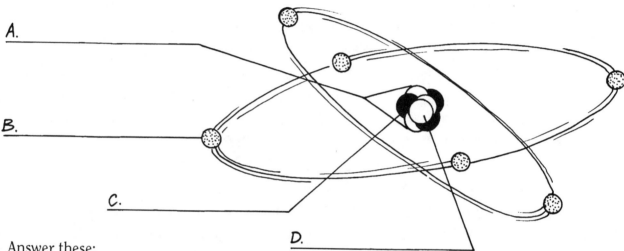

II. Answer these:

_____ 1. the part of the atom that carries no electric charge

_____ 2. the part of the atom that carries a positive charge

_____ 3. the part of the atom that carries a negative charge

_____ 4. the number of electrons that can be held in the first orbit (closest to the nucleus)

_____ 5. the number of electrons that can be held in the second orbit

_____ 6. the number of electrons that can be held in the third orbit

_____ 7. there are the same number of these two particles in an atom

_____ 8. the atomic number is the same as the number of these particles

Draw your own model of an atom with eight protons, eight neutrons, and eight electrons (an oxygen atom).

Name _____

WHICH ATOM IS WHICH?

Every kind of atom has its own unique look. All the atoms of an element have this same look.
Here's a chance for you to look at some atoms and tell what elements they are. Write the name of
the element next to each atom. You may need to use the Periodic Table to help you out. (You can
find one on page 119 of this book.)

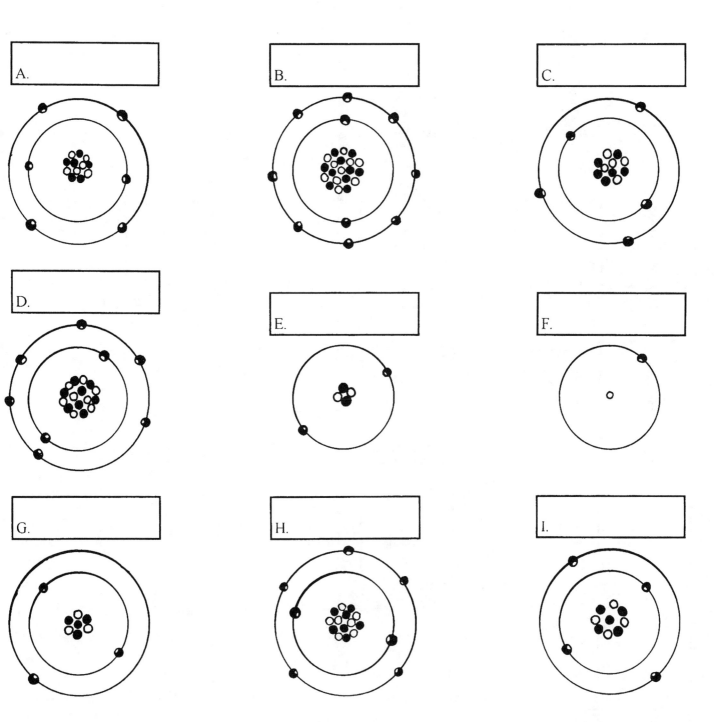

Name

The BASIC/Not Boring Middle Grades Science Book
Copyright ©2002 by Incentive Publications, Inc., Nashville, TN.

A WORLD-FAMOUS TABLE

There is a table (not one for dinner) that's probably the most famous table of science. (You can find it in your physical science book or on page 119 of this book.) If you learn how to read it, you'll have quick access to important stuff about elements. It's called the Periodic Table (because it's written in rows, called periods).

Build your skill at reading the Periodic Table by finding the missing information in the samples below. You can get more practice with the Periodic Table on pages 71, 73, 74, and 75 of this book.

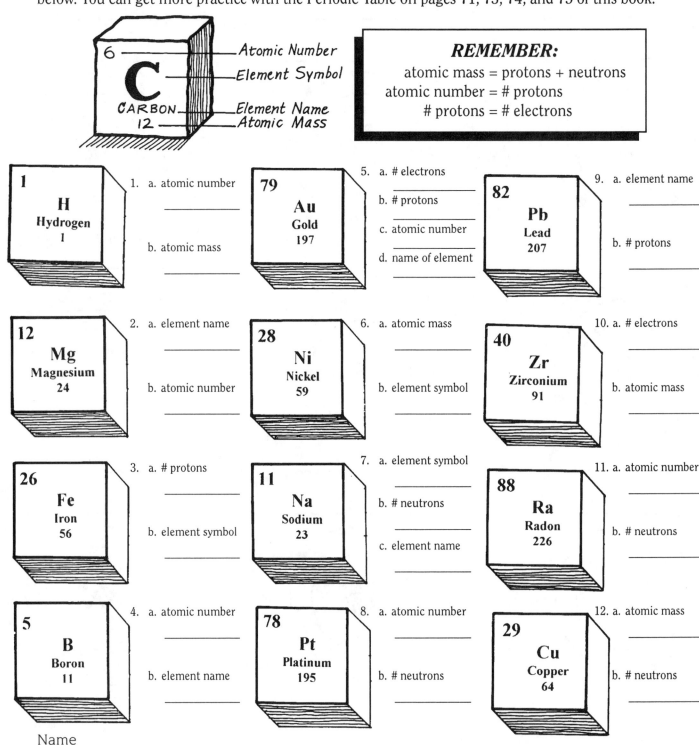

REMEMBER:
atomic mass = protons + neutrons
atomic number = # protons
protons = # electrons

1. a. atomic number
   _____
   b. atomic mass
   _____

2. a. element name
   _____
   b. atomic number
   _____

3. a. # protons
   _____
   b. element symbol
   _____

4. a. atomic number
   _____
   b. element name
   _____

5. a. # electrons
   _____
   b. # protons
   _____
   c. atomic number
   _____
   d. name of element
   _____

6. a. atomic mass
   _____
   b. element symbol
   _____

7. a. element symbol
   _____
   b. # neutrons
   _____
   c. element name
   _____

8. a. atomic number
   _____
   b. # neutrons
   _____

9. a. element name
   _____
   b. # protons
   _____

10. a. # electrons
    _____
    b. atomic mass
    _____

11. a. atomic number
    _____
    b. # neutrons
    _____

12. a. atomic mass
    _____
    b. # neutrons
    _____

Name _____

The BASIC/Not Boring Middle Grades Science Book   Copyright ©2002 by Incentive Publications, Inc., Nashville, TN.

WHO AM I?

These mystery elements are waiting to be identified. The trick is—you'll need the Periodic Table to unmask their identities. Unless you have it memorized, you'll need a copy of the table from your science book or from page 119 of this book. Read the clues about each mystery element, figure out what it is, and then write the name and symbol of the element.

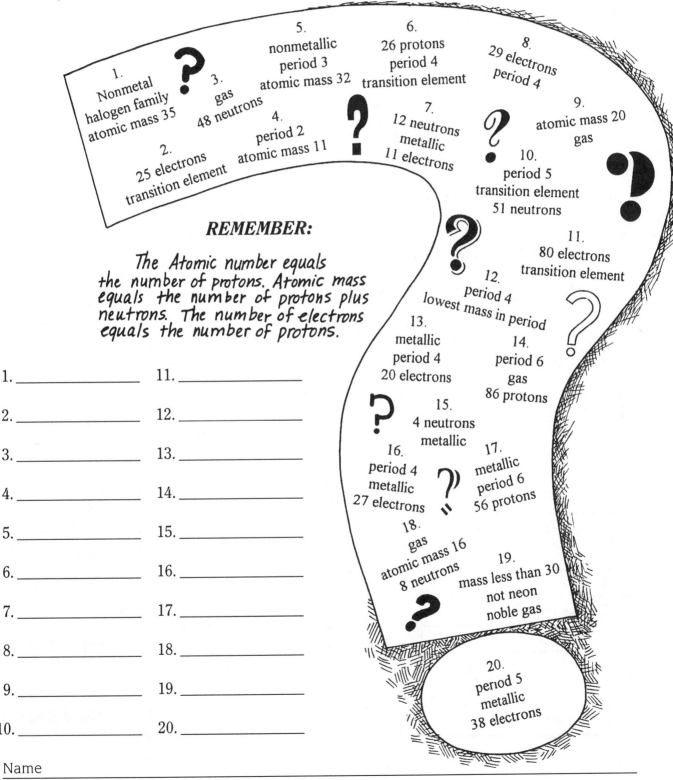

1.
Nonmetal
halogen family
atomic mass 35

2.
25 electrons
transition element

3.
gas
48 neutrons

4.
period 2
atomic mass 11

5.
nonmetallic
period 3
atomic mass 32

6.
26 protons
period 4
transition element

7.
12 neutrons
metallic
11 electrons

8.
29 electrons
period 4

9.
atomic mass 20
gas

10.
period 5
transition element
51 neutrons

11.
80 electrons
transition element

12.
period 4
lowest mass in period

13.
metallic
period 4
20 electrons

14.
period 6
gas
86 protons

15.
4 neutrons
metallic

16.
period 4
metallic
27 electrons

17.
metallic
period 6
56 protons

18.
gas
atomic mass 16
8 neutrons

19.
mass less than 30
not neon
noble gas

20.
period 5
metallic
38 electrons

REMEMBER:

The Atomic number equals the number of protons. Atomic mass equals the number of protons plus neutrons. The number of electrons equals the number of protons.

1. _____   11. _____

2. _____   12. _____

3. _____   13. _____

4. _____   14. _____

5. _____   15. _____

6. _____   16. _____

7. _____   17. _____

8. _____   18. _____

9. _____   19. _____

10. _____   20. _____

Name _____

QUARKS, ISOTOPES, & OTHER CURIOSITIES

Atoms and elements have all kinds of interesting properties and "quirks." One of them is even called a "quark." If you don't know how to answer these questions already from your study of physical science, keep a science book, encyclopedia, or other references handy to help you identify the curiosities of elements and atoms. (See the Periodic Table on page 119 of this book.)

1. Does a neutron have an electric charge? _____

2. What charge does a proton have? _____

3. What charge does an electron have? _____

4. What is the electron cloud of an atom? _____

5. What are the "energy levels" of the electron cloud? _____

6. Which energy level holds no more than 8 electrons? _____

7. Can there be 4 electrons in the first energy level? _____

8. Can there be 20 electrons in the third energy level? _____

9. How many electrons can there be in a level beyond the third? _____

10. If an atom has 16 electrons, how many are in the third level? _____

11. If an atom has 26 electrons, what is the least number of energy levels it has? _____

12. What is an isotope? _____

13. If a hydrogen atom has 2 neutrons, is it an isotope? _____

14. If a hydrogen atom has a mass of 3, is it an isotope? _____

15. What is a quark? _____

CHARGES

POSITIVE

NEGATIVE

NEUTRAL

ENERGY LEVELS

ELECTRON CLOUDS

QUARKS

ISOTOPES

Complete the chart below. Fill in the number of electrons in each energy level.

Element	Total	Level 1	Level 2	Level 3
A. Carbon				
B. Mercury				
C. Calcium				
D. Krypton				
E. Neon				
F. Arsenic				
G. Sodium				

Name _____

 Copyright ©2002 by Incentive Publications, Inc., Nashville, TN.

ELEMENTARY FACTS

Get to know common elements a little better by tracking down the facts that match these clues. They're lurking around the edges of the page; you just have to figure out which one belongs where.

mercury

allotrope

carbon

aluminum

iron

silicon

properties

ore

alkali

organic

metals

_____ 1. vertical columns in the Periodic Table

_____ 2. elements in families have similar _____

_____ 3. family of "salt-producing" elements

_____ 4. family in Group 18 on Periodic Table

_____ 5. horizontal rows on Periodic Table

_____ 6. each element in a period is in a _____ group

_____ 7. elements on left side of Periodic Table

_____ 8. elements on right side of Periodic Table

_____ 9. elements in Groups 3–12 on Periodic Table

_____ 10. number of electrons transition elements have in outer energy level

_____ 11. most reactive metals

_____ 12. most widely used metal

_____ 13. only metal liquid at room temperature

_____ 14. natural material from which metals can be profitably extracted

_____ 15. formed by metals; contains more than one element and has metallic properties

_____ 16. most abundant element in Earth's crust

_____ 17. odorless, tasteless, colorless gas; lightest of all elements

_____ 18. different form of same element due to different arrangements of atoms

_____ 19. second most abundant element in Earth's crust; found in glass and sand

_____ 20. gas element safe to use in balloons

_____ 21. compounds that contain carbon

_____ 22. element contained in 80% of known compounds

different

noble gas

families

two

halogen

hydrogen

periods

transition

helium

nonmetals

alloy

Name

The BASIC/Not Boring Middle Grades Science Book   Copyright ©2002 by INCENTIVE PUBLICATIONS, Inc., Nashville, TN.

SIMPLY SYMBOLS

How sharp is your knowledge of the symbols for elements? This puzzle is already solved, using symbols of common elements. The clues (names of the elements) are missing. See how many you can name without looking for help in any resources. Write the element name next to the matching puzzle number.

Down

1. _____
2. _____
3. _____
4. _____
5. _____
6. _____
7. _____
8. _____
10. _____
11. _____
12. _____
14. _____
15. _____
16. _____
18. _____
19. _____

Across

1. _____
2. _____
3. _____
4. _____
5. _____   15. _____
6. _____   16. _____
7. _____   17. _____
8. _____   18. _____
9. _____   19. _____
10. _____ 20. _____
11. _____ 21. _____
12. _____ 22. _____
13. _____ 23. _____
14. _____ 24. _____

Name _____

A MATTER OF MATTER

You're surrounded! Everything around you is matter because matter is anything that has mass and takes up space. You've learned about the three ordinary states of matter. The difference between these states has to do with how tightly particles are packed together and how they move.

I. Name and describe the three ordinary forms of matter below. Label each circle with its form. Then write a description of the characteristics of each state, and tell something about the motion of the molecules.

A. _____

_____

_____

_____

_____

B. _____

_____

_____

_____

C. _____

_____

_____

_____

_____

II. Match these rules about matter with their meanings.

_____ 1. Boyle's Law

_____ 2. Charles' Law

_____ 3. Archimedes' Principle

_____ 4. Pascal's Principle

_____ 5. Bernoulli's Principle

A. The amount of force a fluid (liquid or gas) uses to push up an object that's been placed in it is equal to the weight of the fluid that was pushed out of the way by the object.

B. When you decrease the size of the container that a gas is in, the gas will exert more pressure on the container.

C. Pressure put on a fluid stays the same throughout the fluid.

D. As long as you don't change the pressure of a sample of gas, the volume of the gas will increase as the temperature rises.

E. Pressure in a fluid is high where the velocity is low and low where the velocity is high.

III. Describe the fourth state of matter (use the back of this sheet or another sheet of paper).

Name _____

MOLECULES ON THE MOVE

There's something that gets molecules in matter moving (or slows their movement) enough to cause changes in states of matter. That "something" is heat—or the absence of it! The state of matter depends on temperature. When temperatures go up or down enough, almost all matter will change.

Show that you understand how temperature changes states of matter by writing an explanation of what happens to cause each of these events below.

1. The punch you poured in the ice cube trays last night is a supply of popsicles today.
   _____
   _____
   _____
   _____

2. You forgot to turn off the teakettle, and now the water is gone.
   _____
   _____
   _____
   _____

3. The cold, hard butter you spread on your toast is now soft and runny. _____
   _____
   _____
   _____

4. The big ice cubes you put in your water are now tiny.
   _____
   _____
   _____
   _____

5. The chicken soup has boiled for half an hour and it seems to have "shrunk."
   _____
   _____
   _____
   _____
   _____

6. When you put the lid on the simmering soup, the inside of the lid gets all wet. _____
   _____
   _____
   _____
   _____

7. The wet sponge you left on the counter last night is dry this morning.
   _____
   _____
   _____
   _____

8. Your little brother is crying because his snowman is shrinking. _____
   _____
   _____
   _____
   _____

9. Your mom hung your jeans outside on the clothesline, the temperature dropped below freezing, and your jeans are cold, hard, and stiff.
   _____
   _____
   _____
   _____

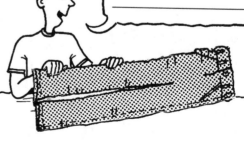

Name _____

     Copyright ©2002 by Incentive Publications, Inc., Nashville, TN.

THE TRUTH OF THE MATTER

Do these scientists know their stuff? They've made a list of "true" statements about some matters of matter. Are all their "pronouncements" really true? Write **T** for the true ones. For erroneous statements, make corrections needed to clear up the errors.

_____ 1. Volume is the amount of space a substance of matter occupies.

_____ 2. Mass and weight of matter are the same thing.

_____ 3. You find the density of a substance by dividing its volume by its weight.

_____ 4. All matter has mass.

_____ 5. In a mixture, elements or compounds are blended without a chemical reaction.

_____ 6. Compounds are chemically bonded together.

_____ 7. A colloid has smaller particles than a solution.

_____ 8. In a suspension, particles cannot be seen through a microscope.

_____ 9. Butter, toothpaste, paint, whipped cream, and fog are all colloids.

I HAVE THE SOLUTION !

_____ 10. Not all matter takes up space.

_____ 11. A boiling point is a chemical property of a substance.

_____ 12. In a homogeneous mixture, particles are spread evenly throughout the mixture.

_____ 13. The ability of metals to rust is a physical property of metals.

_____ 14. The speed of evaporation is a physical property of a liquid.

_____ 15. The density of a substance is a physical property.

_____ 16. Sublimation is the change from a solid to a gas without becoming a liquid first.

_____ 17. Viscosity is a property of a gas.

_____ 18. A solution is a kind of a mixture.

Name _____

The BASIC/Not Boring Middle Grades Science Book   Copyright ©2002 by Incentive Publications, Inc., Nashville. TN.

GREAT COMBINATIONS

Most of the solids, liquids, and gases around you exist because of their ability to combine, or chemically bond, with other elements and make new substances—called compounds. All compounds are created by chemical reactions in which the atoms rearrange themselves and share particles. Once atoms decide to bond, they often hang on tightly to their new arrangement and are not easy to split apart. Each of these groupings of atoms on this page and the next (page 81) shows the atoms that would make up one molecule of a compound. The compound is named, and the atoms are pictured. It's your job to write the formula that shows the makeup of the compound.

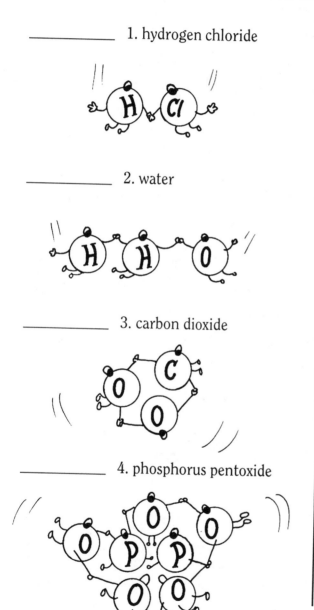

_____ 1. hydrogen chloride

_____ 2. water

_____ 3. carbon dioxide

_____ 4. phosphorus pentoxide

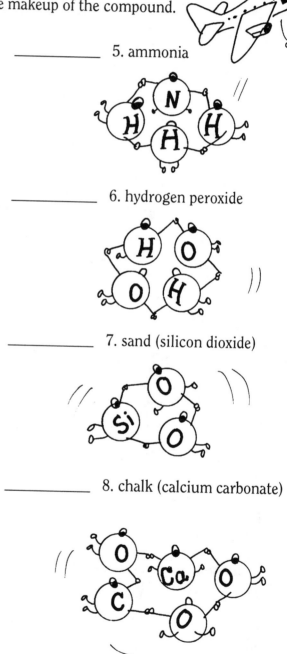

_____ 5. ammonia

_____ 6. hydrogen peroxide

_____ 7. sand (silicon dioxide)

_____ 8. chalk (calcium carbonate)

Use with page 81.

Name _____

GREAT COMBINATIONS, CONTINUED

Use with page 80.
Write the chemical formula for each compound.

_____ 9. baking soda (sodium hydrogen carbonate)

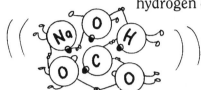

_____ 10. silver nitrate

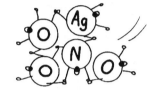

_____ 11. methane

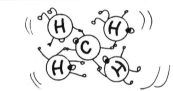

_____ 12. sodium peroxide

_____ 13. carbon monoxide

_____ 14. nitrogen dioxide

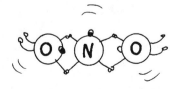

_____ 15. lead monoxide

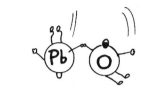

_____ 16. sulfuric acid

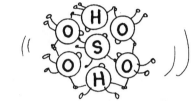

_____ 17. hydrogen bromide

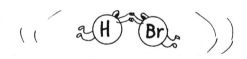

_____ 18. hydrogen fluoride

_____ 19. silver chloride

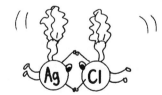

_____ 20. salt (sodium chloride)

Name

The BASIC/Not Boring Middle Grades Science Book   Copyright ©2002 by Incentive Publications, Inc., Nashville, TN.

TWO WAYS TO CHANGE

A melting ice sculpture . . . a spectacular bonfire . . . a cake baking in the oven . . . a milkshake in the making . . . an explosion . . . all of these involve changes in matter. Some are physical changes (changes in shape, color, or state) and others are chemical changes (changes involving chemical reactions). Which are which? For each change described below, write **P** for physical change or **C** for chemical change. Be ready to explain your choices.

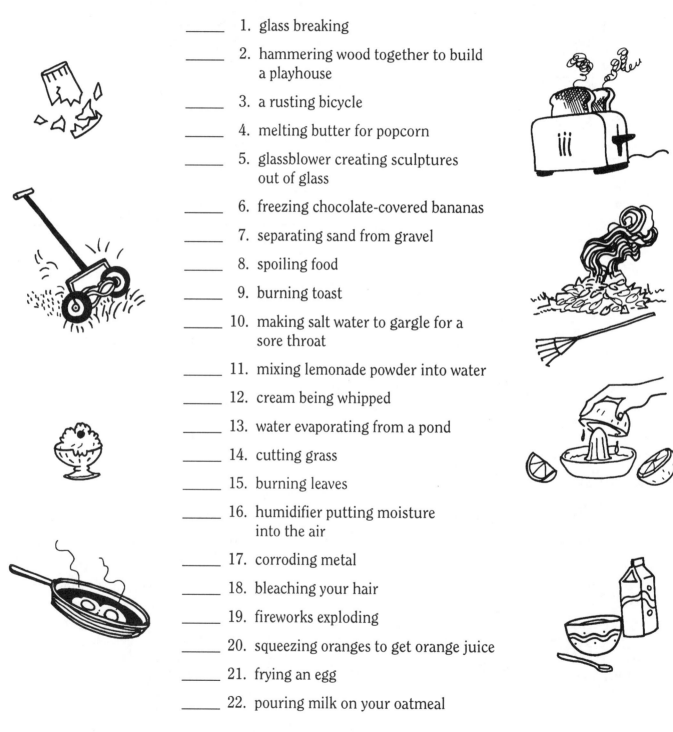

_____ 1. glass breaking

_____ 2. hammering wood together to build a playhouse

_____ 3. a rusting bicycle

_____ 4. melting butter for popcorn

_____ 5. glassblower creating sculptures out of glass

_____ 6. freezing chocolate-covered bananas

_____ 7. separating sand from gravel

_____ 8. spoiling food

_____ 9. burning toast

_____ 10. making salt water to gargle for a sore throat

_____ 11. mixing lemonade powder into water

_____ 12. cream being whipped

_____ 13. water evaporating from a pond

_____ 14. cutting grass

_____ 15. burning leaves

_____ 16. humidifier putting moisture into the air

_____ 17. corroding metal

_____ 18. bleaching your hair

_____ 19. fireworks exploding

_____ 20. squeezing oranges to get orange juice

_____ 21. frying an egg

_____ 22. pouring milk on your oatmeal

Name _____

 Copyright ©2002 by INCENTIVE PUBLICATIONS, Inc., Nashville, TN.

COMPOUNDS WITH CHARACTER

There are hundreds of compounds that are "interesting characters!" Some of them are organic—meaning they contain carbon and often are only found in living organisms. Others are inorganic. They contain no carbon and are not living, but are fascinating and useful just the same. These clues describe some interesting characteristics of a few organic and inorganic compounds. Match the right clue with the right answer. (An answer may be used more than once.)

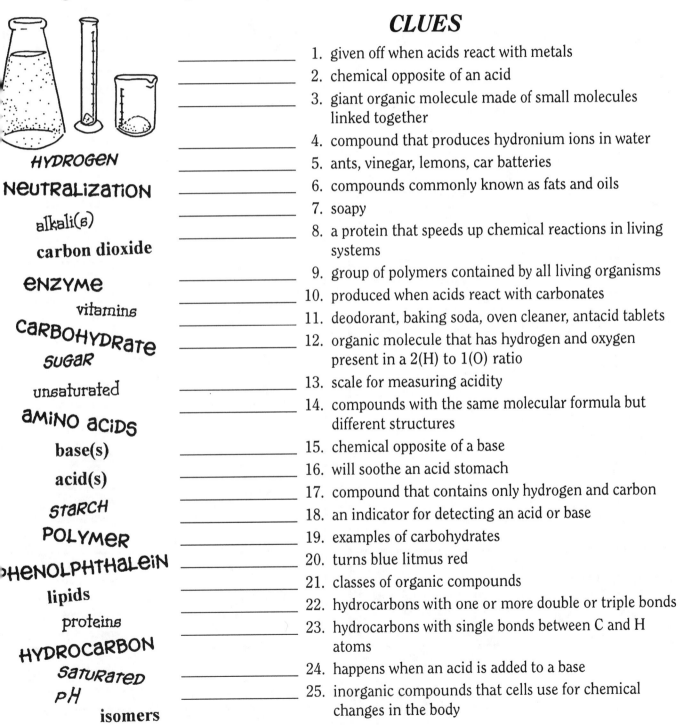

HYDROGEN

NEUTRALIZATION

alkali(s)

carbon dioxide

ENZYME

vitamins

CARBOHYDRATE

SUGAR

unsaturated

AMINO ACIDS

base(s)

acid(s)

STARCH

POLYMER

PHENOLPHTHALEIN

lipids

proteins

HYDROCARBON

SATURATED

pH

isomers

CLUES

1. given off when acids react with metals
2. chemical opposite of an acid
3. giant organic molecule made of small molecules linked together
4. compound that produces hydronium ions in water
5. ants, vinegar, lemons, car batteries
6. compounds commonly known as fats and oils
7. soapy
8. a protein that speeds up chemical reactions in living systems
9. group of polymers contained by all living organisms
10. produced when acids react with carbonates
11. deodorant, baking soda, oven cleaner, antacid tablets
12. organic molecule that has hydrogen and oxygen present in a 2(H) to 1(O) ratio
13. scale for measuring acidity
14. compounds with the same molecular formula but different structures
15. chemical opposite of a base
16. will soothe an acid stomach
17. compound that contains only hydrogen and carbon
18. an indicator for detecting an acid or base
19. examples of carbohydrates
20. turns blue litmus red
21. classes of organic compounds
22. hydrocarbons with one or more double or triple bonds
23. hydrocarbons with single bonds between C and H atoms
24. happens when an acid is added to a base
25. inorganic compounds that cells use for chemical changes in the body

Name

CHEMISTRY CHALLENGE

Take the challenge to win $10,000! Do it by writing the question for every answer on the game board. Questions get harder as the value increases. You win the first amount for a correct answer, but you lose the second amount for each wrong answer. A correct answer for each BONUS square doubles your winnings for that square. (A wrong answer doubles the loss.) Write each answer, in the form of a question, on the answer form on page 86. When you've mastered this challenge, go on to the DOUBLE CHEMISTRY CHALLENGE on page 85. Correct answers on both pages can win $30,000!

MATTER	ELEMENTS	COMPOUNDS	PHYSICAL CHANGES
1. The three states of matter $100 (-$50)	**7.** Smallest particle of an element that has all the properties of that element $100 (-$50)	**13.** Kind of change during which compounds are formed $100 (-$50)	**19.** Point at which matter changes from a solid to a liquid $100 (-$50)
2. BONUS Matter that has no definite shape or volume $200 (-$100)	**8.** Equal to the number or protons in an atom; found on Periodic Table $200 (-$100)	**14.** Group of symbols that represent a compound $200 (-$100)	**20.** Point at which a liquid changes to a gas $200 (-$100)
3. Matter that has a definite volume but no definite shape $300 (-$150)	**9.** Region around the nucleus of an atom occupied by electrons $300 (-$150)	**15.** BONUS Formed when 2 or more atoms bond by sharing electrons $300 (-$150)	**21.** Point at which a liquid changes to a solid $300 (-$150)
4. Matter in which molecules are packed tightly together and move only slightly $400 (-$200)	**10.** Elements with 5 or more electrons in the outer energy level $400 (-$200)	**16.** Charged particle resulting when an atom loses one or more electrons $400 (-$200)	**22.** A change of matter from vapor to liquid $400 (-$200)
5. Repeating pattern arrangement of particles in most solids $500 (-$250)	**11.** The simplest element $500 (-$250)	**17.** A common compound with 2 hydrogen and 2 oxygen atoms $500 (-$250)	**23.** BONUS A change of matter from liquid to gas without boiling $500 (-$250)
6. Property of liquid that describes how it pours $600 (-$300)	**12.** BONUS Elements with 1-2 electrons in the outer energy level $600 (-$300)	**18.** The chemical formula for magnesium chloride $600 (-$300)	**24.** Factor that usually contributes to physical change in the state of matter $600 (-$300)

Take the Chemistry Challenge and win big! Score points by writing the correct question for each answer on the game board. Watch out! The higher you score, the harder the questions become! A BONUS earns double value for a correct question, but you risk losing double as well. So, bone up on your Chemistry trivia.

Name _____

DOUBLE CHEMISTRY CHALLENGE

Take this challenge to win $20,000! Do it by writing the correct question for every answer on the game board. Questions get harder as the value increases. You win the first amount for a correct answer, but you lose the second amount for each wrong answer. A correct answer for each BONUS square doubles your winnings for that square. (A wrong answer doubles the loss.) Write each answer, in the form of a question, on the answer form on page 86. If you combine this with the CHEMISTRY CHALLENGE on page 84, you can win up to $30,000!

MIXTURES & SOLUTIONS	CHEMICAL REACTIONS	ORGANIC CHEMISTRY	ACIDS, BASES, & SALTS
1. Substance in which a solute is dissolved $200 (-$100)	**7.** A factor that speeds up a chemical reaction $200 (-$100)	**13.** Element found in all organic compounds $200 (-$100)	**19.** Substance that produces hydrogen ions in water $200 (-$100)
2. The amount of solute that can be dissolved in an amount of solvent $400 (-$200)	**8.** BONUS Released or absorbed in a chemical change $400 (-$200)	**14.** Compounds that contain only carbon and hydrogen atoms $400 (-$200)	**20.** Blue or red indicator used to test for acids or bases $400 (-$200)
3. When all the solute a solution can hold is dissolved $600 (-$300)	**9.** A factor that slows down a chemical reaction $600 (-$300)	**15.** Compounds with the same molecular formula but different structures $600 (-$300)	**21.** BONUS Measure of acidity in terms of hydroniumn ion concentration $600 (-$300)
4. Mixture in which substances are not spread out evenly $800 (-$400)	**10.** Shows changes that take place during a chemical reaction $800 (-$400)	**16.** Giant molecule made of many small organic molecules linked together $800 (-$400)	**22.** Common household base compound formed from nitrogen and hydrogen $800 (-$400)
5. An insoluble solid in a liquid $1000 (-$500)	**11.** An insoluble substance that crystallizes out of solution $1000 (-$500)	**17.** BONUS Organic molecules with ratio of 2 hydrogen atoms to one oxygen atom $1000 (-$500)	**23.** Strong base commonly known as lye $1000 (-$500)
6. BONUS A way of separating 2 liquids which have different boiling points $1200 (-$600)	**12.** Reaction that combines 2 or more substances into a new compound $1200 (-$600)	**18.** Organic compound with carboxylic acid group and amino group $1200 (-$600)	**24.** Formed from a positive ion from a base and a negative ion from an acid $1200 (-$600)

Name

The BASIC/Not Boring Middle Grades Science Book   Copyright ©2002 by Incentive Publications, Inc., Nashville, TN.

SCORE SHEET FOR CHEMISTRY CHALLENGES

Use with pages 84 and 85.
*—Bonus; doubles value

MATTER   Score

$100 _____

*$200 _____

$300 _____

$400 _____

$500 _____

$600 _____

ELEMENTS   Score

$100 _____

$200 _____

$300 _____

$400 _____

$500 _____

*$600 _____

COMPOUNDS   Score

$100 _____

$200 _____

*$300 _____

$400 _____

$500 _____

$600 _____

PHYSICAL CHANGES   Score

$100 _____

$200 _____

$300 _____

$400 _____

*$500 _____

$600 _____

MIXTURES & SOLUTIONS   Score

$200 _____

$400 _____

$600 _____

$800 _____

$1000 _____

*$1200 _____

CHEMICAL REACTIONS   Score

$200 _____

*$400 _____

$600 _____

$800 _____

$1000 _____

$1200 _____

ORGANIC CHEMISTRY   Score

$200 _____

$400 _____

$600 _____

$800 _____

*$1000 _____

$1200 _____

ACIDS, BASES, & SALTS   Score

$200 _____

$400 _____

*$600 _____

$800 _____

$1000 _____

$1200 _____

TOTAL SCORE _____   TOTAL SCORE _____

TOTAL CHALLENGE & DOUBLE CHALLENGE SCORE _____
Possible Winnings: $30,000

You can play this game with a group, too. You'll need to make up new rules, new
scoring directions, and whatever you need to make it a fun, challenging game.

Name _____

NOTIONS ABOUT MOTIONS

Skydivers leaping out of an airplane, kids doing tricks on skateboards, rollercoasters circling in upside-down loops, commuters riding on subways, people dancing—motion is all around us. In order to describe a motion, you have to know where the object begins. The beginning position (the skydiver in the airplane) is the reference point from which you can describe the distance moved (200 feet into a freefall). Many other terms are used to describe aspects of motion. Many of them are scrambled below. Find the scrambled term that matches each clue. Then unscramble it, and write it next to the clue.

yolevict   deeps   tear   talicecerona

trainie   noctrifi   ster   smas   snotnew

tommemun   nertlaim   ira traicnesse

tridenioc   spira   noholzatir   clatrive

lateptricne   crofe

vragyti   sperruse

_____ 1. the rate of change in velocity
_____ 2. describes the speed and direction of an object
_____ 3. the amount of an object
_____ 4. the greatest velocity a falling object reaches
_____ 5. velocity parallel to Earth's surface
_____ 6. the force on an object pulling toward the center of a circular path
_____ 7. the rate of change in position (or rate of motion)
_____ 8. ratio between two different quantities
_____ 9. property of a body that resists any change in velocity
_____ 10. zero velocity
_____ 11. mass of an object multiplied by its velocity
_____ 12. upward force of air against a moving object
_____ 13. velocity in an up or down direction
_____ 14. unit of measurement for force
_____ 15. a push or pull exerted on one body by another
_____ 16. Forces always come in _____ .
_____ 17. Two objects with the same velocity must be moving in the same _____ .
_____ 18. a force that acts on all objects on Earth
_____ 19. the force that opposes the motion of two touching surfaces
_____ 20. amount of force per unit area

Name _____

WHICH LAW?

We're told that Sir Isaac Newton discovered some things about motion when an apple dropped on his head. Whatever "force" was behind his discoveries, we have benefited from his discoveries.

Here are his three laws of motion. You should be familiar with them. Fill in the missing words in each of the three laws. Then tell which law fits each example below.

Which law? First, Second, or Third?

_____ 1. A frog leaping upward off his lily pad is pulled downward by gravity and lands on another lily pad instead of continuing on in a straight line.

_____ 2. As the fuel in a rocket ignites, the force of the gas expansion and explosion pushes out the back of the rocket and pushes the rocket forward.

_____ 3. When you are standing up in a subway train, and the train suddenly stops, your body continues to go forward.

_____ 4. After you start up your motorbike, as you give it more gas, it goes faster.

_____ 5. A pitched baseball goes faster than one that is gently thrown.

_____ 6. A swimmer pushes water back with her arms, but her body moves forward.

_____ 7. As an ice skater pushes harder with his leg muscles, he begins to move faster.

_____ 8. When Bobby, age 5, and his dad are skipping pebbles on the pond, the pebbles that Bobby's dad throws go farther and faster than his.

_____ 9. When you paddle a canoe, the canoe goes forward.

_____ 10. A little girl who has been pulling a sled behind her in the snow is crying because when she stopped to tie her hat on, the sled kept moving and hit her in the back of her legs.

NEWTON'S FIRST LAW OF MOTION:

An object at _____ stays at _____ or an object that is _____ at a _____ in a straight _____ keeps moving at that _____ unless another _____ acts on it.

NEWTON'S SECOND LAW OF MOTION:

The amount of _____ needed to make an object change its _____ depends on the _____ of the object and the _____ required.

NEWTON'S THIRD LAW OF MOTION:

For every _____ (or force), there is an _____ and _____ action (or force).

Name _____

WHAT'S YOUR MOTION IQ?

Do you know the difference between velocity and inertia? . . . acceleration and rate? . . . speed and velocity? . . . gravity and centripetal force? . . . momentum and inertia? . . . friction and air resistance? If you have those all straight, you'll be able to tell which is operating in each of these examples. Choose from the list of terms. A term may be used more than once.

1. A car hits a tree and doesn't stop, but keeps going until it's severely damaged. Why? _____

2. When a space capsule returns to Earth after a mission, it glows red-hot as it enters the atmosphere because of _____ .

3. Mark and his friends love the Terminator roller coaster because of its two 360° loops. Nobody falls out when the cars are upside-down because of _____ .

rate
distance
inertia
centripetal force
gravity
friction
velocity
acceleration
air resistance
momentum

AND AWAY WE GO!

4. Josh and Ramon head toward each other on their rollerblades at the same, breakneck speed. But, because they are going opposite directions, they do not share the same _____ .

5. The blade of an ice skate melts the ice beneath it and reduces _____ .

6. Joleen shoots an arrow at a target many feet away, but the arrow curves toward the ground before it gets to the target, due to the force of _____ .

7. The sleek shape of a bobsled reduces _____ and allows greater speeds.

8. A pool player hits the eight ball which slams into a second ball. The eight ball stops, but the second ball goes forward, because of _____ .

9. Michael waxes his skis so they'll go faster. He's reducing the force of _____ .

10. Scott falls off his skateboard. He comes to a crashing stop against the sidewalk, but his skateboard rolls on because of _____ .

11. Showing off, Megan swings a bucket of water around in circles, upside-down. No water spills out. Why?_____

12. The snowboard sits at the bottom of the hill, unmoving, until Andrea gets on it and pushes it along. _____ kept it from moving.

13. Jim's little sister isn't swinging very high, so he gives her a huge push to get her higher. This shows an increase in _____ .

14. Kate drops her math paper out of her second floor bedroom window to share with her friend, Evan, who is waiting below. It takes a really long time for the paper to get down to him because of _____ .

15. Tom bragged to Tara that he watched a centipede crawl the whole length of his room in the time he did his homework. His room is 16 feet long and his homework took 2.5 hours, so he's saying the centipede traveled at 6.4 feet per hour. What characteristic of motion has he calculated?_____

Name _____

PROBLEMS WITH TRAINS

What is it about trains that makes them so popular in problems about motion? Well, probably it's the fact that it's usually speeding along or chugging along in a steady motion—going somewhere beyond wherever you are. In keeping with the tradition of train problems, practice your calculations with rate of motion by solving these questions.

> **REMEMBER:**
> Distance = rate x time
> SO: Time = distance ÷ rate
> AND: Rate = distance ÷ time

1. The *Midnight Express* heading west from Chicago to Albuquerque travels at 100 mph for 160 miles. How much time does this take?

2. A train that's heading west leaves a station at the same time that an east-bound train 840 miles away leaves its station. They both travel at an average speed of 120 mph. How long will it take before they meet?

3. If the *West Coast Skyliner* is traveling north at 120 mph and the *Skyliner II* is traveling south at 120 mph, do these trains have the same speed? Do they have the same velocity?

4. The *Black Giant* heads west for 16 hours traveling at an average speed of 120 mph. The *Speed Demon* leaves the same station and heads west on a parallel track, traveling at 95 mph for 20 hours. After these amounts of time, which train will have covered more distance?

5. Two trains leave their stations, which are 2860 miles apart, at the same time—8:00 A.M. central time. They both travel at 110 mph toward each other on the same track. At what time (central time) will they meet?

6. The *Rocky Mountain Cruiser* covers 3105 miles in 27 hours. What is its rate?

7. You are on a train that is going east at 95 mph. You are walking at 5 mph toward the front of the train. In relation to the passengers seated on the train, how fast are you moving?

8. In the same situation above, how fast are you moving in relation to the kid standing beside the railroad track, watching the train go by?

9. The *Appalachian Express* and the *Mississippi Streamer,* starting 2184 miles apart, leave at the same time, heading toward each other. They meet in 12 hours. The *Appalachian Express* has traveled at a rate of 85 mph, and the *Mississippi Streamer* has traveled at a rate of 97 mph. How far has the *Mississippi Streamer* traveled when they meet?

10. The *Quebec Racer* travels for 6 hours at 105 mph. The *Chicago Skyscraper* travels for 8.5 hours at 92 mph. Which train covers more distance? How much more?

Name

THE HEAT IS ON

You reach out to stir the soup and the spoon burns your hand. Your can of soda was icy cold just half an hour ago, but now it's lukewarm. The basement of your house is cool, even on a sweltering hot day. You're sweating in your black shirt on a sunny day, but your friend is comfortable in her white shirt. You ski outside all day on a sub-zero, blizzardy day. You're warm in your living room even though you're 20 feet across the room from the heater. All these things are true because of the amazing talent of heat energy (it can be transferred) and the equally amazing talents of some materials that put up resistance to heat transfer. Use your knowledge about heat energy to do these two tasks:

I. Fill in the diagram below, and write a brief explanation for each method. Be sure to mention what kind of material (metal, wood, water, air, etc.) that method works in.

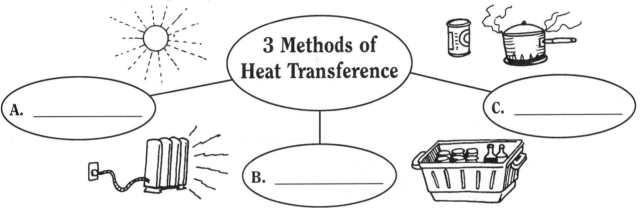

II. Give explanations that answer these questions. Use the back of the page if you need to.

1. How does heat get from the stove burner into your soup?
2. How does a cooler keep drinks cold on a hot day?
3. When two cars sit in the sun all day, the one with the black roof gets hotter than the one with the white, shiny roof. Why?
4. How does the heat from the sun, thousands of miles away, reach your body?
5. Why is the metal spoon in your cup of hot chocolate hot?
6. Why doesn't a plastic spoon in hot chocolate feel hot?
7. Why is your house warm on a cold day, even if you haven't turned on the heat?
8. When you turn on a heater, how does the warmth get to you?
9. Why are you warmer with several layers of clothes than with one heavy jacket?
10. Why do some cooking pots have wooden handles?
11. How does a cold can of soda become warm on a hot day?
12. How does a microwave oven get your food hot?
13. How can a solar heating system heat your water on a day when there's no sun?
14. How is a refrigerator an example of a heat mover?
15. How can temperature (heat) be pollution?
16. Why does clean snow melt more slowly than dirty snow?
17. Why is the attic of a house always warmer than the basement?

Name

SOME FORCEFUL LESSONS

Forces and energy—they're all around you! They keep your feet from slipping out from underneath you. They keep the moon from flying off into space. They make your favorite sports activities possible. They keep the drink in your glass from floating up into your face. They provide the thrills you get at an amusement park or on a water slide.

Make the correct choices about the kinds of forces or energy in these examples. Circle each right answer.

1. What keeps your feet from sliding out from underneath you with every step you take?

    (friction, gravity, work)

2. Why do your hands get warm when you rub them together?

    (potential energy, centripetal force, friction)

3. What kind of energy does the chain have that's pulling the car up to point A?

    (potential, kinetic)

4. What kind of energy does the car itself have at point A?

    (potential, kinetic)

5. At point B, why do the riders pop up out of their seats?

    (gravity, centripetal force, inertia)

6. At point C, what kind of energy does the car have?

    (potential, mechanical, kinetic)

7. At point D, what force is pulling the car down hill?

    (friction, gravity, centripetal)

8. What kind of energy is shown in X, when the boy is pushing by bending back his legs?

    (kinetic, potential)

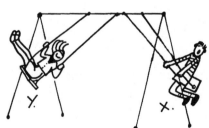

9. What kind of energy is shown in Y, when the girl's legs are extended?

    (potential, kinetic)

Use with page 93.

Name

     Copyright ©2002 by Incentive Publications, Inc., Nashville, TN.

SOME FORCEFUL LESSONS, CONTINUED

Use with page 92.

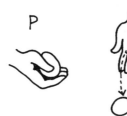

10. What kind of energy is represented by the gasoline pump? (potential, kinetic)

11. What kind of energy is shown in P? (mechanical, potential, kinetic)

12. What kind of energy is shown in Q? (mechanical, potential, kinetic)

13. What type of energy is shown here? (potential, kinetic)

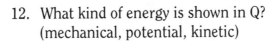

15. What kinds of energy are represented here? (mechanical, potential, kinetic)

16. What type of energy is shown here? (thermal, mechanical)

14. What kind of energy is represented by the food being eaten? (mechanical, potential, kinetic)

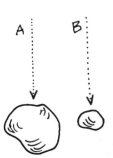

17. Which will reach the ground first, A or B? ____ Why? _____
_____
_____
_____

18. Which will reach the ground first, A or B? ____ Why? _____
_____
_____
_____

19. Where will this astronaut weigh the most? (moon, Earth) Why? _____
_____
_____
_____

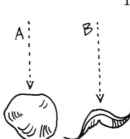

20. How much difference is there between the astronaut's mass on Earth and on the moon?
_____
_____
_____

Name _____

SIMPLE, BUT TOUGH

When you think of machines, you probably think of complex modern machines such as computers, elaborate stereo systems, cars, robots, or spaceships. Actually, machines are not a modern invention. They've been around for thousands of years. And all of them, even the modern ones, are either simple machines or combinations of simple machines.

I. Define these:

A. work _____

B. machine _____

C. simple machine _____

D. mechanical advantage _____

E. resistance force _____

F. effort force _____

II. Name each machine, and tell how it makes work simpler.

1. _____

2. _____

3. _____

4. _____

5. _____

6. _____

Use with page 95.

Name _____

The BASIC/Not Boring Middle Grades Science Book   Copyright ©2002 by Incentive Publications, Inc., Nashville, TN.

SIMPLE, BUT TOUGH, CONTINUED

Use with page 94.

III. Tell what simple machine is represented by each picture.

1. _____ 2. _____ 3. _____ 4. _____

5. _____ 6. _____ 7. _____ 8. _____

9. _____ 10. _____ 11. _____ 12. _____

13. _____ 14. _____ 15. _____ 16. _____

17. _____ 18. _____ 19. _____ 20. _____

Name _____

The BASIC/Not Boring Middle Grades Science Book Copyright ©2002 by Incentive Publications, Inc., Nashville, TN.

PROFILE OF A WAVE

Sound waves, water waves, radio waves, microwaves, electromagnetic waves, light waves, X-rays, gamma rays, and more! These are some (but not all) of the different kinds of waves traveling in the world. A wave is a rhythmic disturbance that carries energy from one place to another. The many different kinds of waves share many characteristics. Some of them are shown on this wave that's being made by kids shaking a rope up and down. Answer the following questions about wave characteristics.

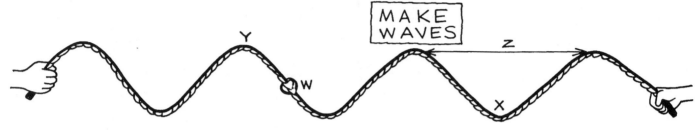

1. What is the distance called that is represented by the arrow Z?_____

2. What letter is labeling the wave's trough?_____

3. What letter is labeling a wave's crest?_____

4. The number of waves that pass the poster per second is called the _____ of the waves.

5. If the knot (W) travels 2 meters in 1 second, we say it has a _____ of 2 m/s.

6. If the wavelengths were shortened, would the frequency be higher or lower?_____

7. The greatest distance the knot (W) travels from its resting position is called the wave's _____ .

8. What kind of waves are these in the rope?_____

9. A wave in which vibrations from the first disturbance set off a series of collisions followed by calm empty spaces is called a _____ wave.

10. Radiation is the transfer of energy by _____ waves.

11. If the kids were wobbling this rope up and down through pudding instead of air, the _____ would change.

12. The rapid, back and forth movements of any object are called _____ .

13. The frequency of a wave is measured with the unit _____ , which is _____ wave per _____ .

14. If the waves in the rope have a frequency of 2 hertz, how many waves pass a point per second?____

Name _____

Copyright ©2002 by Incentive Publications, Inc., Nashville, TN.

GREAT VIBRATIONS

Waves are rhythmic disturbances or vibrations that carry energy from one place to another. The diagram below shows many different waves that are all similar, except for one thing— their lengths. Their similarity starts all of them belonging to a group of electromagnetic waves. Fill in the blanks to reinforce what you've learned about waves.

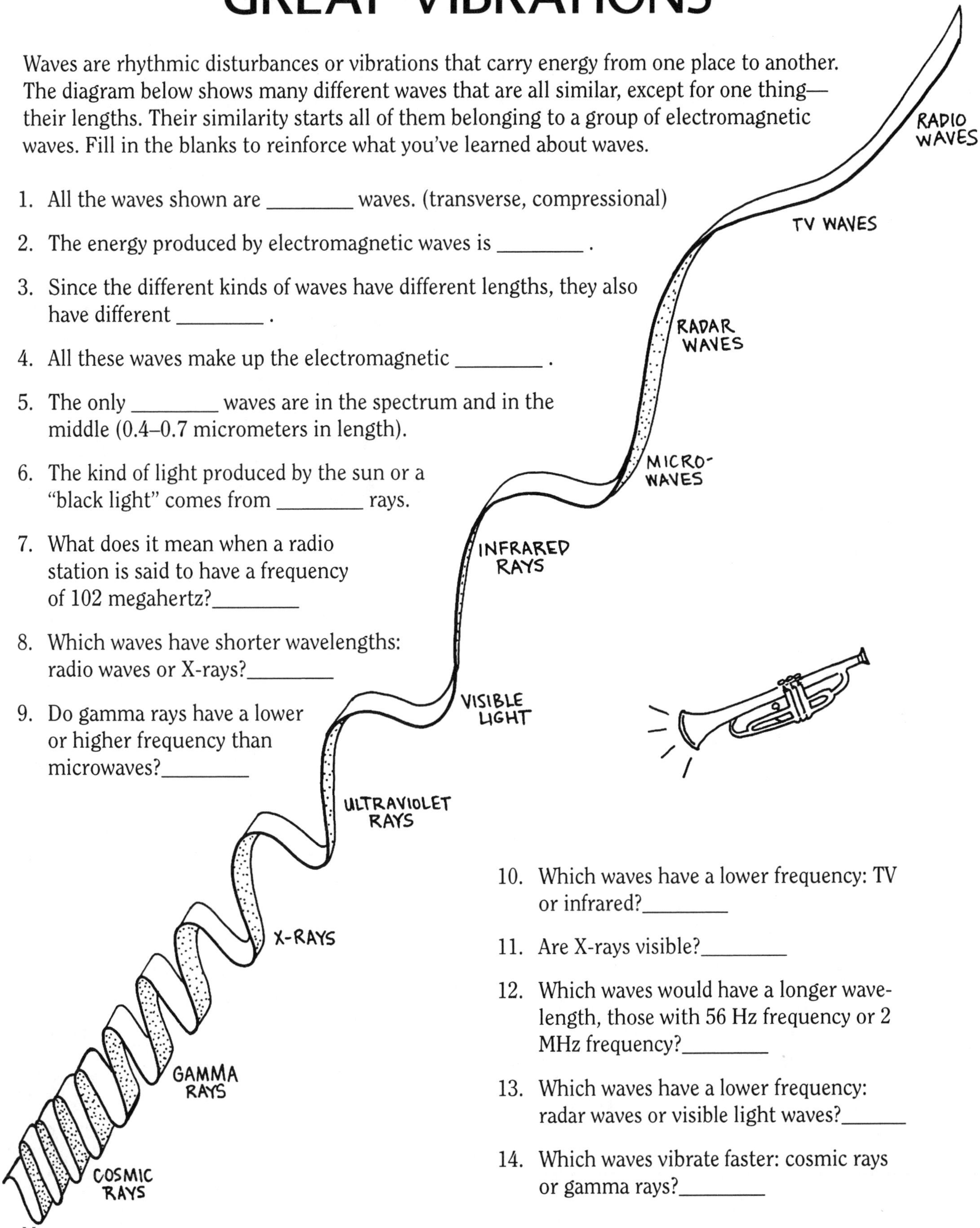

1. All the waves shown are _____ waves. (transverse, compressional)

2. The energy produced by electromagnetic waves is _____ .

3. Since the different kinds of waves have different lengths, they also have different _____ .

4. All these waves make up the electromagnetic _____ .

5. The only _____ waves are in the spectrum and in the middle (0.4–0.7 micrometers in length).

6. The kind of light produced by the sun or a "black light" comes from _____ rays.

7. What does it mean when a radio station is said to have a frequency of 102 megahertz?_____

8. Which waves have shorter wavelengths: radio waves or X-rays?_____

9. Do gamma rays have a lower or higher frequency than microwaves?_____

10. Which waves have a lower frequency: TV or infrared?_____

11. Are X-rays visible?_____

12. Which waves would have a longer wavelength, those with 56 Hz frequency or 2 MHz frequency?_____

13. Which waves have a lower frequency: radar waves or visible light waves?_____

14. Which waves vibrate faster: cosmic rays or gamma rays?_____

RADIO WAVES
TV WAVES
RADAR WAVES
MICRO-WAVES
INFRARED RAYS
VISIBLE LIGHT
ULTRAVIOLET RAYS
X-RAYS
GAMMA RAYS
COSMIC RAYS

Name

The BASIC/Not Boring Middle Grades Science Book — Copyright ©2002 by Incentive Publications, Inc., Nashville, TN.

SOUNDS GOOD TO ME

You probably know that your dog can hear sounds you can't hear. So can elephants! Dogs can hear sounds with frequencies higher than those the human ear can pick up. Elephants and other large animals can hear sounds with very low frequencies. People can hear only sound waves that have frequencies of about 20–20,000 hertz.

The scale below shows the loudness of some sounds, measured in decibels (dB). On this scale, each 10-point span is twice as loud as the 10-point category below it. In other words, a sound of 40 dB is twice as loud as sound of 30 dB. A sound of 50 dB is 16 times as loud as a sound of 10 dB.

Sounds begin with a vibration of matter. These vibrations travel outward in compressional waves. Briefly describe each of these features of sound.

1. decibel _____

2. intensity _____

3. loud sound _____

4. soft sound _____

5. amplitude _____

6. loudness _____

7. music _____

8. pitch _____

9. high pitch _____

10. low pitch _____

11. tone quality _____

12. acoustics _____

13. velocity of sound _____

14. frequency of sound _____

15. the Doppler effect _____

16. noise _____
_____

17. reverberation _____
_____

ELEPHANTS CAN HEAR VERY LOW FREQUENCIES.

DOGS HEAR VERY HIGH FREQUENCIES.

ROCKET LIFT OFF — 170
160
150
140
130
JET TAKE OFF — 120
ROCK MUSIC — 110
THUNDER — 100
POWER MOWER
90
LOUD ORCHESTRA — 80
MOTOR-CYCLE — 70
60
SHOUT
50
40
TALKING — 30
CAT'S PURR — 20
WHISPER
10
PAPER RUSTLE — 0

Name _____

Copyright ©2002 by Incentive Publications, Inc., Nashville, TN.

IT WORKS FOR BATS

You may have heard that bats find things, not with their eyes, but with the use of sounds. They make use of something called the Doppler effect to find their prey. You use it, too, although you may not know it!

The Doppler effect is a change in wave frequency that is caused when the sound source moves, or the person hearing the sound moves. The most frequently occurring instances of this effect in our lives probably are passing sirens and overhead airplanes, but the Doppler effect happens many times a day. Something produces a sound that stays at the same pitch, but to you, because of your motion or the motion of the object, the pitch seems to change (up or down). If you don't already know about the Doppler effect, study it so that you can answer these questions.

1. At which point does the pitch seem higher?

   _____

2. At which point are the sound waves more crowded together? _____

3. At which point does the sound have a lower pitch? _____

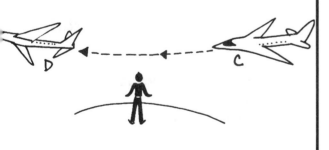

4. Are the sound waves farther apart at point C or D? _____

5. Does the sound have a higher pitch at point C or D? _____

6. Whose movement is contributing to the Doppler effect? _____

7. Are the sound waves closer together at point E or F? _____

8. At which point is the pitch higher? _____

9. Describe the sound waves at point H. _____

   _____

10. At what point is the frequency of the waves lower? _____

11. What happens to the sound as the mower approaches point H? _____

12. What will happen to the sound as the mower turns around and heads back toward the sunbather? _____

   _____

Name _____

ELECTRIFYING FACTS

What is electricity? When electrons move from one atom to another, electricity is produced. Electrons carry negative electric charges. The nucleus of each atom carries positive charges. These charges are attracted to each other, so the electrons want to move where they can join positive charges. Match up these electrifying terms with their descriptions.

_____ A. a circuit with two or more branches for current to flow

_____ B. material that electrons can move through

_____ C. flow of electrons through a conductor

_____ D. made up of series and parallel circuits

_____ E. device to break a circuit

2. static electricity 1. electric charge

3. insulator 4. conductor

7. resistance 6. electric current 5. electroscope

8. battery 9. circuit

_____ F. poor conductor of electricity

_____ G. unit for measuring rate of electron flow in a circuit

_____ H. having too many or too few electrons

_____ I. a temporary source of electric current

11. parallel circuit 10. series circuit

12. complex circuit 13. volt

16. power 15. switch 14. ampere

_____ J. rate at which a device converts electrical energy to another form of energy

_____ K. path of electric conductors

_____ L. electric charge built up in one place

_____ M. device that detects electric charges

_____ N. opposition to the flow of electricity

_____ O. electric circuit where current flows through all parts of the circuit

_____ P. unit to measure electric potential

Name _____

  Copyright ©2002 by Incentive Publications, Inc., Nashville, TN.

NOT JUST IN LIGHTBULBS

Electricity is in lots of places—including some that may surprise you. These are just a few of the things that can produce electricity. Explain how electricity is produced by or related to each one.

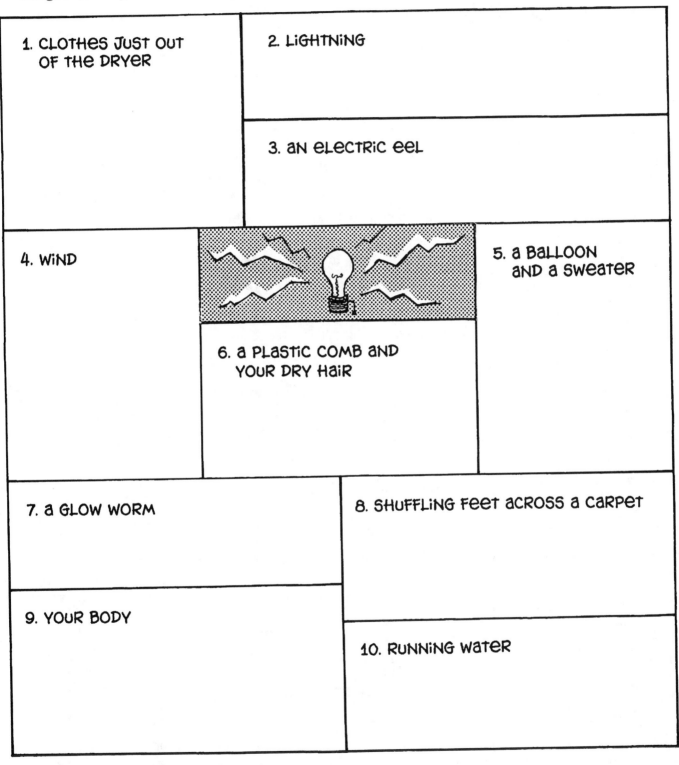

1. CLOTHES JUST OUT OF THE DRYER

2. LIGHTNING

3. AN ELECTRIC EEL

4. WIND

5. A BALLOON AND A SWEATER

6. A PLASTIC COMB AND YOUR DRY HAIR

7. A GLOW WORM

8. SHUFFLING FEET ACROSS A CARPET

9. YOUR BODY

10. RUNNING WATER

Name

     Copyright ©2002 by Incentive Publications, Inc., Nashville, TN.

KEEPING CURRENT

Are you current on your facts about electric currents and circuits? Show how "current" you are by answering these questions about currents and circuits.

I. A. What is an electric current? _____
    _____

    B. What is AC? _____
    _____

    C. What is DC? _____
    _____

II. _____   1. Which pictures represent series circuits?

    _____   2. Which pictures represent parallel circuits?

    _____   3. In which picture will the bulbs not light up?

    _____   4. Will the bulbs in C or E be brighter?

    _____   5. Will the bulbs be dimmer in B or E?

    _____   6. In F, if the circuit is broken at point X, how many bulbs will light?

    _____   7. In F, if the circuit is broken at point Z, how many bulbs will light?

    _____   8. Why do you get a shock if you stick your finger in an electric socket?

Name _____

          Copyright ©2002 by Incentive Publications, Inc., Nashville, TN.

WATTS UP?

Electricity wouldn't be nearly as useful if it stayed in the form of electricity. But ingenious devices have been invented which convert electric energy into other forms that can cook your meals, fly you through the air, dry your hair, run your racing boat—even brush your teeth! This is done with the help of **power,** which has to do with the conversion of electric energy into other forms of energy.

Electric power = the rate at which a device can convert electric energy into another form of energy.

Power is calculated by multiplying the current flow (measured in amperes and represented in the formula by **I**) by the voltage (the potential energy, represented by **V**).

$$P = V \times I$$

Electric power is measured in watts.

Use your great science and math skills—along with the formula—to solve these "power" problems.

_____ 1. A source of 120 V sends a current of 13 A (amperes) to a microwave oven to cook some popcorn. How much power is delivered?

_____ 2. Samantha's hair dryer uses 1500 watts of power from a source of 120 V. What is the current?

_____ 3. A source of 120 V sends a 1.25 A current to a lightbulb. How much power is sent?

_____ 4. If your stereo uses 192 watts of power, and a current of 1.6 A flows through it, what is the voltage of the source?

_____ 5. A turkey dinner is cooking in an oven using 2640 watts of power. If a current of 12 A flows through the oven, what is the voltage of the source?

_____ 6. A source of 120 V delivers a current of 0.63 A to a lightbulb. How much power is delivered?

_____ 7. If your television uses 420 watts of power from a 120 V source, what current is flowing through it?

_____ 8. If Brad shaves with 7.2 watts of power from a 120 V source, what current is flowing past his chin?

WHAT WATTAGE!

Approximate Power of Some Home Devices	
Lamp .... 100 watts	Oven .... 2600 watts
Toaster .... 100 watts	Stereo .... 200 watts
Hair Dryer .... 1600 watts	Microwave .... 1500 watts
Color TV .... 200 watts	Lightbulbs ..... 40 watts, 60 watts,
Refrigerator .... 1000 watts	75 watts, 100 watts, 150 watts
Clock Radio .... 100 watts	

Name _____

PUZZLING PROPERTIES

Show that you're not puzzled by the various properties of light. This puzzle is made up of words that name characteristics, features, devices, or other things related to the study of light. You'll notice that the puzzle is already finished. But something is missing— the clues. For each word in the puzzle, write a clue that is clear and accurate.

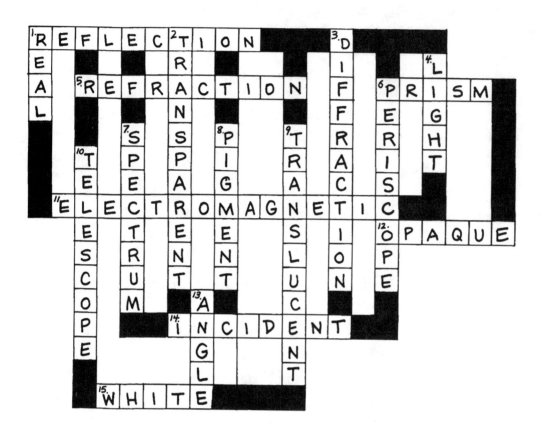

REFRACTION

CLUES

Down

1. _____
2. _____
3. _____
4. _____
6. _____
7. _____
8. _____
9. _____
10. _____
13. _____

Across

1. _____
5. _____
6. _____
11. _____
12. _____
14. _____
15. _____

Name _____

     Copyright ©2002 by Incentive Publications, Inc., Nashville, TN.

WHY WHITE IS WHITE & BLACK IS BLACK

Is an apple red in the dark? Is the coin on the bottom of the pool right where it appears to be? Can everyone see a whole rainbow? Color is a fascinating feature of light. A rainbow may be the most spectacular display of light's colors, but everyday objects and events remind us of the miracles of light and color. Here's a chance for you to show what you understand about some of the behaviors of light and color.

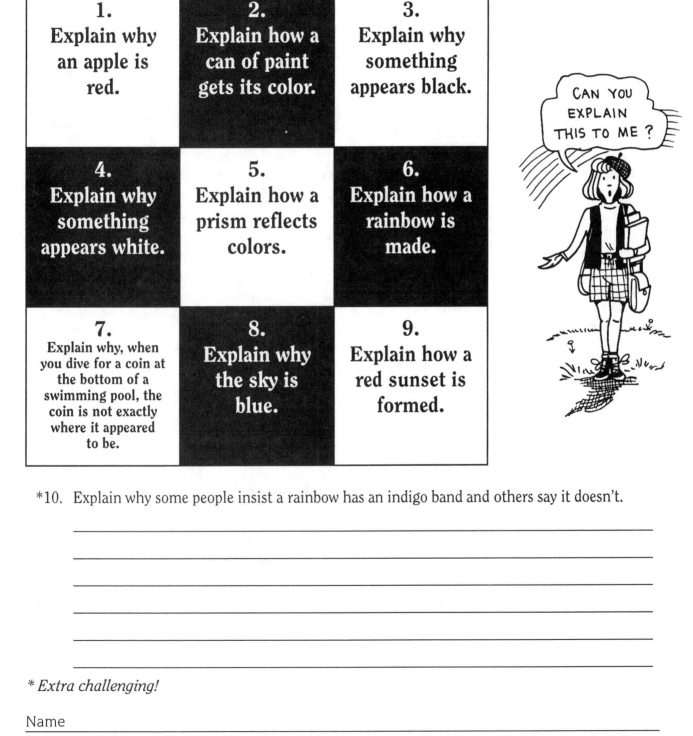

1. Explain why an apple is red.	**2.** Explain how a can of paint gets its color.	**3.** Explain why something appears black.
4. Explain why something appears white.	**5.** Explain how a prism reflects colors.	**6.** Explain how a rainbow is made.
7. Explain why, when you dive for a coin at the bottom of a swimming pool, the coin is not exactly where it appeared to be.	**8.** Explain why the sky is blue.	**9.** Explain how a red sunset is formed.

CAN YOU EXPLAIN THIS TO ME?

*10. Explain why some people insist a rainbow has an indigo band and others say it doesn't.

_____

_____

_____

_____

_____

_____

Extra challenging!

Name _____

LIGHT TRICKS

Light plays some spectacular tricks as it travels through Earth's atmosphere. It can make lakes appear out of nowhere in the desert and ships appear to be floating upside-down above the water. Rainbows, mirages, halos, coronas, blue skies, and red skies are all results of the tricks light plays. Match the descriptions of the tricks with the "happenings" below.

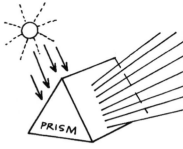

_____ 1. mirage

_____ 2. superior mirage

_____ 3. inferior mirage

_____ 4. borealis

_____ 5. blue sky

_____ 6. sunrise and sunset

_____ 7. rainbow

_____ 8. halo

_____ 9. corona

_____ 10. looming, towering, sinking, stooping

_____ 11. green flash

A. This is the most common mirage. A road appears to be wet, or a lake appears in the desert. It happens when air next to Earth is much warmer than the air just above it. Light rays from the sky are refracted and the observer sees the image of the sky turned upside-down (looking like water).

B. A luminous ring around the sun or moon, this phenomenon is caused by refraction of sunlight or moonlight by ice crystals in high clouds. When it's well-developed, three colors show: red (outer), yellow (middle), and green (inner).

C. This optical effect is caused by refraction of light as it passes through layers of the atmosphere that are not alike.

D. As sun rays pass through the thicker layer of the atmosphere closest to Earth's surface, refraction causes short wavelengths (blues and greens) to be scattered out. Only the longest wavelengths at the red end of the spectrum are visible to the observer.

E. This is a small ring around the moon or sun. Diffraction of light by tiny drops of water in clouds spreads light waves around the sun or moon. The outer edge is brown-red; the inner ring is blue-white. Sometimes one is caused by diffraction of dust after a volcanic eruption; the most famous of these is the "Bishop's Ring."

F. Sunlight entering the atmosphere is reflected by millions of dust particles and water drops (a process called scattering). Short wavelengths on the blue end of the spectrum are scattered most, throwing a lot of blue into the atmosphere.

G. Light shines through millions of raindrops which act like tiny prisms by separating white light by refraction into the colors of the spectrum.

H. These optical phenomena are caused by temperature inversions which refract light in a way that changes appearances of objects. Objects appear to be in a different place (higher above or lower below the horizon) or are stretched or decreased in size.

I. These luminous displays of colors and streaks in the sky occur over the poles. They are thought to be caused as streams of sunlight particles bump into ions in the atmosphere and cause them to glow different colors.

J. An image of a ship at sea appears to be floating above the real ship upside-down, with another upright image above it. This phenomenon occurs during a temperature inversion which causes light rays bounding off the ship to be refracted. It happens over cold land or water.

K. This optical phenomenon happens at sunrise or sunset and is seen best over a body of water. Colors at the blue-green end of the spectrum are refracted most and take longer to disappear below the horizon than the red, yellow, and oranges.

Name

THROUGH LENSES & MIRRORS

When you examine your face in a mirror, take a picture with a camera, look at a bug through a magnifying glass, or spy on your neighbor through a periscope you've made, you're making use of light. In fact, you're counting on light to do some fancy tricks—like reflecting and refracting (bending). Fill in the blanks to complete these simple explanations of the way lenses and mirrors work.

PLANE MIRROR

Light strikes the mirror and is reflected back at an _____ from the silver
1
layer at the back.

CONVEX MAGNIFYING GLASS

A convex lens is _____ in the middle
2
than at the edges. It bends light rays
_____ to a _____ point on the
3   4
other side of the lens. It can
form a real image because
it can _____ light. A
5
convex lens makes the
object appear _____ .
6

CONCAVE LENS

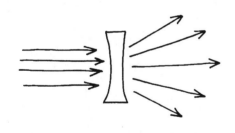

A concave lens is _____ in the middle than at the
7
edges. It bends light rays _____ from each other.
8
It cannot form a real image because it does not
_____ light.
9

PERISCOPE

A periscope is a tube with a _____ (or
10
a prism) at each end, set at a
_____ angle from each
11
other. _____ is reflected
12
from the top _____ to
13
the bottom _____ , so
14
that you can see objects
which are _____ .
15

CAMERA

A camera's opening, called an _____ ,
16
lets light into the camera. A _____
17
focuses the light into an _____ onto
18
light-sensitive _____ . The image
19
projected is in an _____ position.
20

The BASIC/Not Boring Middle Grades Science Book   Copyright ©2002 by Incentive Publications, Inc., Nashville, TN.

THE TRUTH ABOUT MAGNETS

This magnet finds "attractive" only the true statements about magnets and magnetism. Which statements will be attracted to the magnet? Label true statements with a **T**, and label false statements with an **F**. Correct the statements that are false.

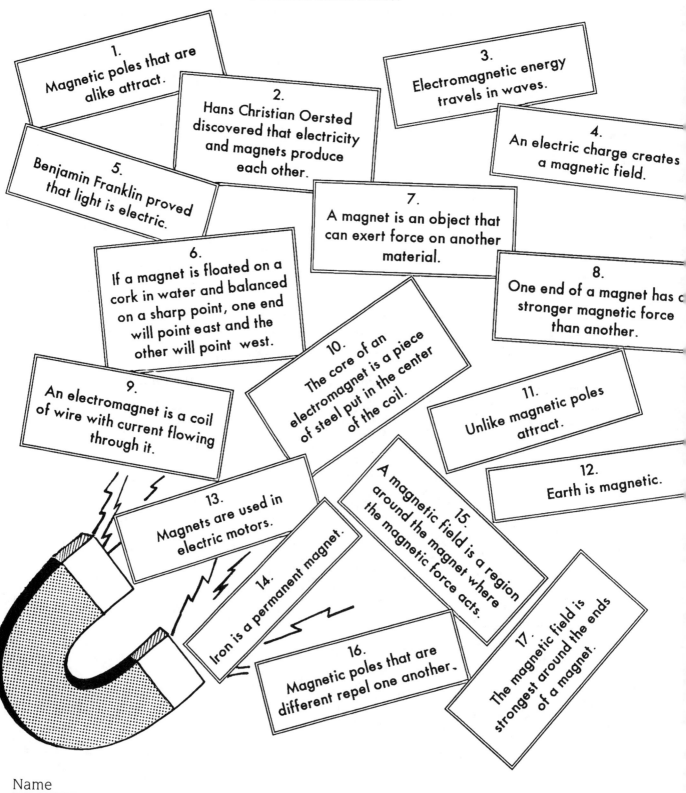

Name

Copyright ©2002 by Incentive Publications, Inc., Nashville, TN.

PHYSICAL SCIENCE
ASSESSMENT AND ANSWER KEYS

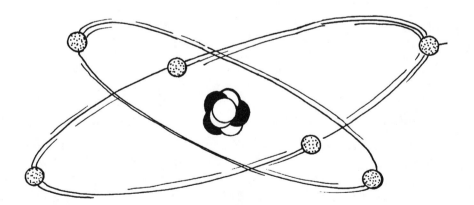

PHYSICAL SCIENCE
SKILLS TEST

Each correct answer is worth 1 point. Total Score Possible = 100 points.

For questions 1–6, use these segments from the Periodic Table to answer the questions.

A.
```
23
Na
11
```

B.
```
64
Cu
29
```

C.
```
1
H
1
```

1. What element is shown in A? _____

2. What is the atomic number of B? _____

3. What is the atomic mass of A? _____

4. How many electrons does hydrogen have? ____

5. What element is shown in B? _____

6. How many neutrons are in element A? _____

For questions 7–16, match the correct term with each definition below. Write the letter of the correct answer.

A. suspension	F. acid
B. pH	G. neutralization
C. condensation	H. base
D. solute	I. viscosity
E. volume	J. electrons

____ 7. amount of mass

____ 8. heterogeneous mixture in which particles can be seen

____ 9. process of combining a base with an acid

____ 10. scale for measuring acidity

____ 11. shared when elements combine to form a compound

____ 12. change from a gas to a liquid

____ 13. compound that produces hydronium ions in water solution

____ 14. ability of liquid to be poured

____ 15. substance dissolved in a solvent

____ 16. the chemical opposite of an acid

For questions 17–19, for each formula show the name of each element and the number of atoms represented by the formula:

Ex: C_2H_2 = 2 carbon atoms + 2 hydrogen atoms

17. $CaSO_4$ _____

18. NH_3 _____

19. NaO_2 _____

For questions 20–22, use the diagram below to answer these questions. Write the letter of the correct answer on the line.

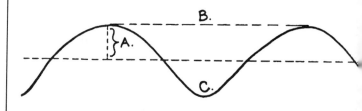

____ 20. Which letter is in the trough?

____ 21. Which letter represents the amplitude of a wave?

____ 22. Which letter represents wavelength?

For questions 23–32, write the letter of the correct answer on the line.

____ 23. The particle in an atom that has no electric charge is the ____ .
   a. electron   c. proton
   b. neutron   d. electron cloud

____ 24. The atomic mass of an element is equal to this:
   a. # of protons
   b. # of neutrons
   c. # of protons + electrons
   d. # of neutrons + protons

____ 25. Groups on the Periodic Table with similar properties are ____ .
   a. families   c. tables
   b. periods   d. compounds

Name _____

Copyright ©2002 by Incentive Publications, Inc., Nashville, TN.

____ 26. Particles found in an atom other than protons, neutrons, and electrons are ____ .
   a. polymers   c. quarks
   b. isotopes   d. acids

____ 27. If an element has 18 electrons, how many would be in the third energy level?
   a. 16   c. 10
   b. 8   d. 2

____ 28. What state of matter has no definite shape and no definite volume?
   a. gas   c. liquid
   b. solid   d. element

____ 29. At what point does a liquid change to a gas?
   a. freezing point   c. dew point
   b. melting point   d. boiling point

____ 30. Molecules will move faster and farther apart when state changes from
   a. liquid to solid   c. gas to solid
   b. gas to liquid   d. liquid to gas

____ 31. When a container decreases in size, what will happen to an amount of gas in the container?
   a. temperature of the gas will decrease
   b. volume of the gas will increase
   c. pressure gas exerts on the container will increase
   d. pressure gas exerts on the container will decrease

____ 32. Two or more elements bonded together chemically form a
   a. mixture   c. compound
   b. colloid   d. suspension

For questions 33–35, write the correct answer for these problems with rate, time, and distance.

_____ 33. Two trains are traveling toward each other from 800 miles apart, each at 80 miles per hour. How long will it be before they meet?

_____ 34. The *Speed Chaser* covers 1350 miles in 15 hours. What is its rate?

_____ 35. The *Silver Streak* travels at a rate of 102 mph for 6 hours. What distance is covered?

For questions 36–47, write the name of the element or compound that is represented by the symbol.

36. Fe _____

37. N _____

38. O_2 _____

39. NaCl _____

40. C _____

41. CO _____

42. Au _____

43. Ca _____

44. He _____

45. HCl _____

46. CO_2 _____

47. Hg _____

For questions 48–50, use the diagrams of circuits to answer these questions.

____ 48. Which circuit(s) is/are parallel?

____ 49. Which circuit(s) is/are series?

____ 50. In which example will a light be unlikely to light up?

For questions 51–60, match the correct term with each definition below. Write the correct letter on the line.

   A. centripetal   F. friction
   B. conduction   G. convection
   C. inertia   H. acceleration
   D. momentum   I. kinetic
   E. velocity   J. mechanical advantage

____ 51. speed and direction of moving object

____ 52. tendency of a body to resist change in velocity

____ 53. mass of an object multiplied by its velocity

____ 54. transfer of energy from particle to particle through matter

____ 55. rate of change in velocity

____ 56. energy of motion

Name _____

___ 57. force that opposes motion of two touching surfaces

___ 58. force pulling toward the center of a circular path

___ 59. transfer of energy through movement of a fluid

___ 60. increase in amount of work done with help of a machine

For questions 61–63, use the diagram below to answer these questions.

___ 61. At which point are the sound waves closer together?

___ 62. At which point is the pitch of the sound lowest?

___ 63. At which point is the pitch of the sound highest?

For questions 64–66, write the correct answer on the line.

___ 64. Jana is drying her hair using a 120 V source of power with a current of 12.5 A. How many watts of power is her hairdryer using?

___ 65. The oven is baking a cake using a current of 12 A and 2640 watts of power. What is the voltage of the power source?

___ 66. If your stereo uses 2 A of current from a power source of 120 V, what is the wattage of power it's using?

For questions 67–69, use the diagram of the electromagnetic wave below to answer these questions.

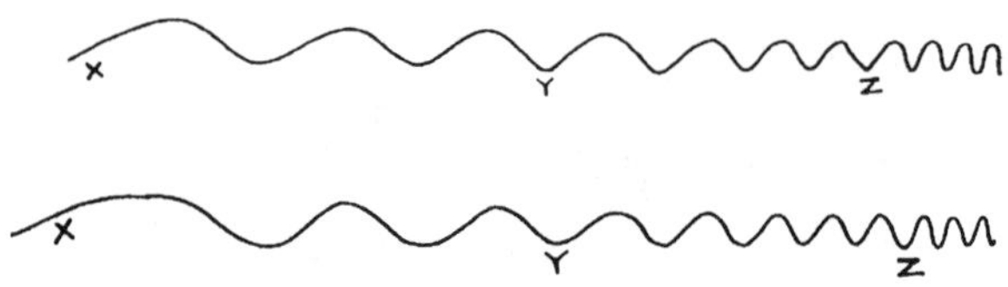

___ 67. Which point would represent visible light waves?

___ 68. Which point would represent gamma rays?

___ 69. Which point would represent radio waves?

For questions 70–78, match the correct term with each definition following.

A. direct current   D. potential   G. filter
B. indicator   E. insulator   H. effort force
C. distillation   F. lipid   I. density

___ 70. energy due to position or condition of matter

___ 71. substance that does not conduct heat or electricity well

___ 72. mass of a material divided by its volume

___ 73. flow of electricity in one direction

___ 74. force applied to a machine

___ 75. separation of liquids by vaporization and condensation

___ 76. device for separating parts of a mixture

___ 77. organic compound which changes color in an acid or base

___ 78. class of organic compounds that contains fats and oils

For questions 79–81, write the chemical formula for each molecule.

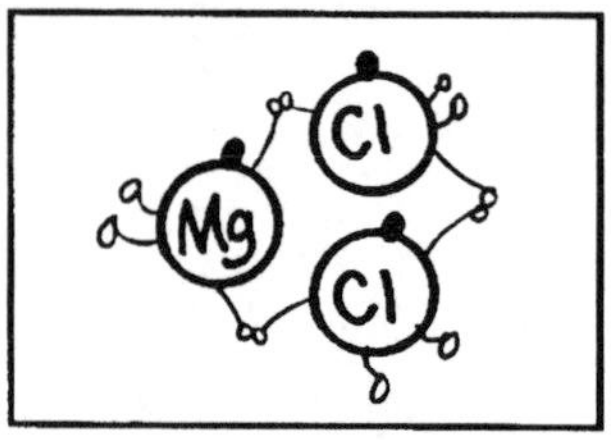

79. _____

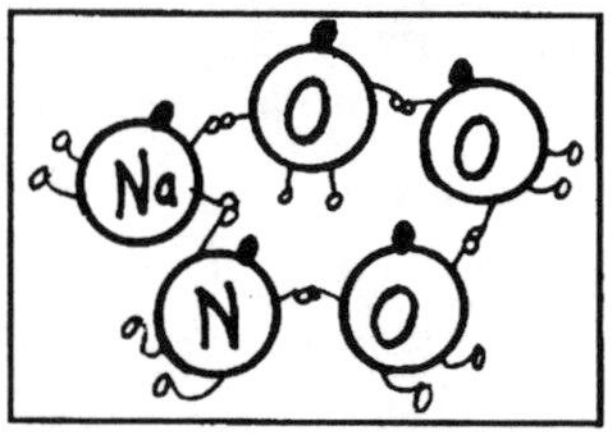

80. _____

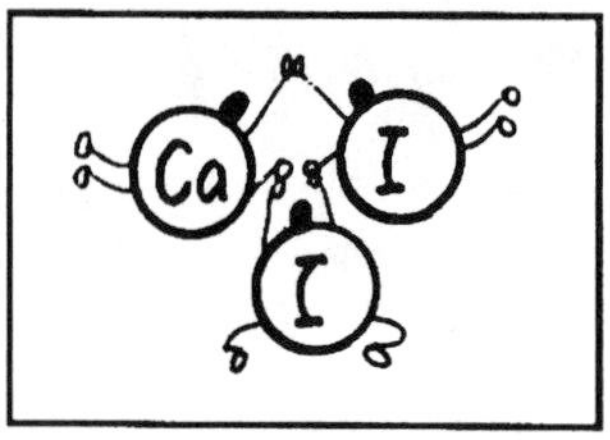

81. _____

Name

For questions 82–91, write the letter of the correct answer on the line.

____ 82. Which is not a physical change?
  a. melting butter
  b. whipping cream
  c. mixing lemonade
  d. molding bread

____ 83. Which is not a chemical change?
  a. boiling, evaporating water
  b. burned toast
  c. rusting nails
  d. bleaching your hair

____ 84. Which is not an organic compound?
  a. vitamin
  b. starch
  c. sulfuric acid
  d. protein
  e. carbohydrate

____ 85. A substance that speeds up a chemical reaction without changing itself is a(n)
  a. catalyst
  b. inhibitor
  c. acid
  d. lipid

____ 86. Which will turn red when dipped in an acidic solution?
  a. red litmus
  b. blue litmus
  c. both
  d. neither

____ 87. What causes a spaceship to get red-hot when reentering Earth's atmosphere?
  a. inertia
  b. friction
  c. pressure
  d. momentum

____ 88. What is the greatest distance a wave travels from its resting position?
  a. pitch
  b. wavelength
  c. amplitude
  d. frequency

____ 89. Which gives opposition to the flow of electricity?
  a. a resistance   c. a conductor
  b. a circuit   d. an ampere

____ 90. What term refers to the bending of light as it passes through an opening or around a bend?
  a. reflecting   c. radiation
  b. refraction   d. diffraction

____ 91. Unit for measuring electric power:
  a. hertz   c. newton
  b. kelvin   d. watt

For questions 92–96, write the correct answer on the line.

92. What happens to a wavelength as the frequency of a wave increases?

  _____

_____ 93. Which has a higher frequency, a TV wave or an X-ray?

_____ 94. What unit is used to measure wave frequencies?

_____ 95. What kind of energy is transferred by electromagnetic waves?

_____ 96. What term means the rapid movement of particles back and forth?

For questions 97–100, use the drawings below to answer these questions.

____ 97. What point is the fulcrum?

____ 98. What point is the effort force?

____ 99. What point is the resistance force?

100. What simple machine is this? _____

SCORE: Total Points _____ out of a possible 100 points

Name _____

PHYSICAL SCIENCE
SKILLS TEST ANSWER KEY

1. sodium
2. 64
3. 11
4. 1
5. copper
6. 12
7. E
8. A
9. G
10. B
11. J
12. C
13. F
14. I
15. D
16. H
17. 1 calcium atom +
    1 sulfur atom +
    4 oxygen atoms
18. 1 nitrogen atom +
    3 hydrogen atoms
19. 1 sodium atom +
    2 oxygen atoms
20. C
21. A
22. B
23. b
24. d
25. a
26. c
27. b
28. a
29. d
30. d
31. c

32. c
33. 5 hours
34. 90 mph
35. 612 miles
36. iron
37. nitrogen
38. oxygen
39. sodium chloride
40. carbon
41. carbon monoxide
42. gold
43. calcium
44. helium
45. hydrogen chloride
46. carbon dioxide
47. mercury
48. B
49. C
50. C
51. E
52. C
53. D
54. B
55. H
56. I
57. F
58. A
59. G
60. J
61. A
62. B
63. A
64. 1500 watts
65. 220 V
66. 240 watts

67. Y
68. Z
69. X
70. D
71. E
72. I
73. A
74. H
75. C
76. G
77. B
78. F
79. $MgCl_2$
80. $NaNO_3$
81. CaI_2
82. d
83. a
84. c
85. a
86. b
87. b
88. c
89. a
90. d
91. d
92. gets shorter
93. X-ray
94. hertz
95. radiation
96. vibration
97. Q
98. R
99. P
100. lever

ANSWERS

Page 70

I. a. nucleus   c. neutron
   b. electron   d. proton

II. 1. neutron   5. 8
   2. proton   6. 18
   3. electron   7. electrons; protons
   4. 2   8. protons (or electrons)

Check to see that student model has 8 protons and 8 neutrons in the nucleus, 2 electrons in the first orbit, and 6 in the second orbit.

Page 71

A. carbon   F. hydrogen
B. neon   G. lithium
C. boron   H. nitrogen
D. oxygen   I. beryllium
E. helium

Page 72

1. a. 1   7. a. Na
   b. 1   b. 12
2. a. magnesium c. sodium
   b. 12   8. a. 78
3. a. 26   b. 117
   b. Fe   9. a. lead
4. a. 5   b. 82
   b. boron 10. a. 40
5. a. 79   b. 91
   b. 79   11. a. 88
   c. 79   b. 138
   d. gold   12. a. 64
6. a. 59   b. 35
   b. Ni

Page 73

1. chlorine; Cl   11. mercury; Hg
2. manganese; Mn 12. potassium; K
3. krypton; Kr   13. calcium; Ca
4. boron; B   14. radon; Rn
5. sulfur; S   15. lithium; Li
6. iron; Fe   16. cobalt; Co
7. sodium; Na   17. barium; Ba
8. copper; Cu   18. oxygen; O
9. neon; Ne   19. helium; He
10. zirconium; Zr 20. strontium; Sr

Page 74

1. no
2. positive
3. negative
4. region around the nucleus that contains electrons
5. different orbits occupied by electrons
6. 2nd
7. no
8. no
9. 32
10. 6

---

11. 3
12. an atom with a number of neutrons different from the usual atom of that element
13. yes
14. yes
15. smaller particles (than atoms) of matter that make up protons and neutrons
   A. 6; 2; 4; 0   E. 10; 2; 8; 0
   B. 80; 2; 8; 18 F. 33; 2; 8; 18
   C. 20; 2; 8; 10 G. 11; 2; 8; 1
   D. 36; 2; 8; 18

Page 75

1. families   12. iron
2. properties   13. mercury
3. halogen   14. ore
4. noble gas   15. alloy
5. periods   16. aluminum
6. different   17. hydrogen
7. metals   18. allotrope
8. nonmetals   19. silicon
9. transition   20. helium
10. two   21. organic
11. alkali   22. carbon

Page 76

Across	Down
1. Th: Thorium	1. Ti: Titanium
2. As: Arsenic	2. Ar: Argon
3. Zr: Zirconium	3. Zn: Zinc
4. Li: Lithium	4. La: Lanthanum
5. Br: Bromide	5. Ba: Barium
6. Sn: Tin	6. Si: Silicon
7. Ca: Calcium	7. Cu: Copper
8. Ni: Nickel	8. Na: Sodium
9. C: Carbon	10. Al: Aluminium
10. Au: Gold	11. Rn: Radon
11. Ra: Radium	12. Kr: Krypton
12. K: Potassium	14. Mg: Magnesium
13. Cl: Chlorine	15. Fe: Iron
14. Mn: Manganese	16. He: Helium
15. Fr: Francium	18. Nb: Niobium
16. Hg: Mercury	19. Po: Polonium
17. N: Nitrogen	
18. Ne: Neon	
19. Pt: Platinum	
20. H: Hydrogen	
21. Pb: Lead	
22. Co: Cobalt	
23. O: Oxygen	
24. F: Fluoride	

Page 77

Student should describe each of the 3 ordinary states of matter:

I. A. Solids—have shape and volume; molecules are packed tightly together and vibrate back and forth only slightly.

   B. Liquids—have volume but no shape; take the shape of their container; molecules are farther apart than in a solid, but still attract each other.
   C. Gases—have no specific volume and no shape; molecules fill whatever space available; molecules and their particles move around very fast and don't necessarily stay very attracted to each other.

II. 1. B   3. A   5. E
   2. D   4. C

III. Plasma can exist only at extremely high temperatures; its particles move very fast

Page 78

Explanations will vary for these changes in matter. See that student explanations include a description of the state changes below, a description of the movement of the particles, a statement of the effects of temperature change.

1. liquid to solid   6. gas to liquid
2. liquid to gas   7. liquid to gas
3. solid to liquid   8. solid to liquid
4. solid to liquid   9. liquid to solid
5. liquid to gas

Page 79

Untrue statements (corrected) are:

2. Mass = amount of a substance;
   Weight = measure of the pull of gravity on a substance
3. Density = mass divided by volume
7. larger particles
8. can be seen with the eye or microscope
10. All matter takes up space.
11. physical property
13. chemical property
17. property of a liquid

Pages 80–81

1. HCl	8. $CaCO_3$	15. PbO
2. H_2O	9. $NaHCO_3$	16. H_2SO_4
3. CO_2	10. $AgNO_3$	17. HBr
4. P_2O_5	11. CH_4	18. HF
5. NH_3	12. Na_2O_2	19. AgCl
6. H_2O_2	13. CO	20. NaCl
7. SiO_2	14. NO_2	

Page 82

1. P	9. C	17. C
2. P	10. P	18. C
3. C	11. P	19. C
4. P	12. P	20. P
5. P	13. P	21. C
6. P	14. P	22. P
7. P	15. C	
8. C	16. P	

Answers

Page 83

1. hydrogen	15. acid
2. alkali or base	16. alkali or base
3. polymer	17. hydrocarbon
4. acid	18. phenolph-thalein
5. acids	
6. lipids	19. sugar, starch
7. alkali or base	20. acid
8. enzyme	21. amino acids,
9. proteins	lipids,
10. carbon dioxide	vitamins
11. alkalis or bases	22. unsaturated
12. carbohydrate	23. saturated
13. pH	24. neutralization
14. isomers	25. vitamins

Page 84

MATTER
1. What are solids, liquids, and gases?
2. What are gases?
3. What are liquids?
4. What are solids?
5. What are crystals?
6. What is viscosity?

ELEMENTS
7. What is an atom?
8. What is an atomic number?
9. What is an electron cloud?
10. What are metals?
11. What is hydrogen?
12. What are transition elements?

COMPOUNDS
13. What is a chemical change?
14. What is a chemical formula?
15. What is a molecule?
16. What is an ion?
17. What is hydrogen peroxide?
18. What is $MgCl_2$?

PHYSICAL CHANGES
19. What is a melting point?
20. What is a boiling point?
21. What is a freezing point?
22. What is condensation?
23. What is evaporation?
24. What is temperature?

Page 85

MIXTURES & SOLUTIONS
1. What is a solvent?
2. What is solubility?
3. What is a saturated solution?
4. What is heterogeneous?
5. What is a suspension?
6. What is distillation?

CHEMICAL REACTIONS
7. What is a catalyst?
8. What is energy?
9. What is an inhibitor?
10. What is a chemical equation?
11. What is a precipitate?
12. What is a synthesis reaction?

ORGANIC CHEMISTRY
13. What is carbon?
14. What are hydrocarbons?
15. What are isomers?
16. What is a polymer?
17. What is a carbohydrate?
18. What is an amino acid?

ACIDS, BASES, & SALTS
19. What is an acid?
20. What is litmus paper?
21. What is pH?
22. What is ammonia?
23. What is sodium hydroxide?
24. What is a salt?

Page 87

1. acceleration	11. momentum
2. velocity	12. air resistance
3. mass	13. vertical
4. terminal	14. newtons
5. horizontal	15. force
6. centripetal	16. pairs
7. speed	17. direction
8. rate	18. gravity
9. inertia	19. friction
10. rest	20. pressure

Page 88

1st: rest; rest; moving; velocity (or speed); line; velocity (or speed); force
2nd: force; speed; mass; acceleration
3rd: action; equal; opposite

1. first	6. third
2. third	7. second
3. first	8. second
4. second	9. third
5. second	10. first

Page 89

1. inertia	8. momentum
2. friction	9. friction
3. centripetal force	10. inertia
4. velocity	11. centripetal force
5. friction	12. Inertia
6. gravity	13. acceleration
7. air resistance or friction	14. air resistance
	15. rate

Page 90

1. 1.6 hours	7. 5 mph
2. 3.5 hours	8. 100 mph
3. yes; no	9. 1020 miles
4. *Black Giant*	10. *Chicago Skyscraper;* 152 miles farther
5. 9 P.M. central time	
6. 115 mph	

Page 91

I. Should include these three. Order is not important.
CONDUCTION: transfer of energy from particle to particle through matter.

Particles at higher temperatures have more energy and vibrate further. They collide with cooler air and spread energy through the material. Heat travels by conduction mainly through solids.
CONVECTION: transfer of energy by the movement of the material, particularly in gases and liquids because they flow. When a fluid (gas or liquid) is heated, it becomes less dense and it is pushed upwards by cooler, more dense fluids that sink. This causes a current that moves heat.
RADIATION: transfer of energy that doesn't need matter. Source of radiant energy is mostly the sun. Radiant energy can travel through space where there is no matter.

II. Answers will vary somewhat.
1. Conduction and convection: Heat from the burner warms the pan by conduction. The liquid soup is warmed by convection currents.
2. The cooler has insulating material—something that is a poor conductor and does not allow thermal energy to transfer well.
3. Black absorbs radiant energy from the sun. White or shiny objects reflect the sun's energy.
4. by radiation
5. Metal is a good conductor of heat. The heat energy moves from the hot liquid through the spoon by conduction.
6. Plastic is a poor conductor of heat energy.
7. Houses are usually insulated with materials that do not transfer thermal energy well. Heat usually flows from warmest spot to cooler spots. The insulating materials hold the heat into the house.
8. The warmth travels through the air by convection.
9. When you wear layers, air is trapped between the layers. Your body heat warms these many pockets of air, and they add extra insulation to keep in your body heat.
10. Wood is a poor conductor of heat; this is a protection to keep hands from burning.
11. Conduction and convection: Heat energy outside the can warms the metal can (a good conductor) by conduction. Warmth from the surface of the can then transfers through the liquid by convection.
12. Microwaves carry radiant energy to the food. This causes the molecules in the food to vibrate rapidly and produce thermal energy (heat).

13. A solar heating system includes containers that store the heat collected on a sunny day. This heat is stored in such materials as hot water or stones.
14. A refrigerator is a heat mover because it removes heat from the food inside a cool space and puts the heat out into the room at a higher temperature (warm air comes out of the back of the refrigerator).
15. Extra heat in the environment is called thermal pollution because it can raise the temperature of the environment and change the ecosystem, causing danger to some life forms.
16. Dirt in the snow is dark in color and absorbs radiant energy from the sun. This causes the snow to melt. Clean snow reflects more of the sun's heat energy away.
17. Air is heated by convection. Warm air is always less dense and lighter. Heavier, denser, cooler air sinks and pushes warmer air upward.

Pages 92–93

1. friction
2. friction
3. kinetic
4. potential
5. inertia
6. kinetic
7. gravity
8. kinetic
9. potential
10. potential
11. potential
12. kinetic
13. potential
14. potential
15. potential (mechanical allowed also)
16. thermal

17. neither; they will both reach the ground at the same time, because gravity exerts the same pull on all objects, no matter what their mass
18. rock; air resistance will slow the feather more than the rock
19. Earth; pull of Earth's gravity is less strong on the moon
20. none, because the astronaut has the same mass, no matter where she is

Pages 94–95

I. A. transfer of energy as the result of the motion of objects
B. a device that makes work easier
C. a machine consisting of only one part
D. number of times a machine multiplies an effort force
E. force exerted by a machine
F. force applied to the machine

II. Explanations of machines may vary.
1. Lever: a bar that pivots on a fixed point a. fulcrum; b. effort force; c. resistance force
2. Pulley: wheel that changes the direction of the effort force

3. Wheel & Axle: large wheel fixed to a smaller wheel or a bar called an axle
4. Inclined Plane: slanted surface used to raise objects
5. Wedge: an inclined plane with one or two sloping sides
6. Screw: an inclined plane wound around a cylinder, usually with a sharp ridge along the edge

III.
1. lever
2. wheel & axle
3. wedge
4. inclined plane
5. pulley
6. lever
7. lever
8. pulley
9. lever
10. wedge
11. screw
12. lever
13. wheel & axle
14. inclined plane
15. wedge
16. lever
17. screw
18. inclined plane
19. lever
20. wheel & axle

Page 96

1. wavelength
2. X
3. Y
4. frequency
5. velocity
6. higher
7. amplitude
8. transverse
9. compressional
10. electromagnetic
11. velocity
12. vibrations
13. hertz; one wave per second
14. 2

Page 97

1. transverse
2. radiation
3. frequencies
4. spectrum
5. visible
6. ultraviolet
7. 102 million waves pass a given point each second
8. X-rays
9. higher
10. TV
11. no
12. 56 Hz
13. radar
14. cosmic

Page 98

Answers may vary somewhat.
1. unit to measure the volume or loudness of sound
2. having to do with the amplitude of a sound wave
3. has a large amplitude
4. has a small amplitude
5. greatest distance a point on a sound wave travels from its rest position
6. a person's response to sound intensity; a sound wave with a large amplitude
7. sounds with pleasing tone quality and pitch

8. a quality of a sound determined by its frequency
9. sound with higher frequency
10. sound with lower frequency
11. differences among sounds of the same pitch and loudness
12. study of the science of sound
13. speed at which sound waves travel through a material or air
14. number of sound waves that pass a point at a given time
15. a change in wave frequency that is caused by the motion of the sound source or the motion of the person hearing it
16. sounds produced by irregular vibrations
17. mixture of many different sounds reflected

Page 99

1. A
2. A
3. B
4. D
5. C
6. Tim's
7. E
8. E
9. They are farther apart.
10. H
11. Pitch gets lower.
12. Pitch will become louder or higher.

Page 100

A. 11	E. 15	I. 8	M. 5
B. 4	F. 3	J. 16	N. 7
C. 6	G. 13	K. 9	O. 10
D. 12	H. 1	L. 2	P. 14

Page 101

1. The process of drying clothes in a dryer often causes them to gain an electric charge. This means that some of the atoms have too many or too few electrons. These atoms with too few and too many electrons attract each other, causing static electricity.
2. Drops of moisture in the air act as conductors to carry electricity across the air.
3. The skin of an electric eel has hundreds of cells that charge up like batteries and hold electric energy.
4. The power of wind can be used to turn a generator and produce electricity.
5. Rubbing a balloon against a sweater can cause some of the atoms in the sweater to lose and be transferred to the balloon. The electrons with too many or too few electrons attract each other, producing static electricity.
6. The comb passing through your hair causes some electrons to be transferred to the comb. The atoms with too few or too many electrons, then, attract each other, producing static electricity.

7. A glow worm produces light through a chemical process that takes place in its body.
8. Feet shuffling across a carpet causes some of the electrons from some atoms to be transferred between objects. The atoms with too few or too many electrons, then, attract each other and produce static electricity.
9. The human body has a complex nervous system that works with electric signals. The electricity is produced through chemical processes in the body.
10. The power of running water can be used to turn a generator and produce electricity.

Page 102

I. A. the flow of charged particles through a conductor
   B. alternating current: flow of particles constantly changing direction
   C. direct current: flow of particles in one direction

II. 1. A, B, C, D
    2. E, F
    3. D
    4. C
    5. B, E
    6. 2
    7. 0
    8. Answers will vary somewhat: because your finger completes a circuit and makes a path for the electricity to flow—it conducts electricity through your body

Page 103

1. 1560 watts	4. 120 V	7. 3.5 A
2. 12.5 A	5. 220 V	8. 0.06 A
3. 150 watts	6. 75.6 watts	

Page 104

Clues will vary somewhat but should contain generally this information:

Across
1. caused by a wave bouncing off an object
5. the bending of waves of light passing from one material into another
6. an object that refracts light twice and produces a visible spectrum
11. Light is a part of this spectrum of waves.
12. material that absorbs light
14. light waves that strike an object
15. color of unseparated light

Down
1. image that can be projected onto a screen
2. material that you can see through
3. bending of light waves as they pass through an opening or around a bend
4. visible part of the electromagnetic spectrum
6. instrument for seeing things not in the line of vision
7. colored bands of visible light
8. colored material that absorbs some colors and reflects others
9. material light passes through but cannot be seen through
10. instrument that uses light to see distant objects
13. ___ of incidence = ___ of refraction

Page 105

1. Only the red waves of the spectrum are reflected off red apples.
2. Pigments are added to paint to give them color. These pigments are colored liquids that absorb some colors and reflect others.

3. Something is black because it reflects no waves from the light spectrum.
4. Something appears white because it reflects all the colors in light together.
5. A prism, because of the angles in the glass, bends the white light. The different colors are refracted at different angles, and so the colors are separated out into a visible spectrum.
6. Raindrops act like tiny prisms. When the sun shines on the raindrops at a certain angle, the raindrops split the light into its many colors.
7. The water bends the light that is reflecting the image of the coin back to you.
8. Sunlight coming through Earth's atmosphere is reflected, or scattered, by millions of dust and water particles in the air. The shortest wavelengths of light are scattered more than the other wavelengths. These are the blue wavelengths. The dust and water scatter so many of these short wavelengths and scatter so much blue light that the sky appears blue.
9. Sunlight, low on the horizon, passes through a thicker layer of atmosphere. Most of the shorter wavelengths (blues and greens) are scattered out, leaving the longer wavelengths toward the red end of the light spectrum. This is why the sky appears red.
10. The indigo wavelengths are difficult to see. Only 1 person in every 1000 can see them.

Page 106

1. C	7. G
2. J	8. B
3. A	9. E
4. I	10. H
5. F	11. K
6. D	

Page 107

1. angle	11. 45°
2. thicker	12. Light
3. together	13. mirror
4. focal	14. mirror
5. focus	15. out of the line of vision
6. larger	16. aperture
7. thinner	17. lens
8. away	18. image
9. focus	19. film
10. mirror	20. inverted

Page 108

These are the corrected false answers.
All other answers are true.

1. Magnetic poles that are UNLIKE attract.
6. One end will point NORTH, the other SOUTH.
8. Both ends have equal force.
10. The core is a piece of IRON.
14. Iron is NOT a permanent magnet.
16. Magnetic poles that are ALIKE REPEL one another . . . or . . . magnetic poles that are DIFFERENT ATTRACT each other.

PERIODIC TABLE

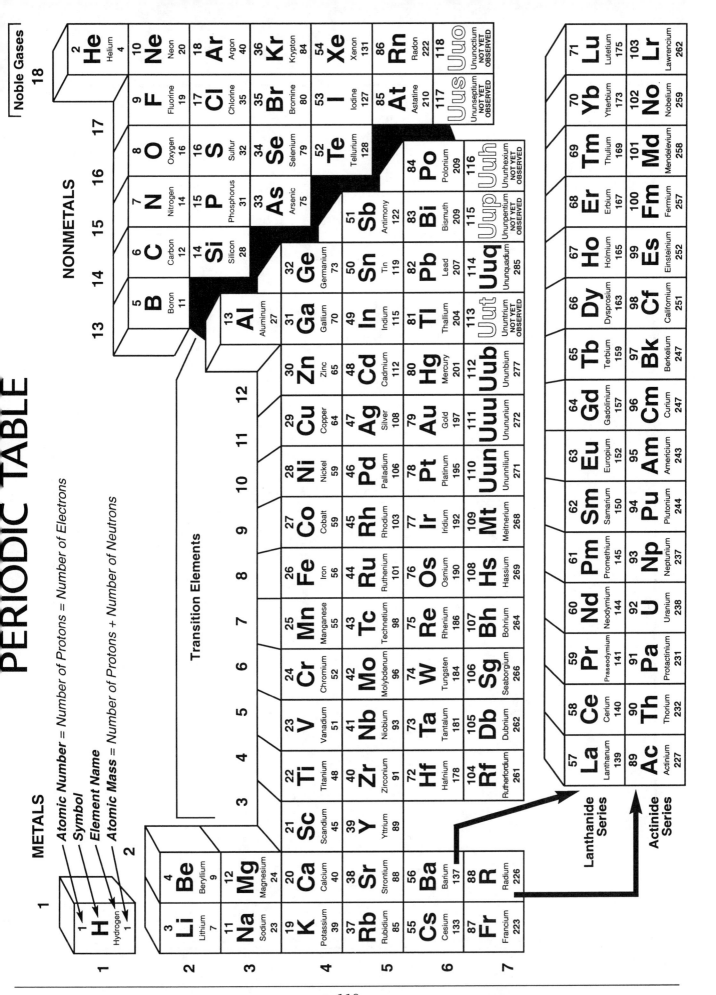

Atomic Number = Number of Protons = Number of Electrons
Symbol
Element Name
Atomic Mass = Number of Protons + Number of Neutrons

METALS

NONMETALS

Noble Gases

Transition Elements

Lanthanide Series

Actinide Series

Copyright ©2002 by Incentive Publications, Inc., Nashville, TN.

EARTH & SPACE SCIENCE

Skills Exercises

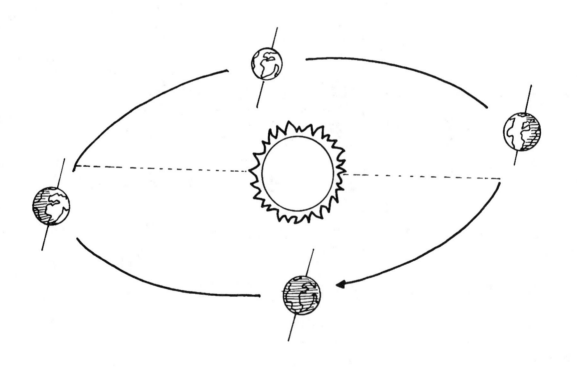

SKILLS CHECKLIST FOR EARTH & SPACE SCIENCE

✔	SKILL	PAGE(S)
	Describe and draw a model of the solar system	122–123
	Identify and describe and compare characteristics of each planet	122–124
	Define and describe features of stellar astronomy	125
	Define and describe characteristics of other objects in the solar system	126
	Define, describe and differentiate among movements of objects in space	127–129
	Explain seasons, equinox and solstice	128
	Describe and diagram the moon's phases and motions	129
	Describe and diagram lunar and solar eclipses	130
	Define and describe several tools of space exploration and travel	131–133
	Identify major accomplishments and events in space exploration	132–133
	Define, describe, and diagram the earth's atmosphere	134
	Define, describe, and illustrate different winds and earth air movements	135
	Define weather and describe factors that contribute to it	136–138
	Identify and describe a variety of weather patterns	136–138
	Define and distinguish among different kinds of precipitation	136–138
	Define and use vocabulary terms related to weather and climate	136–139
	Describe and distinguish among different kinds of weather fronts	138
	Describe factors that influence climate	139
	Describe and define different motions of the ocean	140–143
	Diagram and describe parts and motions of an ocean wave	141
	Explain and diagram causes of high, low, neap, and spring tides	143
	Diagram and describe characteristics of the ocean floor	144
	Define weathering and erosion and explain agents and examples of each	145–149
	Describe effects and processes of wind erosion	145
	Describe effects and processes of water erosion	146–148
	Define and describe characteristics of rivers and riverbeds	146–147
	Define and describe actions and features formed by groundwater	148
	Identify and compare kinds and effects of glaciers	149
	Identify and describe layers and features of the Earth's crust	150
	Identify and describe various landforms on the Earth	151, 160
	Define and explain formation of three classes of rocks	152–153
	List and define characteristics used to identify minerals	154–155
	Identify and distinguish among common minerals	154–155
	Identify features related to volcanoes	156, 159
	Define and illustrate terms and processes related to earthquakes and plate tectonics	157–159
	Investigate some of Earth's most notable earthquakes and volcanoes	159

THE FAMOUS 10

The famous ten—the sun and nine planets—make up our solar system. But ten may not be the right number! Many scientists suspect that there's another planet out there. In any case, we know about nine of them. On the next page, you will make a rough design of the solar system. It will be "rough" because you can't really show the accurate orbits and distances for each planet on a small piece of paper. But you can show that you know where they are.

First, gather the information you need about the solar system by completing the chart below. Then get your markers or colored pencils and draw your own diagram of the solar system on page 123. Follow the directions at the top of page 123.

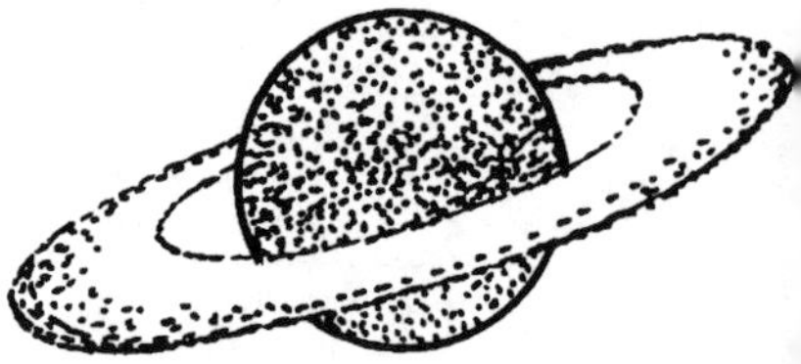

Number in Order from the Sun	PLANET	Number of Known Satellites	Colors, Features, Special Characteristics

Find these solar system facts, and then use them to help you with your design.

1. Johannes Kepler discovered that the paths planets follow are _____ in shape.

2. The point at which a planet is the greatest distance away from the sun in its orbit is called _____ .

3. The point at which the planet is closest to the sun in its orbit is called _____ .

4. The asteroid belt in our solar system is found between the planets _____ and _____ .

5. The inner planets are _____ , _____ , _____ , and _____ .

6. The outer planets are _____ , _____ , _____ , _____ , and _____ .

Use with page 123.

Name

Use with page 122.

Draw the sun in the center of the box below. Add each planet in its orbit. Draw and color the planets to match their characteristics as best you can. Include the moons of each planet. Include the asteroid belt. Label the sun, the planets, and the asteroids.

Name

 Copyright ©2002 by Incentive Publications, Inc., Nashville, TN.

SOLAR SYSTEM SLEUTHING

Space has plenty of mysteries, even the space that we know best—our solar system. Floating around on this page are clues to mystery planets. Figure out which planet matches each clue, and write the code for that planet by the clue.

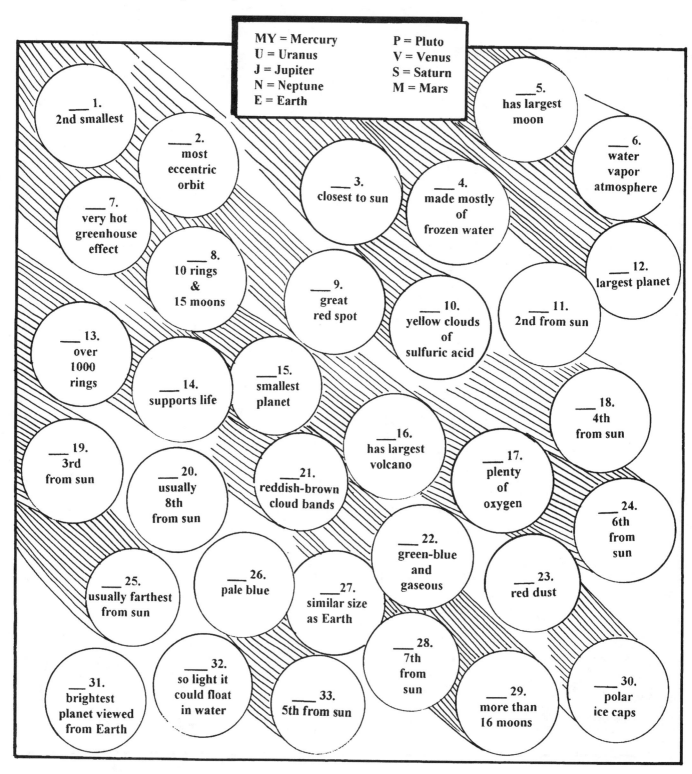

MY = Mercury   P = Pluto
U = Uranus   V = Venus
J = Jupiter   S = Saturn
N = Neptune   M = Mars
E = Earth

___ 1. 2nd smallest

___ 2. most eccentric orbit

___ 3. closest to sun

___ 4. made mostly of frozen water

___ 5. has largest moon

___ 6. water vapor atmosphere

___ 7. very hot greenhouse effect

___ 8. 10 rings & 15 moons

___ 9. great red spot

___ 10. yellow clouds of sulfuric acid

___ 11. 2nd from sun

___ 12. largest planet

___ 13. over 1000 rings

___ 14. supports life

___ 15. smallest planet

___ 16. has largest volcano

___ 17. plenty of oxygen

___ 18. 4th from sun

___ 19. 3rd from sun

___ 20. usually 8th from sun

___ 21. reddish-brown cloud bands

___ 22. green-blue and gaseous

___ 23. red dust

___ 24. 6th from sun

___ 25. usually farthest from sun

___ 26. pale blue

___ 27. similar size as Earth

___ 28. 7th from sun

___ 29. more than 16 moons

___ 30. polar ice caps

___ 31. brightest planet viewed from Earth

___ 32. so light it could float in water

___ 33. 5th from sun

Name _____

 Copyright ©2002 by INCENTIVE PUBLICATIONS, Inc., Nashville, TN.

HOT SPOTS

These sky gazers are viewing some amazing stuff and swapping stories about
what they're seeing. Read the description from each viewer and decide what he
or she is watching. Choose the answers from the box at the bottom of the page.

"I see! (or think I see) . . .

_____ 1. "a mysterious, bright, starlike object in the galaxy core"

_____ 2. "Betelgeuse . . . a large star of high luminosity"

_____ 3. "dark spots on the sun where gas is cooler"

_____ 4. "clouds of dust and gas where stars are born"

_____ 5. "a hot, self-luminous sphere of gas"

_____ 6. "a neutron star that rotates rapidly and gives out a
beam of radiation picked up as a pulse"

_____ 7. "the core of a star left after a supernova explosion"

_____ 8. "billions of stars held together by gravitational attraction"

_____ 9. "a specific pattern of stars"

_____ 10. "a star suddenly exploding with increasing brightness"

_____ 11. "the surface of the sun which emits the radiation we can see"

_____ 12. "2 stars orbiting a common center of gravity"

_____ 13. "a white dwarf which has stopped radiating energy"

_____ 14. "the brightest star in the sky"

_____ 15. "a star explosion which increases the star's luminosity to 1000 times that
of a nova"

_____ 16. "a star that has collapsed after using its fuel"

white dwarf	Andromeda
red supergiant	black dwarf
Milky Way	variable star
quasar	solar flares
neutron star	chromosphere
black hole	Sirius A
binary star	nebulae
constellation	pulsar
galaxy	sunspots
nova	supernova
photosphere	star
corona	

_____ 17. "a star whose brightness changes"

_____ 18. "a nearby galaxy"

_____ 19. "our galaxy"

_____ 20. "very hot gas of the sun visible only
during a total eclipse of the sun"

_____ 21. "sudden increases in brightness of
the chromosphere of the sun"

_____ 22. "a collapsed star from which light
cannot escape"

_____ 23. "bright red layer of sun surface
containing hydrogen gas"

Name _____

The BASIC/Not Boring Middle Grades Science Book   Copyright ©2002 by Incentive Publications, Inc., Nashville, TN.

CLOSE ENCOUNTERS

If you encountered a moving object in space, would you know what you've run into? (Or what has run into you?) Do you know the difference between a **comet** and a **coma**, an **asteroid** and a **meteoroid**, a **meteor** and a **meteorite?** For each of these descriptions, what is it that you've run into when you've encountered . . .

_____ 1. the solid portion of a comet?

_____ 2. a briefly visible meteor?

_____ 3. a meteor that strikes Earth's surface?

_____ 4. the largest asteroid ever found?

_____ 5. long streaks of bright light caused when a meteoroid gets close to the ground as it's burning up?

_____ 6. the large halo made of dust and gas that forms around the nucleus of a comet when it gets close to the sun?

_____ 7. a group of objects orbiting between Mars and Jupiter?

_____ 8. one of several heavenly bodies named for their discoverers?

_____ 9. a mass of frozen gases, cosmic dust, and rocky particles?

_____ 10. a meteoroid that has reached Earth's atmosphere?

_____ 11. fragments of matter similar in composition to planets that orbit the sun?

_____ 12. small fragments of matter (not asteroids) orbiting the sun?

_____ 13. a space curiosity that returns to Earth's view approximately every 76 years?

And, can you answer these?

_____ 14. What do comets orbit?

_____ 15. Where does a comet's tail point?

_____ 16. What shape is a comet's path?

Name _____

COOL MOVES

Earth and its friends in the solar system make some fancy moves. And some of them are not even what they seem to your eyes! Because they watched the sun rise and set every day, people in ancient times thought the sun traveled across the sky or around Earth. They were wrong about this. In the last 500 years, scientists have learned a lot about the movements of Earth, moon, and other planets and bodies in space.

Describe each of these awesome moves or forces:

MOVE or FORCE	DESCRIPTION
RETROGRADE	
REAL MOTION	
APPARENT MOTION	
ROTATION	
REVOLUTION	
EARTH'S GRAVITY	
SUN'S GRAVITY	

Answer these questions about Earth's cool moves:

1. What is caused by Earth's rotation? _____

2. How long does it take for Earth to rotate once? _____

3. Who discovered that things did not revolve around Earth? _____

4. What are Earth's two **real** motions? _____ and _____

5. What is caused by Earth's revolution around the sun? _____

6. How long does it take for one revolution? _____

Name _____

REASONS FOR SEASONS

What's with the seasons? How do they know when to come and go? It all has to do with the movements of Earth in relation to the sun. Here are some reasons. You fill in the blanks to tell what the reason explains.

1. **Reason** for _____:
Because Earth is tilted 23½° from a line perpendicular to its orbit, the length of daylight varies and because of the angle at which the sun's energy strikes a given location through the year.

2. **Reason** for _____ in the Northern Hemisphere:
Because the Northern Hemisphere is tilted toward the sun for a few months.

3. **Reason** for _____ in the Northern Hemisphere and _____ in the Southern Hemisphere: Because Earth's tilt is sideways to the sun, and hours of daylight and darkness are the same in both hemispheres on about September 22.

4. **Reason** for _____ in the Northern Hemisphere:
Because the North Pole is tilted almost directly toward the sun on about June 21.

5. **Reason** for _____ in the Southern Hemisphere:
Because the South Pole is tilted away from the sun on about June 21.

6. **Reason** for _____ in the Southern Hemisphere:
Because the Southern Hemisphere is tilted toward the sun for a few months.

7. **Reason** for _____ in the Northern Hemisphere:
Because the South Pole is tilted almost directly toward the sun on about December 21.

8. **Reason** for _____ in the Northern Hemisphere and _____ in the Southern Hemisphere: Because Earth's tilt is sideways to the sun and hours of daylight and darkness are the same in both hemispheres on about March 20.

9. **Reason** for _____ in the Southern Hemisphere:
Because the South Pole is tilted almost directly toward the sun on about December 21.

10. **Reason** for _____ hours of daylight at the South Pole: Because the South Pole is tilted directly toward the sun on about December 21.

On the diagram at the right, label winter solstice, summer solstice, fall equinox, and spring equinox for the Northern Hemisphere.

Name

MOON TALK

Wax, wane, crescent, gibbous, quarter, full, revolve, rotate, lunar . . . are words you need to know if you're going to speak **moon**. These describe the movements and phases of the moon. Antonia Astronaut, who incidentally is on a moon walk, is telling you some things about the moon. Match each label in the box (A-H) with the correct phase or position of the moon in the diagram. Then match the same labels with Antonia's descriptions below. Write the correct letter on the line.

A. first quarter	C. full moon	E. waxing crescent	G. waning gibbous
B. third quarter	D. new moon	F. waxing gibbous	H. waning crescent

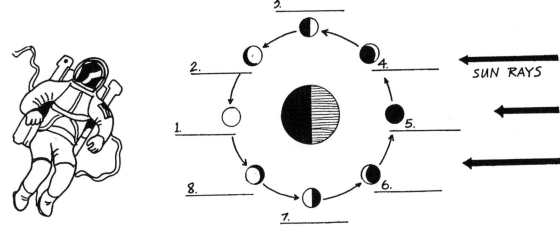

SUN RAYS

_____ 9. "The moon lies between the sun and Earth so the side of the moon facing Earth is dark and the moon is not visible."

_____ 10. "More than a quarter of the moon is visible, and the visible portion is becoming smaller as the moon moves toward the third quarter phase."

_____ 11. "The moon has moved eastward in its orbit from the new moon phase and forms a 90° angle with the sun and Earth, and the moon appears half bright and half dark."

_____ 12. "Although less than a quarter of the moon is visible now, the visible portion is getting larger as the moon moves from the new moon phase toward the first quarter phase."

_____ 13. "The moon is aligned with the sun and Earth, Earth being in the middle. The entire side of the moon facing Earth is bright and visible."

_____ 14. "Less than a quarter of the moon is visible, and the visible part is getting even smaller as the moon moves toward the new moon phase."

_____ 15. "The moon is moving toward the full moon phase, and presently more than a quarter of it is visible on Earth."

_____ 16. "The moon, sun, and Earth are forming a 90° angle, so the side of the moon facing Earth is half dark and half bright. The visible part of the moon will be getting smaller as it moves toward the new moon phase."

Name _____

CASTING SHADOWS

Have you ever seen the sun disappear? Or watched an eerie shadow move across the moon? Imagine what it was like for primitive people when the sky suddenly fell dark in the middle of the day! When three celestial objects fall into alignment, some great shadows are the result. These shadows are called eclipses of the moon or sun, and they're pretty spectacular to watch! These eclipse-watchers have written down some information about eclipses. Do they have all their facts straight? Write T (true) or F (false) next to each statement.

_____ 1. A solar eclipse occurs when Earth falls between the sun and the moon.

_____ 2. All eclipses are visible.

_____ 3. All eclipses are total.

_____ 4. The umbra is the inner part of the shadow.

_____ 5. Eclipses of the sun occur 2–4 times a year.

_____ 6. A lunar eclipse occurs when the moon travels through the shadow of Earth.

_____ 7. There are about 2 lunar eclipses a year.

_____ 8. A lunar eclipse can take place only when the moon is full.

_____ 9. A total solar eclipse lasts a few minutes.

_____ 10. In a solar eclipse, no sunlight penetrates the umbra.

_____ 11. A total lunar eclipse occurs when the moon passes through Earth's penumbra.

_____ 12. Partial lunar eclipses occur more often than total eclipses.

_____ 13. A solar eclipse may last over 3 hours.

_____ 14. A total solar eclipse is visible at all spots on Earth.

_____ 15. All lunar eclipses are total.

_____ 16. In a total solar eclipse, the moon completely covers the sun.

_____ 17. Lunar eclipses occur every 3 years.

_____ 18. A lunar eclipse may last over 3 hours.

_____ 19. The penumbra is the outer part of the shadow.

_____ 20. When the sun's disk is covered in an eclipse, the corona is still visible.

Label the diagrams below **solar eclipse** or **lunar eclipse**.
Label **Earth, moon, umbra,** and **penumbra** on each diagram.

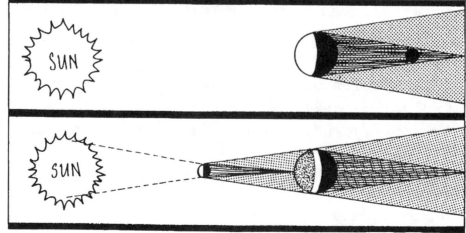

Name

WHAT'S OUT THERE?

For many years, human beings have been snooping around in space, trying to find out what's out there. They've done their snooping using many different methods, instruments, and contraptions. This puzzle is hiding the names of several tools they've used in their quest for information about space. Use the clues to find the answers for each tool. If the answers are right, the letters in the squares will spell the name of a mystery spaceship that has a famous history (# = space between words).

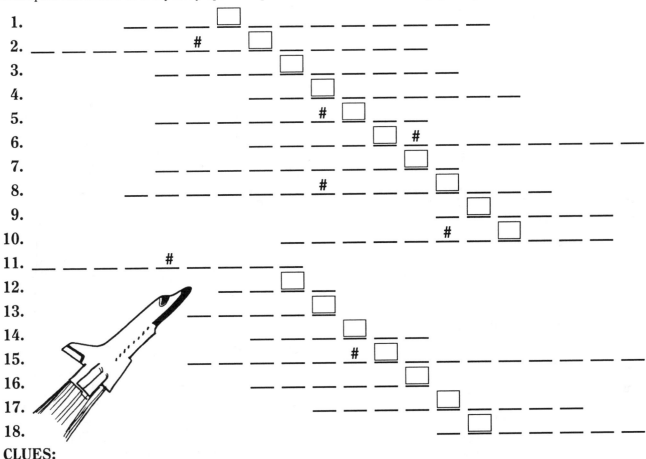

CLUES:

1. an instrument that separates light into various wavelengths
2. a reusable craft for transporting people and supplies to and from space
3. telescope that uses an objective lens to bend light toward the plane where the image is formed
4. instrument that makes small, distant objects visible
5. a workshop in space where astronauts can carry out experiments
6. living and working quarters for astronauts in space
7. telescope that collects light with a mirror
8. U.S. space program that put astronauts on the moon
9. U.S. space project that gave astronauts practice piloting spacecraft and working in space
10. rocket-launched vehicle that carries equipment for gathering data above Earth's atmosphere
11. astronaut Neil Armstrong took one of these on July 16, 1969
12. agency that oversees the U.S. space program
13. instrument that photographs light wavelengths to find movements of space objects (spectro _____)
14. force produced by expansions of gases that pushes a rocket forward
15. reflector disk that collects radio waves
16. action-reaction engines that propel an object forward
17. an object that revolves around another object
18. U.S. space project that gathered data on the basics of space flight

Mystery Spaceship _ _ _ _ _ _ _ _ _ _   _ _ _ _ _ _ _
                   1   2   3   4   5   6   7   8   9 10   12 13 14 15 16 17 18

Name

The BASIC/Not Boring Middle Grades Science Book Copyright ©2002 by Incentive Publications, Inc., Nashville, TN.

SPACE VENTURES

Although people dreamed of venturing into outer space for many years, it was not until the second half of the nineteenth century that anyone actually traveled into space. Some of the most notable discoveries and ventures in space exploration are described below, out of the order in which they occurred. Do some research in your science book, encyclopedia, almanac, or other reference books to find the year that each of these space ventures took place. Then place these ventures onto the timeline on page 133. Add your own space drawings to the timeline, too!

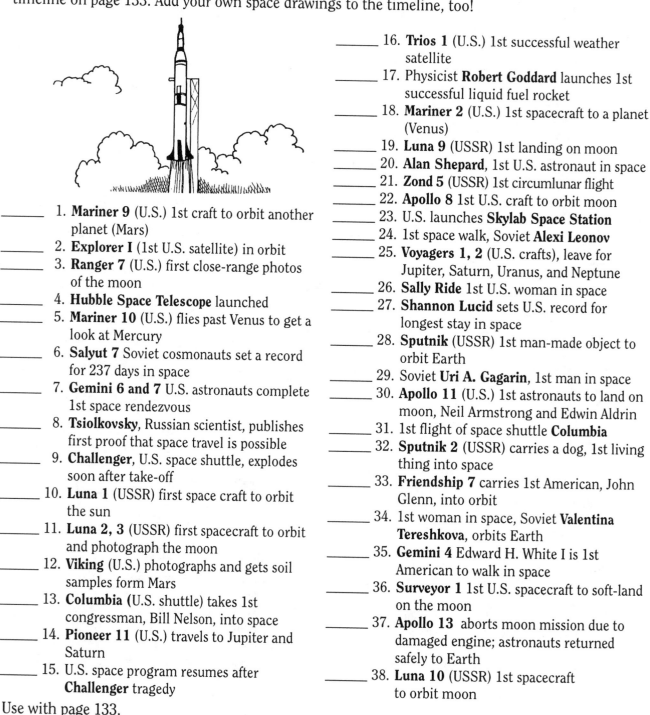

_____ 1. **Mariner 9** (U.S.) 1st craft to orbit another planet (Mars)

_____ 2. **Explorer I** (1st U.S. satellite) in orbit

_____ 3. **Ranger 7** (U.S.) first close-range photos of the moon

_____ 4. **Hubble Space Telescope** launched

_____ 5. **Mariner 10** (U.S.) flies past Venus to get a look at Mercury

_____ 6. **Salyut 7** Soviet cosmonauts set a record for 237 days in space

_____ 7. **Gemini 6 and 7** U.S. astronauts complete 1st space rendezvous

_____ 8. **Tsiolkovsky**, Russian scientist, publishes first proof that space travel is possible

_____ 9. **Challenger**, U.S. space shuttle, explodes soon after take-off

_____ 10. **Luna 1** (USSR) first space craft to orbit the sun

_____ 11. **Luna 2, 3** (USSR) first spacecraft to orbit and photograph the moon

_____ 12. **Viking** (U.S.) photographs and gets soil samples form Mars

_____ 13. **Columbia** (U.S. shuttle) takes 1st congressman, Bill Nelson, into space

_____ 14. **Pioneer 11** (U.S.) travels to Jupiter and Saturn

_____ 15. U.S. space program resumes after **Challenger** tragedy

_____ 16. **Trios 1** (U.S.) 1st successful weather satellite

_____ 17. Physicist **Robert Goddard** launches 1st successful liquid fuel rocket

_____ 18. **Mariner 2** (U.S.) 1st spacecraft to a planet (Venus)

_____ 19. **Luna 9** (USSR) 1st landing on moon

_____ 20. **Alan Shepard**, 1st U.S. astronaut in space

_____ 21. **Zond 5** (USSR) 1st circumlunar flight

_____ 22. **Apollo 8** 1st U.S. craft to orbit moon

_____ 23. U.S. launches **Skylab Space Station**

_____ 24. 1st space walk, Soviet **Alexi Leonov**

_____ 25. **Voyagers 1, 2** (U.S. crafts), leave for Jupiter, Saturn, Uranus, and Neptune

_____ 26. **Sally Ride** 1st U.S. woman in space

_____ 27. **Shannon Lucid** sets U.S. record for longest stay in space

_____ 28. **Sputnik** (USSR) 1st man-made object to orbit Earth

_____ 29. Soviet **Uri A. Gagarin**, 1st man in space

_____ 30. **Apollo 11** (U.S.) 1st astronauts to land on moon, Neil Armstrong and Edwin Aldrin

_____ 31. 1st flight of space shuttle **Columbia**

_____ 32. **Sputnik 2** (USSR) carries a dog, 1st living thing into space

_____ 33. **Friendship 7** carries 1st American, John Glenn, into orbit

_____ 34. 1st woman in space, Soviet **Valentina Tereshkova**, orbits Earth

_____ 35. **Gemini 4** Edward H. White I is 1st American to walk in space

_____ 36. **Surveyor 1** 1st U.S. spacecraft to soft-land on the moon

_____ 37. **Apollo 13** aborts moon mission due to damaged engine; astronauts returned safely to Earth

_____ 38. **Luna 10** (USSR) 1st spacecraft to orbit moon

Use with page 133.

Name

Use with page 132.

SPACE EXPLORATION TIMELINE

Write the key word of each venture from page 132 into the correct date box on the timeline. Some years will have more than one answer.

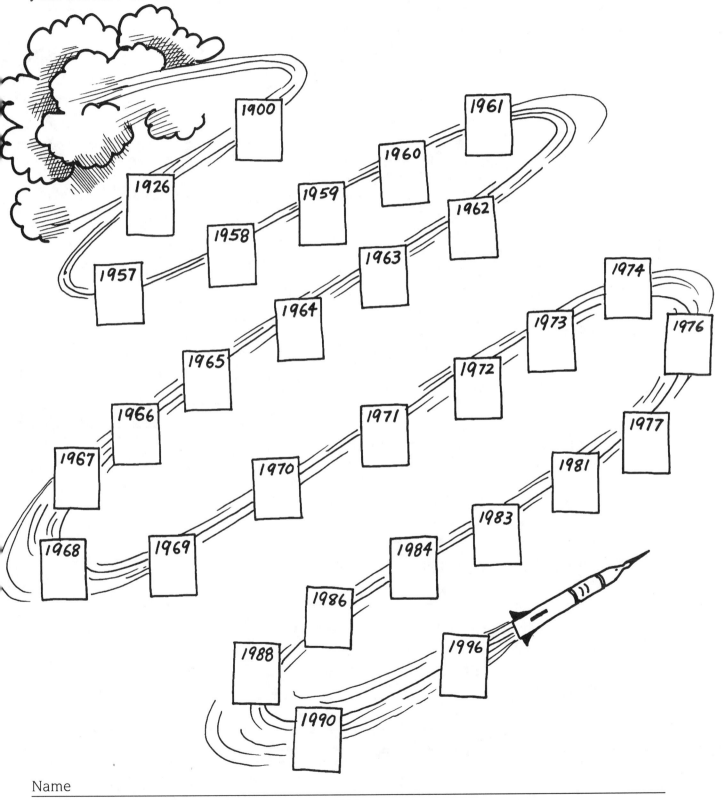

Name

The BASIC/Not Boring Middle Grades Science Book   Copyright ©2002 by Incentive Publications, Inc., Nashville, TN.

THE AIR UP THERE

Zak and Zeke want to explore Earth's atmosphere. They think their amazing balloon can take them high enough to learn all about the atmosphere. Are they right? Here are some things they'll need to learn before they get too far.

1. Label the layers of the atmosphere: **troposphere, thermosphere, stratosphere, mesosphere.**
2. Also label: **tropopause, exosphere, ionosphere.**
3. Tell what layer or feature is described in each phrase below. Write **TR** for **troposphere, TH** for **thermosphere, M** for **mesosphere, S** for **stratosphere, I** for **ionosphere, EX** for **exosphere,** and **TPP** for **tropopause.**

_____ a. contains dust, water vapor, and 75% of all gases
_____ b. extends from 10–20 km above Earth
_____ c. layer with coldest temperatures: –100° C
_____ d. layer extends 85 km above Earth into space
_____ e. temperature decreases with increasing height
_____ f. the ozone layer is in this layer
_____ g. contains the Van Allen Belts of radiation
_____ h. layer where all weather occurs
_____ i. ceiling to the weather zone
_____ j. extends from 15 or 20 km to 50 km above Earth
_____ k. temperatures increase in this layer
_____ l. begins at about 500 km above Earth
_____ m. top portion of troposphere
_____ n. layer has 2 parts
_____ o. lower part has temperatures –50°C; upper temperatures are 0° C
_____ p. jet streams are just below this
_____ q. extends 50–85 km above Earth's surface
_____ r. filled with electronically charged particles

4. What is in the air that makes up Earth's atmosphere? _____

_____

5. What is so important about ozone? _____

_____

6. What is atmospheric pressure? _____

_____

7. Why does air pressure vary? _____

_____

8. Will Zak & Zeke get above the troposphere? _____

Name _____

AIR ON THE MOVE

Amelia Dareheart's plane keeps getting caught in various forms of moving air. For each description, fill in the name of the predicament in which she finds herself. Use the labels in the box to help you with your task.

iii AOHM

doldrums

cyclone

jet stream

hurricane

prevailing westerlies

water spout

front

blizzard

tornado

land breeze

polar easterlies

sea breeze

gale

trade winds

_____ 1. She's caught in a wind that blows toward the equator from about 30° N and 30° S of the equator. What is it?

_____ 2. Ahhhh—relief! She's flying in wind-less _____ along the equator!

_____ 3. Warm air moving toward the poles between 30°–60° latitude in the Northern Hemisphere is pushing her along at a good speed. She's in a _____ .

_____ 4. She's spinning out of control in a low-pressure system where air is whirling counterclockwise toward the center of a _____ .

_____ 5. Warm air over land rises and cool air from the water is moving in, pulling her along in air moving from sea to land. This is a _____ .

_____ 6. Between the North Pole and 60° lati-tude, she's buzzing along in cold, dry, dense, horizontal air currents called _____ .

_____ 7. She's caught in the eye of a storm with warm, moist air rotating around her. She's flying in a _____ . Bad idea!

_____ 8. Now she's in a body of air that got its properties from the place it formed. It is called a _____ .

_____ 9. Moving along quickly, she's in the _____ , the narrow belt of wind near the tropopause that formed when warm tropical air met cold polar air.

_____ 10. Watch out for that _____ , a large mass of moving air.

_____ 11. It's nighttime, and the warm air over the water rises and is replaced by cooler air from the land. This moves her along with the _____ .

_____ 12. She's twisting in hot air spinning upwards; she's caught in the center of a _____ .

_____ 13. This time she's over the sea, in a funnel of water called a _____ .

_____ 14. Oh Amelia! Now it's snow whipped by heavy wind, called a _____ .

Name

WEATHER OR NOT

All the weather forecasters in the town of Secret have this annoying habit of telling about the weather without telling exactly what it is! See if you can give the correct term for the weather condition or event that they describe.

1. "Centers of low pressure are bringing cloudy, wet, windy weather to our area."

2. "Today you can expect the ground to get cold enough for water vapor in the air to condense into water droplets which will be deposited on the ground."

3. "Water droplets are forming and hovering over the ground because the air is being cooled by cool underlying ground."

4. "Whirling funnels of air are expected to form between the bottom of a storm cloud and the ground."

5. "I predict we'll see tiny water droplets in the clouds join together to make drops before the day is over."

6. "This weekend water will freeze on ice pellets in the clouds and make crystals which will join to other crystals."

7. "We'll see lots of electricity released which has built up in thunder clouds by evening."

8. "Hovering over our area is this boundary between two air masses of different composition."

9. "Get prepared for a week of heavy, dense air that sinks."

10. "Centers of high pressure will bring dry, sunny, settled weather for the next several days."

11. "Something will move into the area over the next few days that is formed when tiny droplets of water collected together are suspended in air."

12. "Droplets of water will freeze in layers around a nucleus of ice. These will become larger as air currents toss them up and down during severe thunderstorms."

13. "You can expect to find that cooling ground will cool the air around it, and as the temperature falls, the dew will freeze."

14. "Residents will need to evacuate due to a storm with extremely high winds developing over the warm tropical ocean offshore."

15. "This afternoon, air will expand several times at great speeds and cause booming sounds."

RAIN **LOWS** **FOG** **CLOUDS** **FRONTS**

KSNO

THUNDER **DEW** **FROST** **SNOW** **TORNADO** **HURRICANE** **LIGHTNING** **COLD AIR**

W-WET

HAIL **HIGHS**

K-HOT

Use with page 137.

Name

Copyright ©2002 by Incentive Publications, Inc., Nashville, TN.

Use with page 136.   WARM FRONT   DROUGHT   TORNADO WARNING   ANTICYCLONE

SLEET   # MORE WEATHER OR NOT

CYCLONES

DEW POINT   BLIZZARD

PRECIPITATION

16. "The weather tonight will be dominated by air movement that is caused by air moving from areas of high to low pressure."

17. "You can expect sunlight to shine through rain drops and break up into its many colors."

18. "You can expect some water to fall from the sky in the form of rain, hail, sleet, or snow."

19. "We'll be surrounded for a few days with lighter air that rises."

20. "The measure of the amount of water vapor in the air will be low for the rest of the week."

21. "I'll be right back to report the temperature at which condensation will occur today."

22. "The warm front we had yesterday has stopped moving. It is likely to remain in place for several days."

23. "We're looking here at an area of high pressure where the air is circulating clockwise and causing areas of fair weather."

24. "We're notifying the county that severe tornado conditions exist."

25. "The temperature of the air, rather than getting cooler at higher altitudes, is warmer, and this air is holding the cold air down near the ground, causing fog in the valleys."

26. "Air is flowing out counterclockwise from an area of low pressure and causing a major storm."

27. "We're notifying the county that tornado conditions could develop."

28. "Right now raindrops are falling out there through a layer of air that is less than –3° C. This is causing these drops to freeze."

29. "Get ready for a weekend of high winds and heavy, blowing snow."

30. "The whole Midwest is experiencing a prolonged period without rain or any other precipitation."

31. "This weekend, a cold air mass will invade a warm air mass, bringing rain showers and thunderstorms, followed by cooler temperatures."

32. "Next week, you can expect this warm air mass to meet this cold air mass over the southern part of the state and bring rain and snow."

IND   RAINBOWS
TORNADO WATCH   STATIONARY FRONT
TEMPERATURE INVERSION   RELATIVE HUMIDITY
WARM AIR   COLD FRONT

K-DRY   W-KOOL   W-SMOG

Name

UP FRONT

Where is the front of the front? And does a front have a back, or just a front? What do you know about the fronts that are so dominant in forming the weather around you? See if you can tell one front from another.

I. Fill in all the blanks to show that you understand the characteristics of each type of front.

II. Then label each drawing correctly: **warm front, cold front, stationary front,** or **occluded front.**

A **warm front** develops when a _____ air mass
1
meets a _____ air mass. The _____ air is less
2   3
_____ than the _____ air and slides up over
4   5
it. One of the first signs of a warm front is _____
6
clouds. _____ clouds form as the front continues to
7
move. _____ clouds may develop and produce
8
precipitation in the form of _____ or _____ .
9   10

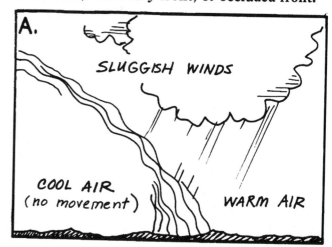

A **cold front** develops when a _____ air mass
11
invades a _____ air mass. The _____ air
12   13
forces the _____ air rapidly upward along a steep
14
incline. The kinds of clouds that tend to form along a
cold front are _____ and _____ . These
15   16
produce _____ . The passage of a cold front brings
17
_____ temperatures and _____ weather.
18   19

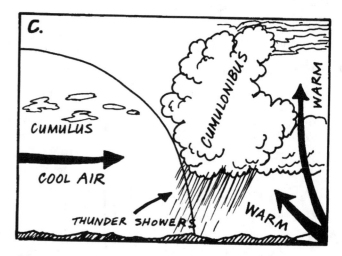

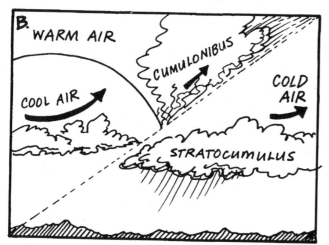

A **stationary front** develops when either a cold front
or a warm front _____ . This could remain in place for
20
_____ and often brings _____ across the region.
21   22

An **occluded front** develops when two _____ air
23
masses merge, forcing the _____ air to rise. This type
24
of front generally brings _____ and _____ .
25   26

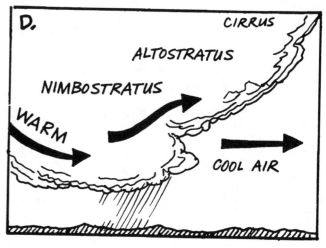

Name

        Copyright ©2002 by Incentive Publications, Inc., Nashville, TN.

WHAT DIFFERENCE DOES IT MAKE?

Of course you know that climate is the average long-range weather of a place. You probably also know that different areas of the world have different climate conditions. This means differences in temperature, amounts of rain or snow, humidity, or cloudiness. But . . . do you know why? Brush up on climate causes by finding out how each of these factors affects climate conditions. Write phrases or sentences to explain the effects of each one on climate.

latitude	Earth's revolution around the sun
tilt of Earth	bodies of water
ocean currents	altitude (elevation)
topography	large land masses
prevailing winds	large, permanent ice surfaces
cultural factors such as cities	

Name

139

Copyright ©2002 by INCENTIVE PUBLICATIONS, Inc., Nashville, TN.

OCEAN MOTIONS

Currents and tides . . . rolling waves and breakers . . . upwellings and tsunamis. The ocean never stops moving—that one thing is for sure! There are constant motions on the ocean. Some of them you want to be in. Some you want to watch. Others you want to hide from.
Define each of these motions. Write your definitions on the back of this page.

A. surface current   **B. density current**   **C. waves**   **D. tides**
E. upwellings   **F. tsunami**   **G. surf**

Answer these questions or complete these statements about ocean motions.

1. Upwellings bring _____ to the surface of the ocean.

2. Surface currents are caused by _____.

3. What ocean movements are affected by the moon's gravity?_____

4. What direction do most surface currents north of the equator move? _____

5. What direction do most surface currents south of the equator move? _____

6. How do cold currents affect climate? _____

7. How do warm currents affect climate? _____

8. What causes circulation in deep water? _____

9. What two things affect the density of water? _____ and _____

10. Does evaporation of salt water cause density to (increase) or (decrease)? _____

11. Another name for a thermohaline current is _____.

12. Is very salty water more or less dense than less salty water? _____

13. Is cold ocean water more or less dense than warmer water?_____

14. Does polar water diluted by melting ice become more or less dense?_____

15. Does heavy rainfall make ocean water more or less dense? _____

16. Which ocean motion is caused by earthquakes?_____

17. Which ocean motion occurs when a wave strikes the bottom of the ocean? _____

Name _____

CATCH A WAVE

These surfers and swimmers are having a great time catching and riding waves. Show how well you know waves by answering the questions about which surfer or swimmer is where.

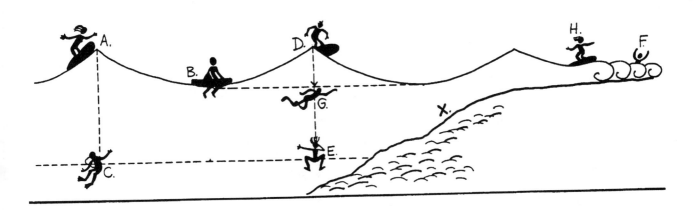

1. Which surfers are on the crests of waves? _____

2. Which surfers/swimmers are in deep-water waves? _____

3. Which surfers/swimmers are in shallow-water waves? _____

4. Where is surfer B? _____

5. The distance between surfers A and D is called the _____.

6. Which swimmers are at the wave base? _____

7. Which surfers/swimmers are in the surf or breakers? _____

8. The distance between which 2 surfers/swimmers is equal to the wave height? _____

9. The time it takes the waves A and B to pass any point is called the _____.

10. The distance between surfer A and swimmer C is equal to ½ the _____.

11. What is a wave, anyway? _____

12. How do particles of water in a wave move? _____

13. What happens when a deep-water wave strikes the bottom of the ocean? _____

    _____

14. What kind of a wave is caused by seismic activity? _____.

15. A wave moving in water that is deeper than ½ its wavelength is called a _____.

Name _____

The BASIC/Not Boring Middle Grades Science Book   Copyright ©2002 by Incentive Publications, Inc., Nashville, TN.

WHICH TIDE IS WHICH?

Isaac Newton discovered that everything in the universe exerts a pull on everything else. So what does this have to do with ocean water? Well, the sun and moon are both large enough and close enough to Earth that their gravitational forces pull ocean water into a bulge. This causes tides.

But . . . different locations of the sun, moon, and Earth in relationship to each other result in different kinds of tides. Show the sharpness of your TIDE IQ by telling which tide is which in the diagrams below.

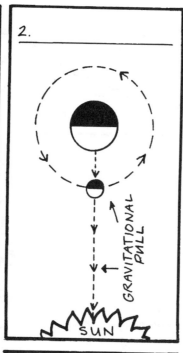

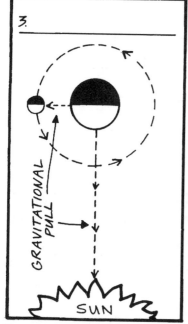

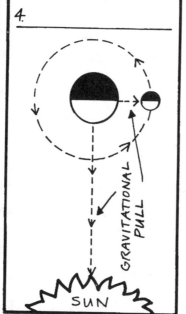

Name and describe the tide caused by each position.

1. _____

_____

_____

_____

2. _____

_____

_____

_____

3. _____

_____

_____

_____

4. _____

_____

_____

_____

Name _____

   Copyright ©2002 by Incentive Publications, Inc., Nashville, TN.

TIDE TALK

If the tide is out, is this a good place to set up your beach blanket? See if you know enough about tides to solve the puzzle. After you finish all the circles, the vertical word will answer the problem at the bottom of the page.

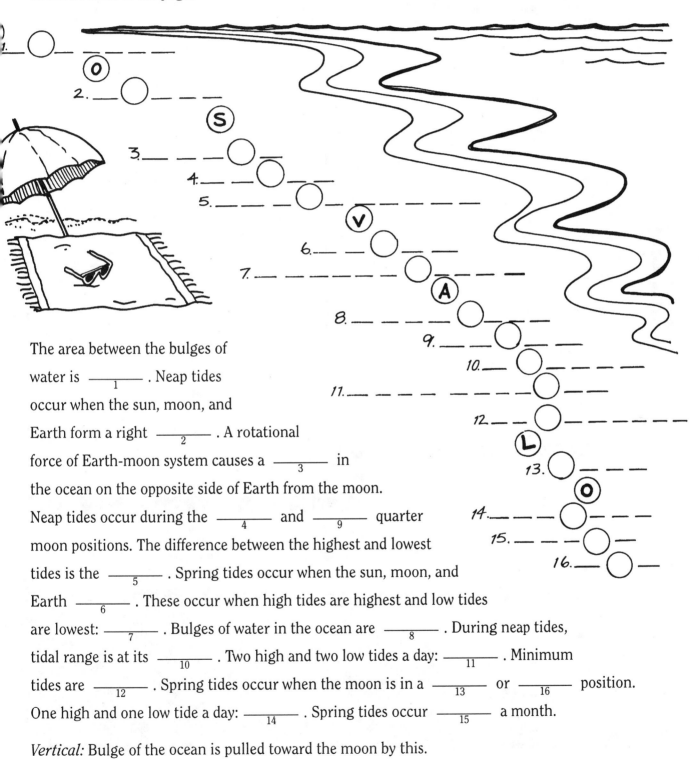

The area between the bulges of water is ———— . Neap tides occur when the sun, moon, and Earth form a right ———— . A rotational force of Earth-moon system causes a ———— in the ocean on the opposite side of Earth from the moon. Neap tides occur during the ———— and ———— quarter moon positions. The difference between the highest and lowest tides is the ———— . Spring tides occur when the sun, moon, and Earth ———— . These occur when high tides are highest and low tides are lowest: ———— . Bulges of water in the ocean are ———— . During neap tides, tidal range is at its ———— . Two high and two low tides a day: ———— . Minimum tides are ———— . Spring tides occur when the moon is in a ———— or ———— position. One high and one low tide a day: ———— . Spring tides occur ———— a month.

Vertical: Bulge of the ocean is pulled toward the moon by this.

Name _____

The BASIC/Not Boring Middle Grades Science Book   Copyright ©2002 by Incentive Publications, Inc., Nashville, TN.

UPS & DOWNS AT THE BOTTOM

Most people never see much of the ocean floor. But if you did get a good look at it, you'd see that it's not just a flat, bland floor. The ocean floor has a topography like the dry surface of Earth—with mountains and valleys and plains. But the features of the underwater surface are even more spectacular and pronounced than the ones above water.

These are some topographical features of the ocean floor. Write the letter (A–G) that gives the correct description for each one. Then find the letter on the diagram below (S–Z) that shows an example of the feature.

FEATURE	DEFINITION	EXAMPLE
1. continental shelf	_____	_____
2. continental slope	_____	_____
3. abyssal plain	_____	_____
4. mid-ocean range	_____	_____
5. oceanic trench	_____	_____
6. seamount	_____	_____
7. island	_____	_____

A. steeply sloping edge of continental shelf that drops to the ocean basin

B. volcano that does not rise above sea level

C. mountain that rises above sea level

D. relatively flat part of continent covered by sea water

E. deep ocean trough

F. flat, almost level, area of ocean basin

G. underwater mountain chain

Name

    Copyright ©2002 by Incentive Publications, Inc., Nashville, TN.

DISAPPEARING ACT

Four agents are responsible for a powerful earthwide act that changes or carries away parts of earth's materials—even tough ones like mountains. These are the agents of weathering or erosion.

Name these agents:

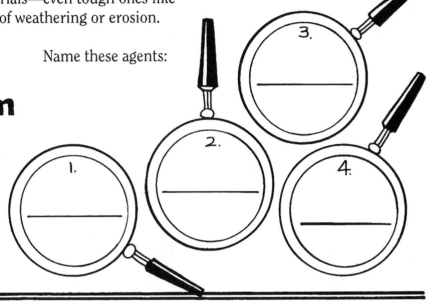

decomposition

disintegration

loess

talus

abrasion

deflation

weathering

oasis

creep

landslides

erosion

mudflows

slump

dune

rockfalls

gravity

Use the clues below to find out which processes and results these agents are using to do their disappearing acts.

CLUES

1. physical weathering; breakup of rocks into fragments
2. force that pulls material down a slope
3. process by which weathered materials are carried away
4. fertile green area in desert where winds have eroded land to a depth where water is present
5. material that accumulates at the bottom of a steep slope
6. blowing sand dropped by wind when an obstacle is met
7. windblown deposit of fine dust
8. rapid downslope movements of debris and dirt mixed with rain
9. loose material in layers slipping down a slope
10. scouring action of particles carried by wind
11. rapid movement of large amounts of material downslope
12. large masses of fallen rock
13. removal of loose material by wind
14. rocks formed from new substances
15. changes that rocks undergo near Earth's surface
16. slow downslope movements of materials

Name

WATER ON THE MOVE

Moving water is Earth's major agent of erosion—responsible for some of the most spectacular changes and landforms on the surface of Earth.

Here are some things that moving water can do. Tell which term is associated with each great feat of water.

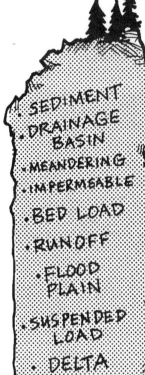

1. Rivers move at different speeds.

2. Water is drained from areas that share a system of channels.

3. Moving rivers roll heavy materials along the river bottom.

4. Moving rivers pick up lighter sediment and carry it along.

5. When the river profile flattens or the river meets an obstacle, it begins to wander from side to side across the flood plain.

6. As a moving river drags material along, it cuts a path into the rock.

7. A river deposits fertile soil on either side of its banks during floods.

8. Precipitation flows across Earth's surface and back into the ocean.

9. Water runs off rapidly from rocks that have no spaces for water to soak in.

10. Precipitation soaks into the ground and into rocks that have spaces between grains.

11. Moving water moves soil, particles, rocks, and debris— then drops it along the way.

12. Runoff carries loose material to the foot of a slope and drops the heaviest sediment first, then carries lighter sediment farther, dropping sediment in a triangular shape.

13. Water from high elevations flows in a network of rills, creeks, and streams into a river.

14. Rivers deposit sediment in their mouths in a fan shape as they empty into other bodies of water.

Terms (on the column):
- SEDIMENT
- DRAINAGE BASIN
- MEANDERING
- IMPERMEABLE
- BED LOAD
- RUNOFF
- FLOOD PLAIN
- SUSPENDED LOAD
- DELTA
- CHANNEL
- PERMEABLE
- VELOCITY
- ALLUVIAL FANS
- DRAINAGE SYSTEM

Name _____

MOSTLY WATER

The surface of Earth is mostly water. Oceans, lakes, rivers, streams, ponds, icebergs, and glaciers cover ¾ of Earth's surface. Wiley Will Waters claims he's an expert on world water features. He's describing his visits to some of these places. Does he really know what he's talking about? For each of his descriptions, write YES or NO. If he's got his terms and features mixed up and an answer is NO, circle his misstatement and correct it on the line underneath.

_____ 1. "Today, I'm on the shores of the world's largest lake, Lake Superior."

_____ 2. "Here we are at the source of the Amazon River, the place where it empties into the Atlantic Ocean."

_____ 3. "This network of rills and creeks and streams which flow into the river is called a floodplain."

_____ 4. "Here the river has overflowed its banks and deposited silt in the river channel."

_____ 5. "The deposit dropped by this river in its mouth is called an aquifer."

_____ 6. "This river, the Nile, is the world's longest river."

_____ 7. "Sometimes a river wanders out of its bed and becomes a meandering river."

_____ 8. "Some of Earth's water is under the surface, called groundwater."

_____ 9. "The source of this river is the place where it began."

_____ 10. "The Niagara River takes a steep plunge over this drop called a delta."

_____ 11. "Rivers flow into their tributaries all over the world."

_____ 12. "This oxbow lake was formed when a curve of a meandering river got cut off."

_____ 13. "Here's the Pacific—the world's largest ocean."

_____ 14. "This drainage system is the place where the river empties into a larger body of water."

_____ 15. "This river has not flooded for a long time; it has stayed in its channel."

Name _____

The BASIC/Not Boring Middle Grades Science Book Copyright ©2002 by Incentive Publications, Inc., Nashville, TN.

WHAT'S TRUE ABOUT GROUNDWATER?

Earth is actually a lot like a giant sponge. Water not only flows and moves around on the surface in rivers and lakes and oceans, it also collects and moves beneath the surface. The water that sinks into Earth's crust is called groundwater. Jocelyn has just taken a TRUE-FALSE test about groundwater. Grade her test. Give her 5 points for each correct answer. What is her final score?

_F_ 1. Groundwater flows faster than surface water.

_F_ 2. Water seeps into the ground until it reaches a rock layer with no pores.

_T_ 3. Gravity causes groundwater to move through connecting pores of Earth's crust.

_T_ 4. Some groundwater returns to the surface in springs.

_F_ 5. Often groundwater must be pumped to the surface to be used.

_F_ 6. Hot springs forced through small openings in Earth's crust are geysers.

_F_ 7. Groundwater is water that runs along Earth's surface.

_T_ 8. Stalactites are deposits hanging from cave roofs caused by dripping groundwater.

_F_ 9. Groundwater stops moving downward when it meets permeable rock.

_T_ 10. Some groundwater returns to the surface in swamps.

_T_ 11. Groundwater sometimes flows out of the surface in artesian wells.

_F_ 12. A funnel-shaped depression of limestone dissolved by rain is called a cave.

_F_ 13. Groundwater moves through permeable rock.

_T_ 14. Rainwater is weak acid that dissolves limestones and rock and creates caves.

_F_ 15. Calcium carbonate deposits on cave floors build up stalactites.

_T_ 16. Aquifers are permeable rock layers that are filled with water.

_F_ 17. Gravel and sand are good aquifers.

_F_ 18. Sinkholes are formed by meteors striking Earth's surface.

_F_ 19. The water table is just below the layer of impermeable rock.

_T_ 20. The water table is part of the zone of saturation.

Jocelyn's Score _____

AWESOME ICE

Six million square miles of Earth's surface is covered by glaciers! That's 10% of Earth. Glaciers are huge masses of ice that move slowly on land. A glacier can carry massive amounts of rocks and other debris as it moves.

This glacier is filled with mixed-up glacial trivia. Match up the pairs that belong together. On the back of this page write the numbers 1–46. Beside each number, write the number of the trivia that matches it. (Each pair will be listed twice.)

1
movement of glacial ice

2
melting water at base of glacier helps the ice move over land

3
layered deposits of glacial debris

4
large, deep crack in glacier surface

5
high, deep valleys formed by glaciers

6
glacial flow

7
ridges of debris left by melting water

8
horn

9
erosion

10
pressure causing ice layers to slide over each other

11
massive glaciers in polar regions that cover nearly all of Greenland and Antarctica

12
melt water

13
iceberg

14
basal flow

15
kettle lake

16
cirque

17
striations

18
crevasse

19
plucking

20
peak sharpened by glaciers

21
valley glacier

22
till

23
ice shelf

24
ground moraine

25
outwash

26
terminal moraine

27
plastic flow

28
abrading

29
debris dropped from base of glacier as it melts

30
small basins formed when blocks of ice surrounded by debris melt

31
scouring of bedrock surface by glacier

32
glaciers that extend onto a plain at the foot of a mountain

33
long, parallel scratches made by rocks dragged along by glaciers

34
mass of ice broken off a glacier

35
piedmont glacier

36
thick floating ice sheet attached to a continent

37
continental glaciers

38
moraines

39
hanging valleys

40
a process by which glacial water freezes around rocks as it moves

41
first material dropped by glacier—boulders, sand, clay

42
a hollow in which snow accumulates to form a valley glacier

43
alpine glacier formed in valleys at high elevations

44
water resulting from melting glaciers

45
ridges deposited at edges of glacier

46
how glaciers change Earth's surface

Name

DIGGING IN

No one has ever been able to dig into all the layers of Earth. If you could do it, you'd find things very different from what you see on the surface. Scientists have never gotten below the crust—so they can only use instruments to guess about what's inside. But they have some good ideas about Earth's layers. Pretend you are in the process of digging all the way to the center of Earth by answering these questions as you go! You'll need a science text or encyclopedia to help you answer some of the questions. Others can be answered from studying the diagram below.

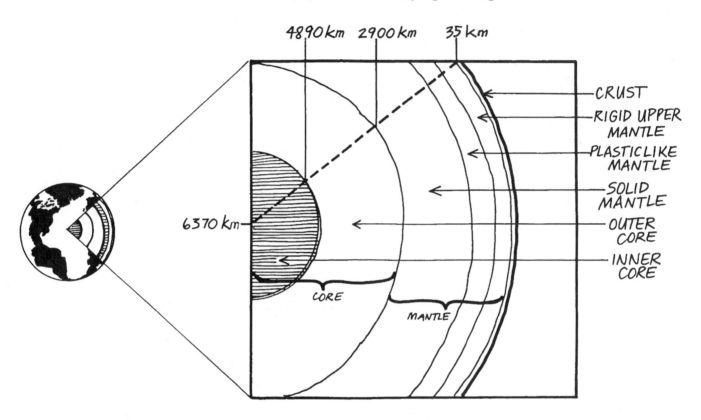

1. You're digging through the outermost layer. Where are you?_____

2. You reach the point where the mantle begins. What is it called? _____

3. You've gotten to about 100 km below the surface. Where are you?_____

4. The inside of Earth is very plasticlike here. Could you be in the mantle?_____

5. You're in a rocky, rigid layer. Where are you?_____

6. You're at the Gutenberg Discontinuity. Where are you? _____

7. You're close to the center, in a solid area. Where are you? _____

8. You're close to the center, but in a liquid area. Where are you? _____

9. You're in the crust, but only 5 km below the surface. What are you under?_____

10. You're in a near-fluid area about 200 km down. Where are you?_____

Name _____

THE AMAZING CRUST

A crust doesn't sound very exciting, does it? But the crust of Earth is a pretty amazing place. It is loaded with spectacular stuff. Get an atlas, an almanac, or an encyclopedia, and get to work finding out about some of the wonders of Earth's crust.

FIND EACH OF THESE:

1. the largest sand dunes
   Where? _____
   Height? _____

2. the biggest continent _____
   Area? _____

3. the largest volcanic crater
   Where? _____
   Area? _____

4. the highest mountain_____
   Height? _____

5. the highest active volcano
   Where? _____
   Height? _____

6. the longest glacier _____
   Where? _____

7. the deepest mine
   Where? _____
   Depth? _____

8. the biggest island _____
   Area? _____

9. the oldest rock
   Age? _____

10. the largest coral reef_____
    Length? _____

11. the largest lake _____
    Area? _____

12. the highest waterfall? _____
    Height? _____

13. highest sea wave
    Height? _____

14. largest cave system_____
    Length? _____

15. lowest point of land _____
    Depth below sea level? _____

16. deepest ocean trench _____
    Depth? _____

17. largest ocean_____
    Area? _____

18. largest tsunami
    Height? _____

Name _____

TAKEN FOR "GRANITE"

Spewing, erupting volcanoes . . . high temperatures . . . tons of pressure . . . deposits of buried and hard-ened fragments . . . all of these lead to something we take for granted—the common (or not so common) ROCK! You might think rocks are pretty ordinary, not worth a lot of attention. Or you may be a serious rock hound (someone who loves, collects, and studies rocks). Whichever you are, it's good to know about rocks, because they're a pretty fundamental part of your world.

Show that you don't take rocks for granted by answering the questions on these two pages (152 and 153). You'll find some help on the rocks at the bottom of both pages. An answer may be used more than once.

1. What are the three big groups of rocks? _____

_____

2. Which rocks are formed from hardened lava that flowed from volcanoes? _____

3. What is the name of a very porous igneous rock that is so light that it floats? _____

4. What are the hollow ball-like objects, such as quartz, which are found in sedimentary rocks? _____

5. Which kind of metamorphic rocks are massive and lack banding?

_____

6. What happens to rock fragments that get buried after a long time?

_____

7. Which rocks have a name that means "fire"?

_____

8. What are the remains of once-living organisms found in sedimentary rocks?

_____

9. What are wavy features found on some sandstones? _____

10. What rocks are changed by high temperatures and high pressure?

_____

11. Name 4 kinds of sedimentary rocks._____

_____

12. What term is used to describe metamorphic rocks with a banded texture?

_____

EXTRUSIVE MARBLE DARK Anthracite FOSSILS FELSITE CEMENTATION

Siltstone PUMICE Intrusive Metamorphic FELDSPAR Limestone SAND-STONE Quartzite RIPPLE MARKS

Use with page 153.

Name _____

Use with page 152.

13. What kinds of rocks are similar to layers of cake? _____

14. Basaltic magma would form what color of igneous rock? _____

15. What 2 groups of rocks are formed from all 3 kinds of rocks? _____

_____

16. What class of sedimentary rocks is made of fragments of rocks, minerals, and shells?

_____

17. Which igneous rocks are coarse-grained due to slow cooling? _____

18. Name 4 kinds of metamorphic rocks. _____

_____

19. What kinds of rocks are caused by weathering? _____

20. Name 4 kinds of igneous rocks. _____

_____

21. What is the class that includes sedimentary rocks which are deposited from a solution made by organic processes? _____

22. What metamorphic rock is commonly known as "coal"? _____

23. Which igneous rocks are fine-grained due to fast cooling? _____

24. What process happens when mud or silt is buried and water and air are squeezed out, producing such rocks as shale? _____

25. What process happens when minerals are precipitated out of water and hold particles of rock together? _____

26. What rocks are a mix of rounded pebbles and sand? _____

27. What rocks are a mix of sharp, angular pebbles? _____

28. What sedimentary rock is formed from thin layers of clay compacted very tightly together? _____

29. Where is the precipitate calcite commonly found to create interesting formations in the ground? _____

30. What animals secrete calcite around their bodies, forming massive reefs?

_____

harden GEODES BRECCIA CONGLOMERATE Granite CORALS IGNEOUS SHALE CAVES SEDIMENTARY

nonfoliated FOLIATED COMPACTION LIGHT CLASTIC SLATE basalt NON-CLASTIC

Name _____

TREASURES IN THE EARTH

Earth's crust is loaded with minerals—some of them common, some of them very rare. Even those that don't cost hundreds or thousands of dollars in the gem variety are valuable and useful. All minerals are natural, inorganic solids which have interesting crystalline structures. Each mineral is a specific combination of elements. Minerals are usually identified by certain physical properties such as hardness, streak, luster, mass, form, cleavage, feel, smell, and taste.

Erik and Erika, two young mineral fanatics, have discovered some treasures. Answer the questions on these two pages (154 and 155) about what they have found. To do this you will need to pay attention to the hardness scale below. You will also need the chart of "Physical Properties of Some Common Minerals" found on page 162.

1. Erika has found a mineral that scratches quartz. Could it be gypsum? _____

2. The searchers are thrilled to find a handful of pale yellow, shiny nuggets. They are sure they have found gold! The mineral leaves a greenish-black streak, and cannot be scratched by fluorite. Have they struck it rich? _____

3. Erik has a handful of whitish-gray stones with a nonmetallic luster that leave a colorless streak. They can be scratched by a steel file but not by a knife. What does he have? _____

4. Both kids have found samples of a red mineral which leaves a gray streak. It can be scratched with a fingernail and with a penny, and it can be easily cut with a knife. What is it?_____

5. Erika is holding a very soft mineral that leaves black "grease" on her fingers. It makes a black streak and has a shiny luster. What is it? _____

6. Erik has found a metallic, gray mineral that leaves a gray streak. The crystals appear cubic. When it breaks, it breaks with clear, clean cleavage. It scratches gypsum. Is it graphite?_____

7. Erika has a pile of white, nonmetallic stones that leave a white streak. They can be scratched with a fingernail. What are they? _____

8. Erik has some yellow stones that leave a yellow streak. They can be scratched with a fingernail. He wonders if they could be gold, but they do not have a metallic luster. What might they be?

9. A pale white stone is found at Erik's feet. It has hexagonal crystals, leaves a white streak, and can be scratched by a knife, but not by a fingernail. Could it be dolomite? _____

HARDNESS SCALE

Hardness	Characteristics and Example
1	soft, greasy, flakes on fingers (talc)
2	can be scratched by fingernail (gypsum)
3	can be cut easily with a knife or nail, or scratched by a penny (calcite)
4	can be scratched easily by a knife (fluorite)
5	can be scratched by a knife with difficulty (apatite)
6	can be scratched by a steel file (orthoclase)
7	scratches a steel file (quartz)
8	scratches quartz (topaz)
9	scratches anything lower on scale (corundum)
10	scratches anything lower on scale (diamond)

Use with page 155.

Name _____

     Copyright ©2002 by Incentive Publications, Inc., Nashville, TN.

Use with page 154.

10. Erik has picked up a mineral which feels soapy and leaves a white, powdery residue on his hands. It is very soft and flakes off. What has he probably found? _____

11. Meanwhile, Erika has a colorless chunk that breaks apart into cubes. It has no luster and is soft enough to be scratched by fluorite. When she gets it wet, it starts to dissolve. What has she found? _____

12. Right away, Erika finds another colorless chunk of mineral. It cannot be scratched by calcite. It has no shine to it, and seems to break apart in many directions. What has she probably found? _____

13. The two have stumbled upon a large amount of a mineral that has various colors. Some of it is almost clear. It appears to have hexagonal crystals and is hard enough to scratch a steel file. What could it be? _____

14. Erik has found a deep red mineral that looks like a gem. It leaves a colorless streak and is harder than quartz. Could it be a garnet? ___

15. A brown mineral that leaves a brown streak is in Erika's basket. It fractures irregularly, and can be scratched by a steel file but not by a knife. It has a nonmetallic luster. What might it be? _____

16. Erika is especially excited about a find of whitish mineral that glows when she puts it under ultraviolet light. It leaves a colorless streak and cannot be scratched with a penny, but can be scratched with a knife. What might it be? _____

17. Erik's mother has let him examine a gem she has. It is blue, leaves a colorless streak, and cannot be scratched with anything they find. It does scratch quartz. What might it be?

_____

DRUSY QUARTZ

CITRINE QUARTZ

SMOKY QUARTZ

ROSE QUARTZ

AMETHYST QUARTZ

18. Erica thinks she's found some copper. The mineral looks coppery-red, and can be scratched by fluorite. It has a metallic luster. Is this probably copper? _____

19. Another black mineral is in Erik's basket. It leaves a black streak and has a metallic luster. It cannot be scratched by a fingernail, knife, or penny. Is it galena? _____

20. A yellow gem that Erika has seems to be a topaz. If it is, will it scratch a steel file? _____

21. The pair has happened upon a small amount of a shiny, silvery-white mineral that leaves a light gray streak. It is hard enough to scratch calcite. Could it be silver? _____

22. Erika has a green, nonmetallic mineral that leaves a colorless streak. It can be scratched by a penny, but not easily by a fingernail. Could it be muscovite? _____

Name _____

 Copyright ©2002 by Incentive Publications, Inc., Nashville, TN.

WHICH VOLCANO?

One volcano is not necessarily like every other volcano. Did you know that there are different sorts of volcanoes? There are—because not all volcanoes look or behave alike or throw out the same stuff at the same speed. Read up on volcanoes so you can decide which description and which picture belongs with which kind of volcano. (A volcano is a crack or vent in Earth's crust through which lava or magma is expelled.)

LABELS:

STRATOVOLCANO
Description #: _____ Picture #: _____

SHIELD VOLCANO
Description #: _____ Picture #: _____

CINDER CONE VOLCANO
Description #: _____ Picture #: _____

DOME VOLCANO
Description #: _____ Picture #: _____

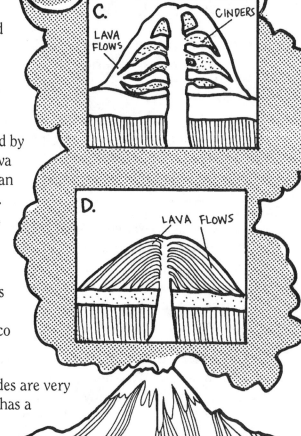

1. The most common form of volcano, this kind is made of layers of lava and ash, cinders and rock fragments. A quiet lava flow seals off solid lava inside. The pressure builds up and results in violent eruptions. Mt. Fuji in Japan and Mt. Vesuvius in Italy are examples of this kind of volcano.

2. This kind of volcano has a low, broad look. It is formed by basalt flowing quietly out of a central opening. The lava flows out over gently sloping sides. These volcanoes can grow to be very large and spread out over a huge area. The Hawaiian Islands are built of this kind of volcano.

3. These are cone-shaped hills that are very steep. This kind of volcano is formed by violent eruptions that blow out fragments of lava in fine cinders. The cinders build up around the vent to make a very steep cone. Mt. Pelee in Martinique and Mt. Capulin in New Mexico are examples of this kind of volcano.

4. This volcano has slower-flowing lava. Although the sides are very steep, the volcanoes are smaller. This kind of volcano has a dome-shaped mass in the crater.

Name _____

FOLDS & FAULTS & QUAKES

Are you puzzled by the folds and cracks and quivers and shakes of Earth's surface? Well, you don't have to be for long. Get out your science book or an encyclopedia and brush up on the features and terms related to faults, folds, and earthquakes. Then take a hard look at this puzzle. You'll notice that the puzzle is already done for you! Oh, but something is missing—the clues to the puzzle. It's your job to create them. Use the spaces provided at the bottom.

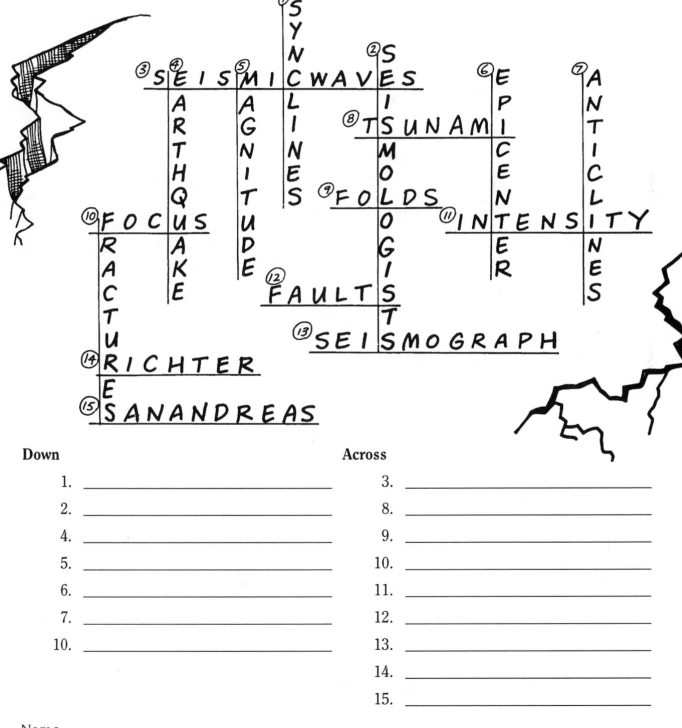

Down

1. _____

2. _____

4. _____

5. _____

6. _____

7. _____

10. _____

Across

3. _____

8. _____

9. _____

10. _____

11. _____

12. _____

13. _____

14. _____

15. _____

Name _____

 Copyright ©2002 by Incentive Publications, Inc., Nashville, TN.

GIANT PLATES

Earth's crust is made up of many huge pieces like a gigantic jigsaw puzzle. Each piece is a giant plate. Continents and oceans rest on these plates, which are always on the move. They are constantly being pulled apart or pushed together, or they are colliding with each other.

Fit together the puzzle pieces that belong. There are eleven pairs of matching terms and descriptions in the puzzle pieces below. For each number (1–22), list the matching puzzle piece. (Each pair will be listed twice.)

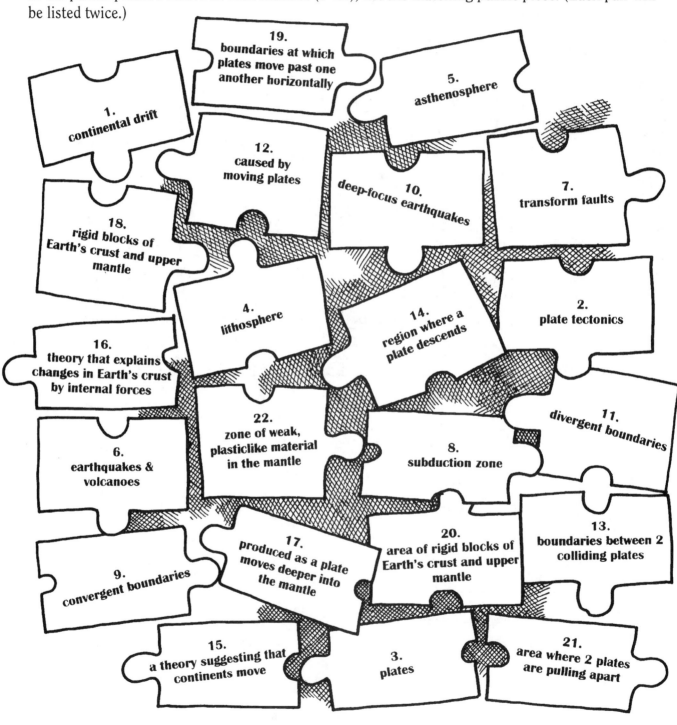

Name

GREAT QUAKES & ERUPTIONS

Can you find out about some of Earth's most devastating earthquakes, most damaging volcanoes, longest earthquakes, most active volcanoes? Get a good almanac or encyclopedia, and see what you can learn about these earthquakes and volcanoes.

EARTHQUAKES

Write what you can find out about the magnitude, length, and damage of each "quake."

1923   Tokyo _____

1927   China _____

1939   Chile _____

1970   Peru _____

1976   China _____

1980   Italy _____

1989   San Francisco _____

1992   Turkey _____

1993   India _____

1994   California _____

1995   Japan _____

VOLCANOES

Write what you can find out about these eruptions and their damage.

A.D. 79   Mt. Vesuvius, Italy _____

1669   Mt. Etna, Sicily _____

1792   Mt. Unzen, Japan _____

1815   Mt. Tambora, Indonesia _____

1883   Mt. Krakotoa, Indonesia _____

1902   Mt. Pelée, Martinique _____

1906   Mt. Vesuvius, Italy _____

1980   Mt. St. Helens, Oregon, USA _____

1984   Mt. Mauna Loa, Hawaii _____

1985   Nevado del Ruiz, Colombia _____

Name _____

SUCH ODD STUFF!

There are some strange, mysterious features on and just below Earth's surface. Find out what these mysteries are. (See the list below.) Which mysterious sight would you be near in each of these examples?

A. HOT SPRINGS

B. FUMORALE

C. GEYSER

D. LACCOLITH

E. VOLCANIC NECK

F. SINKHOLE

G. CALDERA

H. MUDSPOTS

I. SOLFATARAS

J. BATHOLITH

K. DIKE

SPLURP

_____ 1. You take a swim in a lake-filled crater formed when a volcano blew its top and the volcano's cone collapsed into the vent.

_____ 2. You are filming a natural hot spring that is shooting hot water high up into the air through a small opening in Earth's surface.

_____ 3. Your cousin is videotaping you as you relax in a steaming hot pool of underground water which was heated by magma in a thermal region before it rose through cracks into the pool.

_____ 4. You're recording the strange popping noises as you watch the plopping, spurting patterns made by hot water squirting up through mud.

_____ 5. You hold your nose because this spot smells like rotten eggs. It's an outlet in Earth's surface where steam, chlorides, sulfurs, and other gases are given off by cooling magma. The rocks around the edges are yellow from the sulfur, and wow! Does it smell!

_____ 6. More rotten eggs! This dying volcano gives off sulfur vapors all the time.

_____ 7. You have to envision this one, because it's beneath the surface. A large mass of intrusive igneous rock forms the core of a mountain you're admiring. This solid mass extends far down into Earth.

_____ 8. You saw it with your own eyes! A road disappeared, and a truck with it—into a funnel-shaped depression in the earth caused by dissolving limestone beneath the surface.

_____ 9. Another underground marvel—a mushroom-shaped body of igneous rock, formed as lava hardens in this strange shape.

_____ 10. The earth has eroded away to leave a tall skinny mass of rock that was formed underground when magma entered a vertical crack and hardened.

_____ 11. An inactive volcano had magma solidified in its pipe. As the softer, outer rock wore away, this remained resistant to erosion.

Name

EARTH & SPACE SCIENCE
ASSESSMENT AND ANSWER KEYS

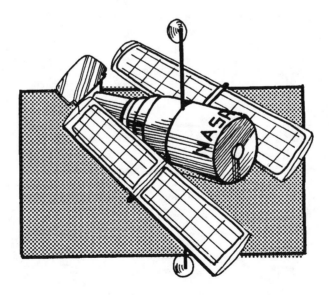

PHYSICAL PROPERTIES OF SOME COMMON MINERALS

Metallic Luster

MINERAL	COLOR	STREAK	HARDNESS	CRYSTALS	BREAKAGE
GRAPHITE	black to gray	black to gray	1–2	hexagonal	scales
SILVER	silvery, white	light gray to silver	2.5	cubic	hackly
GALENA	gray	gray to black	2.5	cubic	perfect, cubic
GOLD	pale-golden yellow	yellow	2.5–3	cubic	hackly
COPPER	copper red	copper red	3	cubic	hackly
CHROMITE	black or brown	brown to black	5.5	cubic	irregular
MAGNETITE	black	black	6	cubic	conchoidal
PYRITE	light brassy yellow	greenish black	6.5	cubic	uneven

Nonmetallic Luster

MINERAL	COLOR	STREAK	HARDNESS	CRYSTALS	BREAKAGE
TALC	white, greenish	white	1	monoclinic	in 1 direction
BAUXITE	gray, red, brown, white	gray	1–3	—	—
GYPSUM	colorless, gray, white	white	2	monoclinic	basal cleavage
SULFUR	yellow	yellow to white	2	orthorhombic	conchoidal
MUSCOVITE	white, gray, yellow, rose, green	colorless	2.5	monoclinic	basal cleavage
HALITE	colorless, red, white, blue	colorless	2.5	cubic	cubic
CALCITE	colorless, white	colorless, white	3	hexagonal	in 3 directions
DOLOMITE	colorless, white, pink, green, gray	white	3.5–4	hexagonal	in 3 directions
FLUORITE	colorless, white, blue, green, red, yellow, purple	colorless	4	cubic	cleavage
HORNBLENDE	green to black	gray to white	5–6	monoclinic	in 2 directions
FELDSPAR	gray, green, white	colorless	6	monoclinic	2 planes
QUARTZ	colorless, colors	colorless	7	hexagonal	conchoidal
GARNET	yellow-red, green, black	colorless	7.5	cubic	conchoidal
TOPAZ (gemstone)	white, pink, yellow, blue, colorless	colorless	8	orthorhombic	basal
CORUNDUM (gemstone)	colorless, blue, brown, green, white, red, pink	colorless	9	hexagonal	fracture

EARTH & SPACE SCIENCE
SKILLS TEST

Each correct answer is worth 1 point.

Questions 1–20: Match each term with its definition.

_____ 1. loess
_____ 2. core
_____ 3. gibbous
_____ 4. geyser
_____ 5. salinity
_____ 6. front
_____ 7. impermeable
_____ 8. sediment
_____ 9. latitude
_____ 10. delta
_____ 11. trough
_____ 12. aquifers
_____ 13. erosion
_____ 14. diurnal
_____ 15. neap
_____ 16. umbra
_____ 17. corona
_____ 18. equinox
_____ 19. meteorites
_____ 20. fault

a. boundary where two air masses meet
b. distance north or south of the equator
c. time of year when day and night are the same length
d. meteors that strike the ground
e. crack in Earth's crust
f. innermost layer of Earth
g. phase where more than ¼ of the moon is visible
h. tides that occur when sun, moon, and Earth are at right angles
i. Earth's materials are carried away
j. hot springs that regularly erupt water & steam
k. sediment deposit at mouth of river
l. inner shadow in an eclipse
m. windblown deposit of dust
n. low point of a wave
o. outer zone of the sun's surface
p. occurs daily
q. permeable rocks containing water
r. water cannot soak in
s. concentration of salt
t. loose earth material resulting from weathering

21. What moon phase is shown in the diagram below?

_____

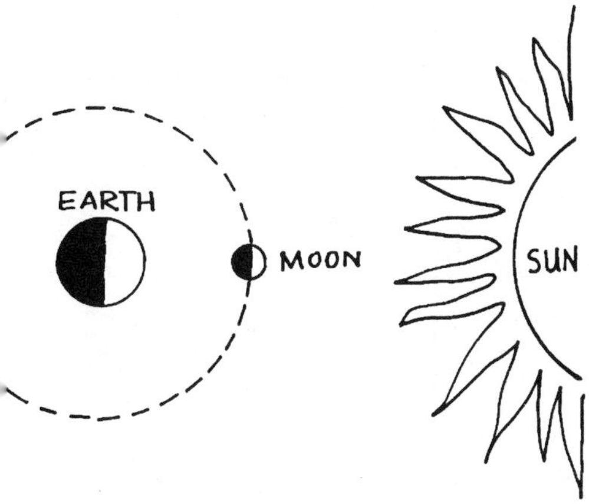

For 22–32, fill in the word that is being defined.

_____ 22. type of rock formed by volcanic activity

_____ 23. planet noted for thousands of rings

_____ 24. largest planet; has cloud bands and red spot

_____ 25. scale used to measure earthquakes

_____ 26. outermost layer of Earth

_____ 27. usually farthest known planet from sun

_____ 28. billions of stars held together by gravity

_____ 29. objects orbiting sun between Mars & Jupiter

_____ 30. agency that oversees U.S. space program

_____ 31. 3 agents of erosion

_____ 32. theory explaining moving of continents and internal Earth processes

Name _____

The BASIC/Not Boring Middle Grades Science Book   Copyright ©2002 by Incentive Publications, Inc., Nashville, TN.

For 33-35, use the diagram below to answer the questions.

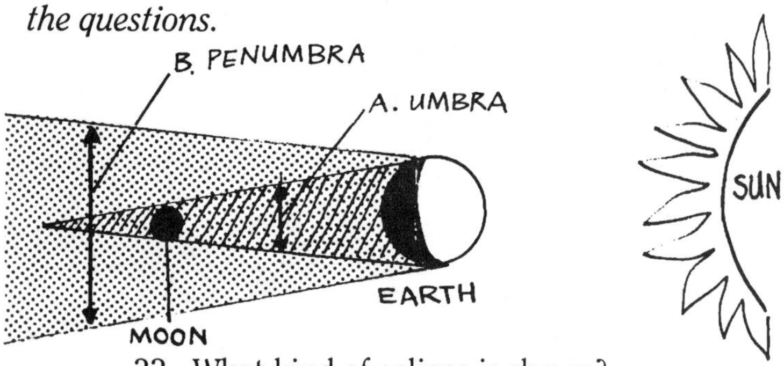

B. PENUMBRA
A. UMBRA
SUN
EARTH
MOON

_____ 33. What kind of eclipse is shown?

_____ 34. Which letter represents the penumbra?

_____ 35. Which letter represents the umbra?

For 36-52, write the letter of the correct answer.

_____ 36. A ___ is a hot, glowing sphere of gas.
a) corona   c) star
b) solar flare   d) black hole

_____ 37. The first man-made object to orbit
Earth was   e) Apollo   g) Lun
            f) Sputnika   h) Pioneer

_____ 38. A ___ is a funnel of water spinning over
the ocean.
a) cyclone   c) water spout
b) hurricane   d) tornado

_____ 39. Prevailing winds can affect climate by
e) cooling   g) bringing moisture
f) warming   h) e, f, and g

_____ 40. During ___ in the Northern Hemisphere,
the North Pole is tilted toward the sun on
about June 21.
a) spring equinox   c) fall equinox
b) winter solstice d) summer solstice

_____ 41. ___ results when water vapor condenses in
water droplets on the ground.
e) Fog   f) Dew   g) Snow   h) Frost

_____ 42. Which climate would NOT be found
above 30° latitude?
a) semi-arid tropical
b) dry subtropical
c) Mediterranean subtropical
d) dry continental

_____ 43. A boundary of two air masses meeting is a
e) front   g) low pressure area
f) hurricane   h) high pressure area

_____ 44. A ___ is a reusable craft for transporting
people & equipment into space.
a) space probe   c) space shuttle
b) rocket   d) space station

_____ 45. Which does NOT make water more dense?
e) higher salt content g) melting ice
f) colder temperatures h) great evaporatio

_____ 46. Which is NOT a feature of the sun?
a) chromosphere c) photosphere   e) sola
b) corona   d) quasar   flar

_____ 47. The moon is ___ when it is less than ¼
visible and getting smaller
f) waxing crescent   h) waning crescent
g) waning gibbous   i) waxing gibbous

_____ 48. A wave in water less deep than ½ its wave
length is a ___ .
a) tidal wave   c) upwelling
b) shallow-water wave   d) deep-water wav

_____ 49. A ___ is a briefly visible meteor.
e) meteorite   g) asteroid
f) shooting star   h) comet

_____ 50. ___ are the prevailing winds in 30°–60°
latitude in the Northern Hemisphere.
a) Trade winds   c) Easterlies
b) Doldrums   d) Westerlies

_____ 51. Which of these do NOT influence climate?
e) latitude   g) altitude
f) longitude   h) topography

_____ 52. The motion of an object relative to the
position of its observer is ___ .
a) apparent motion   c) rotation
b) real motion   d) retrograde motio

For 53-56, use the
diagram of Earth's
atmosphere to
answer these.

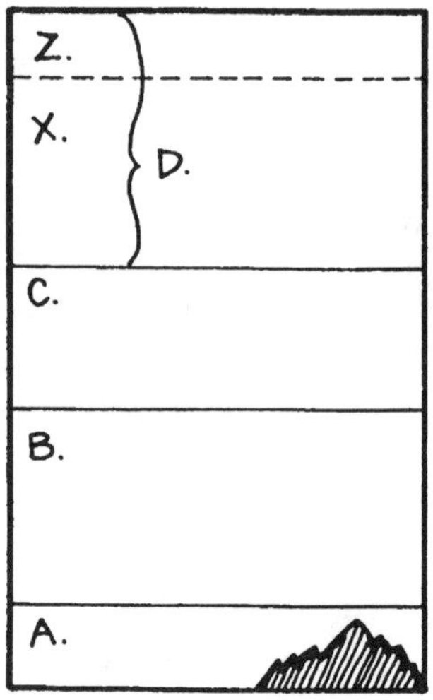

Z.
X.
D.
C.
B.
A.

Name

_____ 53. Which letter represents the stratosphere?

_____ 54. Which layer is labeled D?

_____ 55. Which layer is the mesosphere?

_____ 56. In which layer does weather take place?

For 57-62, write the answer.

_____ 57. What wind blows from land to sea at night?

_____ 58. What do comets orbit?

_____ 59. What part of Earth's atmosphere absorbs harmful ultraviolet rays?

_____ 60. What causes surface currents on the ocean?

_____ 61. Which is more dense: cold or warm ocean water?

_____ 62. What kind of a front is pictured below?

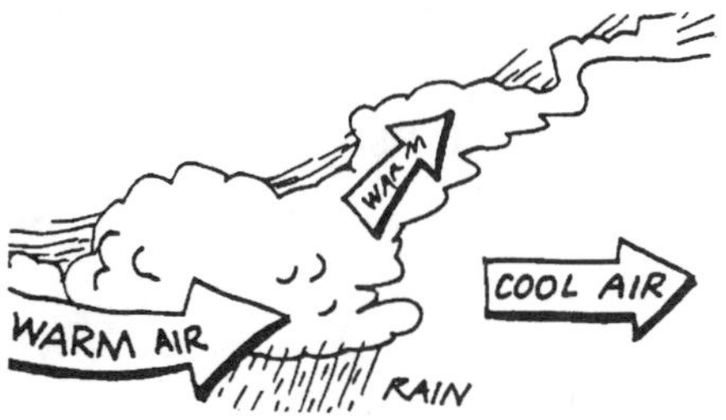

For 63–67, write the word that is being defined.

_____ 63. fog mixed with pollution

_____ 64. the outer, incomplete shadow formed during an eclipse

_____ 65. magma that is released at Earth's surface during volcanic eruptions

_____ 66. thick mass of ice in motion

_____ 67. water that falls to Earth's surface from the atmosphere as rain, snow, hail, or sleet

For 68–72, use the diagram below.

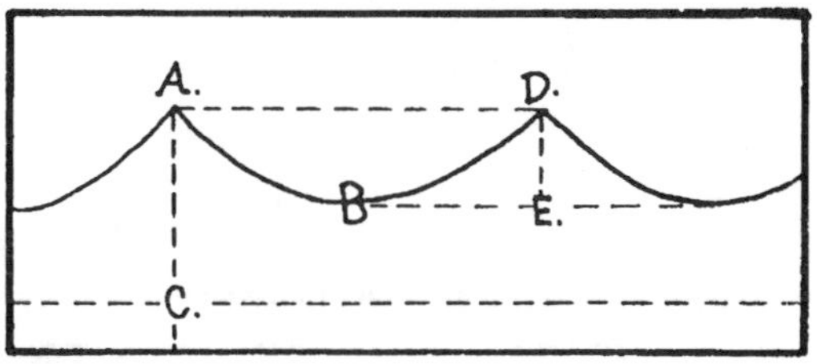

_____ 68. What part of the wave is A?

_____ 69. Which letter is at the wave base?

_____ 70. What does the distance A-D represent?

_____ 71. Which letter is in the trough?

_____ 72. What does the distance D-E represent?

For 73-74, use the diagram below.

_____ 73. Which diagram below pictures a spring tide?

_____ 74. Which diagram below pictures a neap tide?

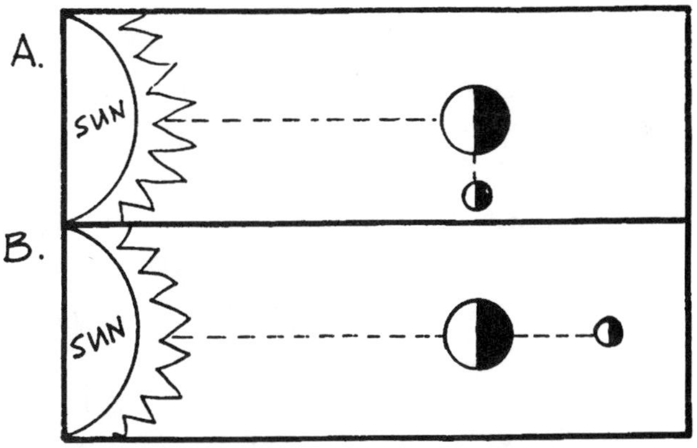

For 75–95, fill in the letter of the correct answer.

_____ 75. The ___ is the distance between the crests of two successive waves.
    a) wave height   c) wavelength
    b) wave period   d) wave base

_____ 76. The area between two tidal bulges is ___ .
    e) low tide   g) high tide
    f) spring tide   h) trough

_____ 77. A _____ occurs when the moon, sun, and Earth are aligned, with the moon on the opposite side of Earth from the sun.
    a) new moon   c) first quarter moon
    b) full moon   d) third quarter moon

_____ 78. In a(n) _____ , water is under pressure from the weight of water in an aquifer in the layers above.
    e) geyser   g) permeable rock
    f) sinkhole   h) artesian well

Name

_____ 79. The difference between the highest and lowest tide is the ___ .
    a) tidal range   c) neap tide
    b) spring tide   d) bulge

_____ 80. Precipitation that returns to the ocean is ___ .
    e) a flood   g) runoff
    f) rain   h) water vapor

_____ 81. When Earth, moon, and sun are aligned, which is NOT happening?
    a) neap tide   c) high tides are highest
    b) spring tide   d) low tides are lowest

_____ 82. The distance between the crest of a wave and the wave base is equal to ½ of ___ .
    e) the wavelength   g) the wave base
    f) the wave period   h) the wave width

_____ 83. Which is NOT associated with wind erosion?
    a) loess   c) talus
    b) dune   d) deflation

_____ 84. Which is a cause of tides?
    e) winds   g) temperature changes
    f) gravitational force   h) ocean storms

_____ 85. The ___ is the steeply sloping edge of the continental shelf.
    a) abyssal plain   c) continental slope
    b) seamount   d) ocean basin

_____ 86. ___ is the slow, downslope movement of earth material.
    e) rockfalls   g) deflation
    f) mudflows   h) creep

_____ 87. A ___ is a funnel-shaped depression in the ground caused when limestone dissolves along cracks
    a) stalactite   c) cave
    b) sinkhole   d) fumarole

_____ 88. The original hollow in which snow accumulates to form a valley glacier is a ___ .
    e) cirque   g) oxbow lake
    f) moraine   h) striation

_____ 89. Which term(s) are associated with glaciers?
    a) flow   c) outflow   e) cirque
    b) piedmont   d) crevasse   f) all of these

_____ 90. Which feature is not ordinarily used to identify a mineral?
    g) hardness   i) luster   l) mass
    h) shape of crystals   j) melting point   m) smell
    k) streak

_____ 91. The ___ is the point on Earth's surface where the seismic activity is strongest in a earthquake.
    a) focus   c) epicenter
    b) fracture   d) fold

_____ 92. Which group of rocks are rocks changed b high temperature and pressure?
    e) metamorphic   g) igneous
    f) sedimentary   h) f and g

_____ 93. A geographic feature formed when a volcano erupts and the peak collapses into the hole created is a ___ .
    a) dome   c) magma flo
    b) cinder conew   d) caldera

_____ 94. Which is (are) NOT igneous rock(s)?
    e) limestone   g) pumice   i) e and h
    f) basalt   h) marble   j) f and h

_____ 95. Sediment carried along by river or stream (not dragged) is ___ .
    a) runoff   c) suspended load
    b) channel   d) bedload

For 96-100, write the number of the feature from the diagram below.

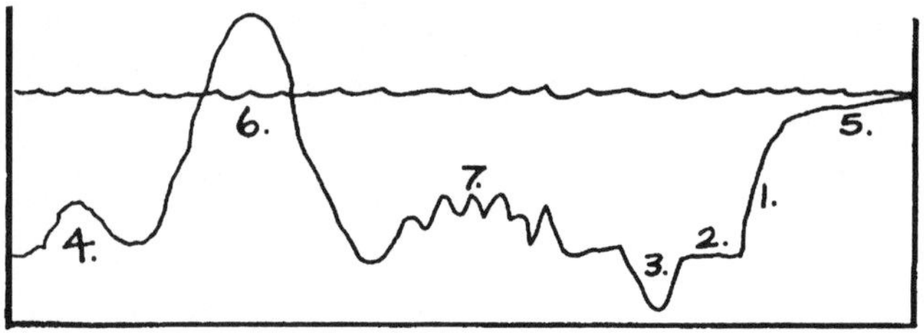

_____ 96. seamount

_____ 97. continental shelf

_____ 98. ocean trench

_____ 99. abyssal plain

_____ 100. continental slope

SCORE: Total Points _____ out of a possible 100 points

Name _____

EARTH & SPACE SCIENCE
SKILLS TEST ANSWER KEY

1. m
2. f
3. g
4. j
5. s
6. a
7. r
8. t
9. b
10. k
11. n
12. q
13. i
14. p
15. h
16. l
17. o
18. c
19. d
20. e
21. new
22. igneous
23. Saturn
24. Jupiter
25. Richter
26. crust

27. Pluto
28. galaxy
29. asteroids
30. NASA
31. any 3 of these: water, wind, gravity, ice
32. plate tectonics
33. lunar
34. B
35. A
36. c
37. f
38. c
39. h
40. d
41. f
42. a
43. e
44. c
45. g
46. d
47. g
48. b
49. f
50. d

51. f
52. a
53. B
54. thermosphere
55. C
56. A
57. land breeze
58. sun
59. ozone layer
60. wind
61. cold
62. warm
63. smog
64. penumbra
65. lava
66. glacier
67. precipitation
68. crest
69. C
70. wavelength
71. B
72. wave height
73. B
74. A
75. c

76. e
77. b
78. h
79. a
80. g
81. a
82. e
83. c
84. f
85. c
86. h
87. b
88. e
89. f
90. j
91. c
92. e
93. d
94. i
95. c
96. 4
97. 5
98. 3
99. 2
100. 1

The BASIC/Not Boring Middle Grades Science Book   Copyright ©2002 by Incentive Publications, Inc., Nashville, TN.

ANSWERS

Page 122

Features given may vary.
Order of planets:
1. Mercury / 0 moons / 2nd smallest, heavily cratered, dark color
2. Venus / 0 moons / cloud cover, yellow color
3. Earth / 1 moon / water vapor atmosphere, sustains life
4. Mars / 2 moons / polar caps, craters, clouds & fog, red color
5. Jupiter / 20 known moons / largest planet, gaseous, reddish-brown & white cloud bands, large red spot
6. Saturn / 17 moons / gaseous, many rings
7. Uranus / 15 moons / gaseous, dark rings
8. Neptune / 2 moons / gaseous, rings
9. Pluto / 1 moon / made of frozen water and gases

Bottom:
1. elliptical
2. aphelion
3. perihelion
4. Mars & Jupiter
5. Mercury, Venus, Earth, Mars
6. Jupiter, Saturn, Uranus, Neptune, Pluto

Page 123

Student-drawn solar systems may vary some. Check to see that planets are in the right order, have accurate coloring, and are drawn with accurate proportions.

Page 124

1. MY
2. P
3. MY
4. P
5. J
6. E
7. V
8. U
9. J
10. V
11. V
12. J
13. S
14. E
15. P
16. M
17. E
18. M
19. E
20. N
21. J
22. U
23. M
24. S
25. P
26. N
27. V
28. U
29. S
30. M
31. V
32. S
33. J

Page 125

1. quasar
2. red supergiant
3. sunspots
4. nebulae
5. star
6. pulsar
7. neutron star
8. galaxy
9. constellation
10. nova
11. photosphere
12. binary stars
13. black dwarf
14. Sirius A
15. supernova
16. white dwarf
17. variable star
18. Andromeda
19. Milky Way
20. corona
21. solar flares
22. black hole
23. chromosphere

Page 126

1. nucleus
2. shooting star
3. meteorite
4. Ceres
5. fireball
6. coma
7. asteroid belt
8. comets
9. comet's tail
10. meteor
11. asteroids
12. meteoroids
13. Halley's comet
14. the sun
15. away from the sun
16. elliptical

Page 127

Retrograde: apparent westward movement of a planet as seen from Earth
Real motion: actual movement of an object
Apparent motion: motion of an object relative to the position of its observer
Rotation: turning motion of an object on its axis
Revolution: circling of one object around another
Earth's gravity: attraction of object to Earth
Sun's gravity: attraction of object to the sun
1. day and night
2. about 24 hrs
3. Copernicus
4. rotation and revolution
5. seasons
6. 1 year/365 days

Page 128

1. seasons
2. summer
3. fall equinox; spring equinox
4. summer solstice
5. winter solstice
6. summer
7. winter solstice
8. spring equinox; fall equinox
9. summer solstice
10. 24 hours of
1. spring equinox
2. summer solstice
3. fall equinox
4. winter solstice

Page 129

1. C
2. F
3. A
4. E
5. D
6. H
7. B
8. G
9. D
10. G
11. A
12. E
13. C
14. H
15. F
16. B

Page 130

1. F
2. F
3. F
4. T
5. T
6. T
7. T
8. T
9. T
10. T
11. F
12. T
13. F
14. F
15. F
16. F
17. F
18. T
19. T
20. T

See that students have accurately labeled the diagrams of the eclipses.

Page 131

1. spectroscope
2. space shuttle
3. refracting
4. telescope
5. space lab
6. space station
7. reflecting
8. Apollo program
9. Gemini
10. space probe
11. moon walk
12. NASA
13. graph
14. thrust
15. radio telescope
16. rocket
17. satellite
18. Mercury
Mystery: Challenger Space Shuttle

Pages 132-133

1. 1971
2. 1958
3. 1964
4. 1990
5. 1973
6. 1984
7. 1965
8. 1903
9. 1986
10. 1959
11. 1959
12. 1976
13. 1986
14. 1974
15. 1988
16. 1960
17. 1926
18. 1962
19. 1966
20. 1961
21. 1968
22. 1968
23. 1973
24. 1965
25. 1977
26. 1983
27. 1996
28. 1957
29. 1961
30. 1969
31. 1981
32. 1957
33. 1962
34. 1963
35. 1965
36. 1966
37. 1970
38. 1966

Page 134

1-2. See that students have accurately labeled diagram as shown.

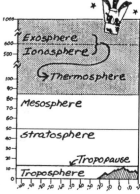

3. a. TR
   b. S
   c. M
   d. TH
   e. TR
   f. S

g. EX
h. TR
i. TPP
j. S
k. TH
l. I
m. TPP
n. TH
o. S
p. TPP
q. M
r. I
4. nitrogen, oxygen, argon, carbon dioxide, water vapor, traces of other gases
5. Ozone absorbs harmful ultraviolet radiation.
6. The force of air pressing down on Earth's surface
7. because of differences in air's density
8. no

Page 135
1. trade winds
2. doldrums
3. prevailing westerlies
4. cyclone
5. sea breeze
6. polar easterlies
7. hurricane
8. gale
9. the jet stream
10. front
11. land breeze
12. tornado
13. water spout
14. blizzard

Page 136-137
1. lows
2. dew
3. fog
4. tornado
5. rain
6. snow
7. lightning
8. fronts
9. cold air
10. highs
11. clouds
12. hail
13. frost
14. hurricane
15. thunder
16. wind
17. rainbows
18. precipitation
19. warm air
20. relative humidity
21. dew point

22. stationary front
23. anticyclone
24. tornado warning
25. temperature inversion
26. cyclones
27. tornado watch
28. sleet
29. blizzard
30. drought
31. cold front
32. warm front

Page 138
A. stationary
B. occluded
C. cold
D. warm
1. warm
2. cold
3. warm
4. dense
5. cold
6. cirrus
7. stratus
8. nimbostratus
9. rain
10. snow
11. cold
12. warm
13. cold
14. warm
15. cumulonimbus
16. cumulus
17. rain storms
18. cooler
19. clear
20. stops moving
21. several days
22. precipitation
23. cool
24. warm
25. wind
26. precipitation

Page 139
Answers will vary.
latitude—climates are cooler farther away from the equator
revolution—different stars are seen in the night sky at different orbital positions
tilt of Earth—seasons change; climate warmer when Earth tilts toward sun
water—milder, sometimes wetter effects
ocean currents—can warm or cool land, depending on the current temperatures

altitude—colder temperatures, affects precipitation
topography—causes variations in temperatures, winds, & moisture
land masses—tends toward colder, drier, hotter, or more extreme climates
prevailing winds—can cool or warm, depending on the wind
ice surfaces—cool temperatures
cultural factors—cities can increase pollution or humidity

Page 140
A. surface current—movement of water caused by wind
B. density current—movement of water from areas of more to less density
C. waves—movement in which water rises and falls regularly
D. tides—shallow water waves caused by gravitational forces of the sun, moon, and Earth
E. upwellings—rising of cold, deep water toward the surface
F. tsunami—sea waves caused by earthquake activity
G. surf—result of the forming and breaking of many waves
1. nutrients
2. winds
3. tides
4. clockwise
5. counterclockwise
6. cooler temperatures
7. warmer temperatures
8. density currents
9. temperature; salinity
10. increase
11. density current
12. more
13. more
14. less
15. less
16. tsunamis
17. surf

Page 141
1. A, D
2. A, B, C, D, E, G
3. H, F
4. trough
5. wavelength
6. C, E
7. H, F
8. D, G
9. wave period
10. wavelength
11. rise and fall of water
12. in a circular motion
13. waves are slowed, get higher, curve over their tops, and break
14. tsunami
15. deep-water wave

Page 142
1. full moon spring tide: The moon, Earth, and sun are lined up with Earth between the sun and moon. The lined-up gravitational force pulls on bulge on the side of Earth towards the moon and the side opposite the moon causing spring tides. The high tides are highest during spring tide, and the low tides are lowest, giving the greatest tidal range.
2. new moon spring tide: The moon, Earth, and sun are lined up with moon between Earth and the sun. The lined-up gravitational force pulls on bulge on the side of Earth towards the moon and the side opposite the moon causing spring tides. The high tides are highest during spring tide, and the low tides are lowest, giving the greatest tidal range.
3. third quarter neap tide: The moon is in the third quarter position, forming a right angle with Earth and the sun. The gravitational forces are not all pulling together, so the tides are minimal.

4. first quarter neap tide: The moon is in the first quarter position, forming a right angle with Earth and the sun. The gravitational forces are not all pulling together, so the tides are minimal.

Page 143
1. low tide
2. angle
3. bulge
4. first
5. tidal range
6. align
7. spring tides
8. high tides
9. third
10. lowest
11. semidiurnal
12. neap tides
13. full
14. diurnal
15. twice
16. new
Vertical: moon's gravitational force

Page 144
1. D . . . . S, Z
2. A . . . . T
3. F . . . . U
4. G V
5. E . . . . W
6. B X
7. C . . . . Y

Page 145
1-4. wind, water, ice, gravity
Bottom:
1. disintegration
2. gravity
3. erosion
4. oasis
5. talus
6. dune
7. loess
8. mudflows
9. slump
10. abrasion
11. landslides
12. rockfalls
13. deflation
14. decomposition
15. weathering
16. creep

Page 146
1. velocity
2. drainage basin

Answers

3. bed load
4. suspended load
5. meandering
6. channel
7. flood plain
8. runoff
9. impermeable
10. permeable
11. sediment
12. alluvial fans
13. drainage system
14. delta

Page 147

1. NO . . . Caspian Sea
2. NO . . . mouth
3. NO . . . drainage system
4. NO . . . floodplain
5. NO . . . delta
6. YES
7. YES
8. YES
9. YES
10. NO . . . waterfall
11. NO . . . tributaries flow
      into rivers
12. YES
13. YES
14. NO . . . mouth
15. YES

Page 148

Jocelyn has these wrong:
   2, 5, 6, 13
Her final score is 80%.

Page 149

1-6	24-29
2-14	25-3
3-25	26-45
4-18	27-10
5-39	28-31
6-1	29-24
7-38	30-15
8-20	31-28
9-46	32-35
10-27	33-17
11-37	34-13
12-44	35-32
13-34	36-23
14-2	37-11
15-30	38-7
16-42	39-5
17-33	40-19
18-4	41-22
19-40	42-16
20-8	43-21
21-43	44-12
22-41	45-26
23-36	46-9

Page 150

1. crust
2. MOHO
   (Mohorovicic
   Discontinuity)
3. mantle
4. yes
5. upper mantle
6. line between mantle and core
7. inner core
8. outer core
9. an ocean
10. mantle

Page 151

1. Sahara Desert . . .
      1410 ft
2. Asia . . .
      174,00,000 square miles
3. Indonesia . . .
      685 square miles
4. Mt. Everest . . .
      29,022 ft
5. Mt. Guallatiri (in Chile) . . .
      19,882 ft
6. Lambert Glacier . . .
      Antarctic
7. South Africa . . .
      12,467 ft
8. Greenland . . .
      840,000 square miles
9. 3800 million years
10. Great Barrier Reef . . .
      1200 miles
11. Caspian Sea . . .
      146,100 square miles
12. Angel Falls . . .
      3212 ft
13. 112 ft
14. Mammoth Caves . . .
      350 miles
15. Dead Sea . . .
      1286 ft
16. Marianas . . .
      35,837 ft
17. Pacific . . .
      64,000,000 square ft
18. 278 ft

Pages 152-153

1. igneous, metamorphic,
   sedimentary
2. igneous
3. pumice
4. geodes
5. nonfoliated
6. harden
7. igneous
8. fossils
9. ripple marks
10. metamorphic
11. sandstone, limestone, shale,
   siltstone
12. foliated
13. sedimentary
14. dark
15. metamorphic, sedimentary
16. clastic
17. intrusive
18. slate, marble, quartzite,
   anthracite
19. sedimentary
20. granite, pumice, feldspar,
   basalt, felsite
21. nonclastic
22. anthracite
23. extrusive
24. compaction
25. cementation
26. conglomerate
27. breccia
28. shale
29. caves
30. corals

pages 154-155

Answers may vary.
1. no
2. no
3. feldspar
4. bauxite
5. graphite
6. no
7. gypsum
8. sulfur
9. yes
10. talc
11. halite (salt)
12. calcite
13. quartz
14. yes
15. chromite
16. fluorite
17. corundum (sapphire)
18. yes
19. no
20. yes
21. no
22. yes

Page 156

1. cinder cone ....Example B
2. stratovolcano ......Example C
3. shield..................Example D
4. dome...................Example A

Page 157

Clues may vary somewhat; should
generally follow definitions below.

DOWN

1. troughs (downward folds)
   between folds in Earth's crust
2. scientists who study
   earthquakes and seismic
   activity
4. vibrations caused by sudden
   movement of surface rocks
5. strength of an earthquake
6. point on surface where
   seismic activity is strongest
7. ridges; upward fold in Earth's
   crust
10. breaks in rocks

ACROSS

3. vibrations resulting when a
   rock suddenly breaks and
   moves
8. seismic sea wave
9. bends in rock layers
10. point on fault deep below
   surface where movement
   occurs
11. measure of how much damage
   an earthquake causes
12. fractures along which
   movement takes place
13. instrument that records
   earthquakes
14. scale that measures
   earthquake magnitude
15. significant fault which runs
   most the length of California

Page 158

1-15	9-13	17-10
2-16	10-17	18-3
3-18	11-21	19-7
4-20	12-6	20-4
5-22	13-9	21-11
6-12	14-8	22-5
7-19	15-1	
8-14	16-2	

Page 159

Information students gather will
vary according to reference
materials used.

Page 160

1.	G	caldera
2.	C	geyser
3.	A	hot springs
4.	H	mudspots
5.	B	fumorale
6.	I	solfataras
7.	J	batholith
8.	F	sinkhole
9.	D	laccolith
10.	K	dike
11.	E	volcanic neck

Copyright ©2002 by INCENTIVE PUBLICATIONS, Inc., Nashville, TN.

LIFE SCIENCE
Skills Exercises

SKILLS CHECKLIST FOR LIFE SCIENCE

✔	SKILL	PAGE(S)
	Describe and distinguish between cell processes	173
	Describe the system of classification of life	174–176, 182, 184–195
	Describe and distinguish between simple organisms	175, 176
	Identify features of plant structure and explain their functions	177, 179
	Define, describe, and distinguish between plant processes	178
	Identify flower parts and their functions	179
	Describe pollination and fertilization in angiosperms	179
	Define and use vocabulary terms related to plants	180, 181
	Describe the system of classification of animals	182, 184–195
	Identify characteristics of vertebrates	182, 192–195
	Describe and distinguish between different kinds of symmetry	183
	Identify characteristics of different animal phyla	184–190, 192–195
	Identify characteristics of simple invertebrates	186
	Identify characteristics of mollusks and echinoderms	187
	Identify and distinguish among characteristics of different arthropods	188–191
	Identify characteristics of arachnids	189
	Identify characteristics of insects	190
	Describe complete and incomplete metamorphosis in insects	191
	Identify characteristics of cold-blooded vertebrates	192
	Identify characteristics of warm-blooded vertebrates	193
	Identify terms and characteristics related to animal behavior	196
	Define and use vocabulary terms related to animals	197
	Describe, identify, and give examples of different habitats	198, 199
	Define and identify characteristics of different biomes	200, 201
	Explain the relationships in food chains	202
	Explain concepts related to ecosystems	203
	Identify a variety of relationship[s ion ecosystems	203, 204
	Explain CO_2–O_2, nitrogen, and water cycles	205
	Define and use vocabulary terms related to ecology	206
	Identify concepts related to the use of natural resources	207
	Identify the parts of a light microscope and their functions	208

OSMOSIS IS NOT A DISEASE

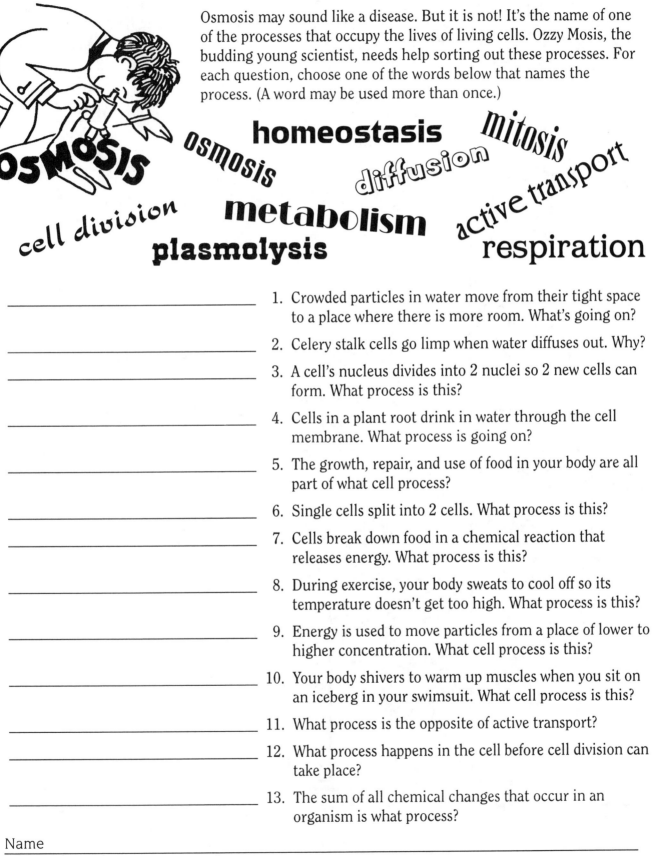

Osmosis may sound like a disease. But it is not! It's the name of one of the processes that occupy the lives of living cells. Ozzy Mosis, the budding young scientist, needs help sorting out these processes. For each question, choose one of the words below that names the process. (A word may be used more than once.)

homeostasis   *osmosis*   **mitosis**
OSMOSIS   *osmosis*   *diffusion*   *active transport*
cell division   **metabolism**   **respiration**
plasmolysis

_____ 1. Crowded particles in water move from their tight space to a place where there is more room. What's going on?

_____ 2. Celery stalk cells go limp when water diffuses out. Why?

_____ 3. A cell's nucleus divides into 2 nuclei so 2 new cells can form. What process is this?

_____ 4. Cells in a plant root drink in water through the cell membrane. What process is going on?

_____ 5. The growth, repair, and use of food in your body are all part of what cell process?

_____ 6. Single cells split into 2 cells. What process is this?

_____ 7. Cells break down food in a chemical reaction that releases energy. What process is this?

_____ 8. During exercise, your body sweats to cool off so its temperature doesn't get too high. What process is this?

_____ 9. Energy is used to move particles from a place of lower to higher concentration. What cell process is this?

_____ 10. Your body shivers to warm up muscles when you sit on an iceberg in your swimsuit. What cell process is this?

_____ 11. What process is the opposite of active transport?

_____ 12. What process happens in the cell before cell division can take place?

_____ 13. The sum of all chemical changes that occur in an organism is what process?

Name _____

WELCOME TO THE KINGDOM

Living things are classified into five kingdoms. Has the mighty Leo named them correctly? Cross out any incorrect labels and write in the correct ones. Then, write the correct kingdom next to each phrase that describes one of the characteristics of its members (items 6-15). Some will have more than one answer.

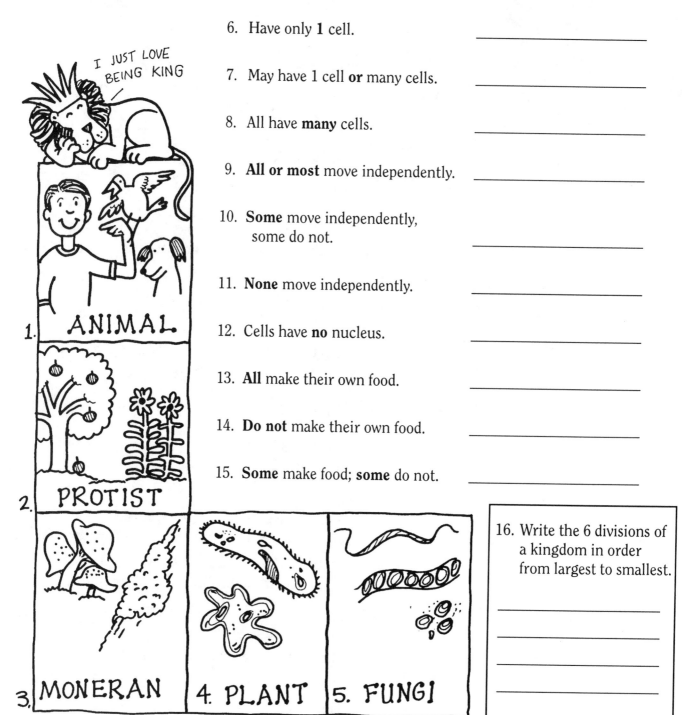

6. Have only **1** cell. _____

7. May have 1 cell **or** many cells. _____

8. All have **many** cells. _____

9. **All or most** move independently. _____

10. **Some** move independently, some do not. _____

11. **None** move independently. _____

12. Cells have **no** nucleus. _____

13. **All** make their own food. _____

14. **Do not** make their own food. _____

15. **Some** make food; **some** do not. _____

I JUST LOVE BEING KING

1. ANIMAL

2. PROTIST

3. MONERAN   4. PLANT   5. FUNGI

16. Write the 6 divisions of a kingdom in order from largest to smallest.

_____
_____
_____
_____
_____
_____

Name _____

   Copyright ©2002 by Incentive Publications, Inc., Nashville, TN.

A VISIT FROM A VIRUS

You've probably been visited by a virus or some bacteria, so you are qualified to answer these questions. Write your answers on the lines preceeding the questions.

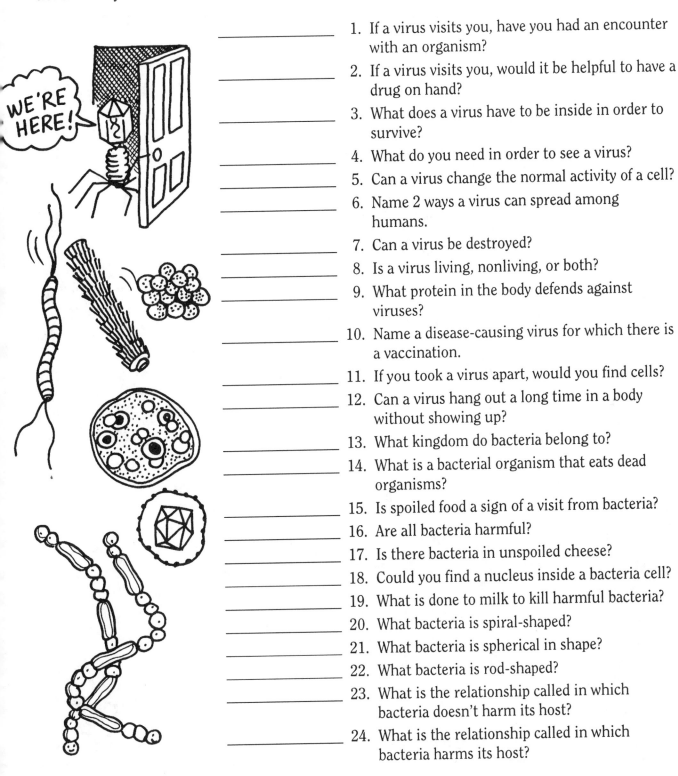

1. If a virus visits you, have you had an encounter with an organism?

2. If a virus visits you, would it be helpful to have a drug on hand?

3. What does a virus have to be inside in order to survive?

4. What do you need in order to see a virus?

5. Can a virus change the normal activity of a cell?

6. Name 2 ways a virus can spread among humans.

7. Can a virus be destroyed?

8. Is a virus living, nonliving, or both?

9. What protein in the body defends against viruses?

10. Name a disease-causing virus for which there is a vaccination.

11. If you took a virus apart, would you find cells?

12. Can a virus hang out a long time in a body without showing up?

13. What kingdom do bacteria belong to?

14. What is a bacterial organism that eats dead organisms?

15. Is spoiled food a sign of a visit from bacteria?

16. Are all bacteria harmful?

17. Is there bacteria in unspoiled cheese?

18. Could you find a nucleus inside a bacteria cell?

19. What is done to milk to kill harmful bacteria?

20. What bacteria is spiral-shaped?

21. What bacteria is spherical in shape?

22. What bacteria is rod-shaped?

23. What is the relationship called in which bacteria doesn't harm its host?

24. What is the relationship called in which bacteria harms its host?

Name _____

Copyright ©2002 by Incentive Publications, Inc., Nashville, TN.

The BASIC/Not Boring Middle Grades Science Book

STRANGE CHOICE OF FRIENDS

Fungi and protists don't get a lot of respect from most people. They are not exactly plants or animals. But Lorena thinks they're rather interesting characters. So she's listing impressive facts about protists and fungi.

But is she right? Use your knowledge about protists and fungi to decide if each thing she's written is true (T) or false (F).

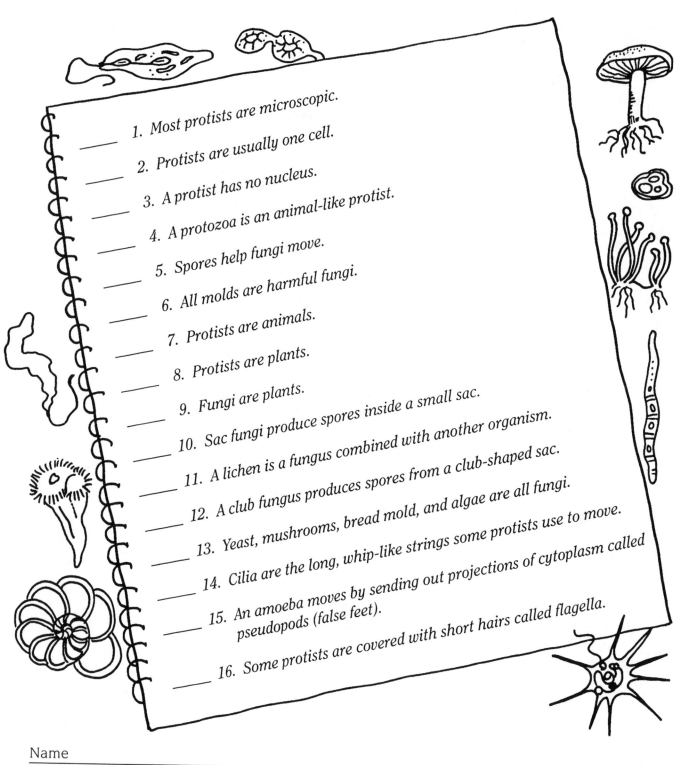

_____ 1. Most protists are microscopic.

_____ 2. Protists are usually one cell.

_____ 3. A protist has no nucleus.

_____ 4. A protozoa is an animal-like protist.

_____ 5. Spores help fungi move.

_____ 6. All molds are harmful fungi.

_____ 7. Protists are animals.

_____ 8. Protists are plants.

_____ 9. Fungi are plants.

_____ 10. Sac fungi produce spores inside a small sac.

_____ 11. A lichen is a fungus combined with another organism.

_____ 12. A club fungus produces spores from a club-shaped sac.

_____ 13. Yeast, mushrooms, bread mold, and algae are all fungi.

_____ 14. Cilia are the long, whip-like strings some protists use to move.

_____ 15. An amoeba moves by sending out projections of cytoplasm called pseudopods (false feet).

_____ 16. Some protists are covered with short hairs called flagella.

Name _____

     Copyright ©2002 by Incentive Publications, Inc., Nashville, TN.

PLANT PARTS, INC.

Cat A. Pilar tried going into the auto parts business. But she had a bit of trouble getting customers to believe she could replace a carburetor or repair brake systems. So she switched to plant parts. Here's a list of broken parts her customers have brought in. Tell what each part is by writing a brief description.

1. leaf _____

2. xylem _____

3. taproot system _____

4. epidermis _____

5. cuticle _____

6. phloem _____

7. vessels _____

8. cambium _____

9. blade _____

10. stomata _____

11. petiole _____

12. fibrous root system _____

13. root hairs _____

14. roots _____

FLOWER PETALS? OR BIKE PEDALS?

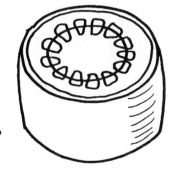

A.

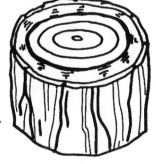

B.

Woodruff Woodchuck brought in these two stems to be fixed.

15. Which stem is woody? _____

16. Which is herbaceous? _____

Name _____

PLANT ANTICS

So you thought plants just stood around all day doing nothing? Not so! They breathe, eat, grow, make food, sweat, and move stuff around inside all the time. There are four plant processes pictured here. Use the phrases below to help you write a description of each of these four processes. You might use some of the phrases in more than one place.

- tiny openings called stomata
- opposite of photosynthesis
- sugar and oxygen are produced
- green plants trap light
- water vapor is lost through stomata
- stomata open during the day
- takes place in cells with chlorophyll
- oxygen, carbon dioxide, & water vapor
- energy is released from food

- light energy is used to make food
- gases are lost by diffusion
- water and carbon dioxide are produced
- stomata are closed at night
- carbon dioxide and water combine
- energy is stored in food
- light energy used for chemical reactions
- opposite of respiration

Name

WHAT DO BEES KNOW?

This know-it-all bee thinks he can describe the pollination and fertilization that takes place in this flower. Does he know as much as he thinks? Read through his explanation and find the errors. Cross out and fix anything that is not correct.

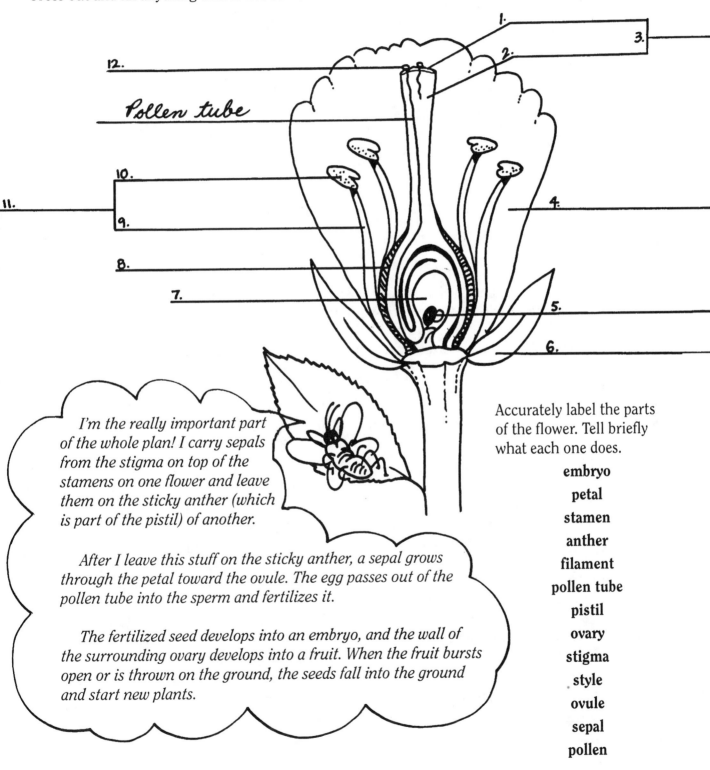

Pollen tube

I'm the really important part of the whole plan! I carry sepals from the stigma on top of the stamens on one flower and leave them on the sticky anther (which is part of the pistil) of another.

After I leave this stuff on the sticky anther, a sepal grows through the petal toward the ovule. The egg passes out of the pollen tube into the sperm and fertilizes it.

The fertilized seed develops into an embryo, and the wall of the surrounding ovary develops into a fruit. When the fruit bursts open or is thrown on the ground, the seeds fall into the ground and start new plants.

Accurately label the parts of the flower. Tell briefly what each one does.

embryo

petal

stamen

anther

filament

pollen tube

pistil

ovary

stigma

style

ovule

sepal

pollen

Name

Copyright ©2002 by INCENTIVE PUBLICATIONS, Inc., Nashville, TN.

WOULD YOU SLEEP ON A MONOCOT?

"Would you sleep on a mono-cot?" ...."No, but I might sleep on a di-cot."

"What kind of a plant does a daily workout?" ...."A gym-nosperm!"

"Have you ever seen a gameto-fight?" ...."No, but I've seen a sporophyte!"

"Is it legal for a flower to carry a gun?" ...."No, but they can carry pistils!"

The vocabulary terms on the plant on page 181 are all answers to plant "riddles" on this page. Write the number of each of the following questions on the matching answer leaf on page 181.

1. I come in green, brown, and red, and have no roots, stems, or leaves.
2. Water vapor is lost from leaves through me.
3. I anchor plants in soil.
4. You'll find me holding a moss or liverwort in the ground.
5. I am not found in mosses, algae, or liverworts.
6. Conifers hide their seeds in me.
7. When you eat an apple, you are eating me.
8. Plants use me from the atmosphere to make food.
9. I'm the female reproductive organ of an angiosperm.
10. I'm the reason plants are green.
11. My flower petal parts come in sets of 4 or 5.
12. Visit me if you're looking for a frond.
13. I'm a seed plant that has no fruit.
14. I am formed from sporophytes.
15. I am formed from gametophytes.

16. I'm a growing young plant that rests during dormancy.
17. Plants get me from the soil.
18. My flower parts come in sets of 3.
19. I am the young leaves inside the embryo of a seed.
20. I have soft, green stems.
21. You're eating me when you eat a cob of corn.
22. Plants get nitrogen from me.
23. This is how some plants are like your circulatory system.
24. I cause production of food using light.
25. We are the male reproductive organs of angiosperms.
26. Plants add me to the atmosphere.
27. I grow, reproduce, and die within one season.
28. Chlorophyll traps me.
29. The purpose of seeds is to produce more of me.
30. I'm a plant with no vessels.

Use with page 181.

Name

Use with page 180.

A   a pistil
D   a plant embryo
B   an algae
O   a cotyledon
E   herbaceous
H   a gymnosperm
R   stomata
G   oxygen
P   carbon dioxide
Q   vessels
C   a fern
F   nonvascular
U   an annual
L   photosynthesis
N   light energy
M   Both have vessels.
X   stamens
T   endosperm
Y   nitrogen
S   gametes
Z   spores
ZZ   an angiosperm
V   new plants
BB   chlorophyll
AA   cones
W   soil
XX   a rhizoid
I   roots
J   a monocot
K   a dicot

Name

The BASIC/Not Boring Middle Grades Science Book

Copyright ©2002 by Incentive Publications, Inc., Nashville, TN.

BONES OR NO BONES?

Some animals have them. Some do not. A backbone may not seem like a big deal to you, but it is a major feature in the classification of animal species. Look at all the characteristics and animals in this list. Write the number of each one where it belongs—either in the BONES (vertebrates) or the NO BONES (invertebrates) category.

1. salamander
2. 95% of known species
3. toad
4. phylum chordata
5. snail
6. coral
7. pelican
8. turtle
9. soft bodies
10. internal skeleton
11. snake
12. sponge
13. tarantula
14. humans
15. exoskeletons
16. earthworm
17. wasp
18. clam
19. goldfish
20. ostrich
21. dolphin
22. spinal cord
23. skeletons made of bone
24. spider
25. slug
26. whale
27. skeletons made of cartilage
28. shark
29. closed circulatory systems
30. fly
31. zebra
32. crocodile

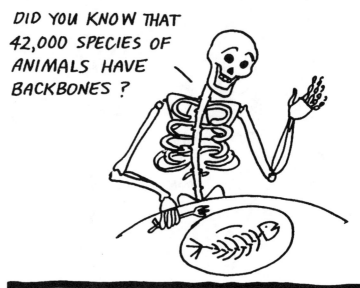

DID YOU KNOW THAT
42,000 SPECIES OF
ANIMALS HAVE
BACKBONES ?

BONES

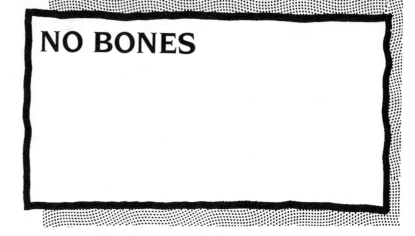

NO BONES

Name

A SIDE VIEW

Bertram Bi Olly Gist wants to classify these animals according to their **symmetry.** Help him out.
Label each animal with *B* for **bilateral,** *R* for **radial,** or *N* for **no symmetry.**

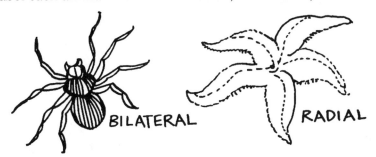

NO SYMMETRY

Symmetry is a similarity or likeness of two parts.

An organism with **bilateral symmetry** has two sides or parts that are alike.

An organism with **radial symmetry** has an arrangement of similar parts around a central axis like spokes of a wheel.

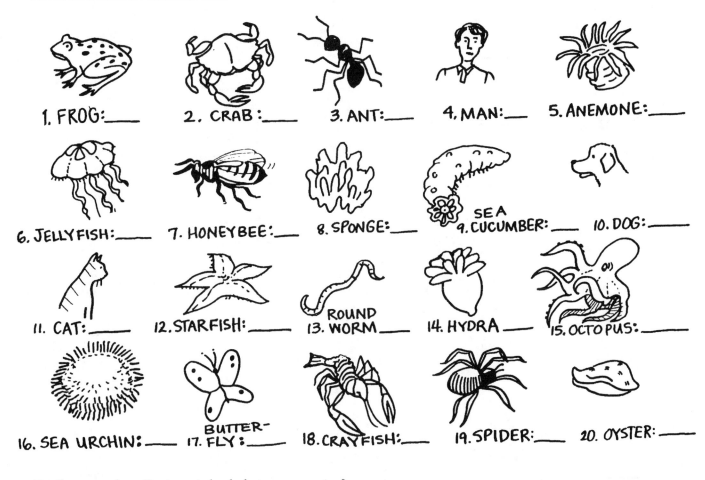

1. FROG:____   2. CRAB:____   3. ANT:____   4. MAN:____   5. ANEMONE:____

6. JELLYFISH:____   7. HONEYBEE:____   8. SPONGE:____   9. SEA CUCUMBER:____   10. DOG:____

11. CAT:____   12. STARFISH:____   13. ROUND WORM____   14. HYDRA____   15. OCTOPUS:____

16. SEA URCHIN:____   17. BUTTER-FLY:____   18. CRAYFISH:____   19. SPIDER:____   20. OYSTER:____

By the way, does Bertram's body have symmetry? _____

Name _____

FILE INTO PHYLA

A **phylum** is kind of like a file. It is a way to group animals with similar characteristics together. There are many different animal **phyla.** The nine major phyla are represented by animals pictured on the next page (page 185). Your job is to make sure that Zak (the zookeeper) has 1 or more animals for each phylum in his "file." Write the name of each animal onto the correct file card. Also, find the description on page 185 which matches each phylum, and write that letter on the file card.

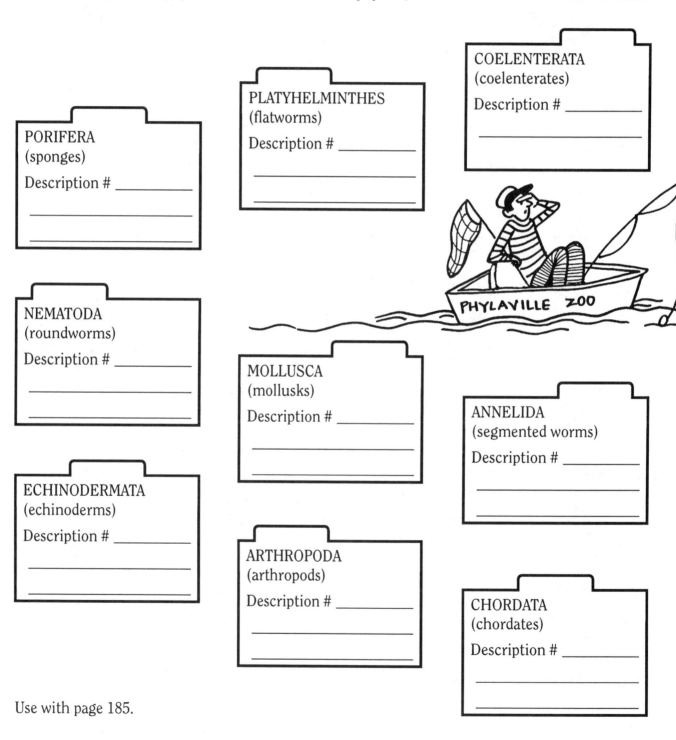

COELENTERATA
(coelenterates)

Description # _____

_____

PLATYHELMINTHES
(flatworms)

Description # _____

_____

_____

PORIFERA
(sponges)

Description # _____

_____

_____

NEMATODA
(roundworms)

Description # _____

_____

_____

MOLLUSCA
(mollusks)

Description # _____

_____

_____

ANNELIDA
(segmented worms)

Description # _____

_____

_____

ECHINODERMATA
(echinoderms)

Description # _____

_____

_____

ARTHROPODA
(arthropods)

Description # _____

_____

_____

CHORDATA
(chordates)

Description # _____

_____

_____

Use with page 185.

Name

Use with page 184.

Name

The BASIC/Not Boring Middle Grades Science Book   Copyright ©2002 by INCENTIVE PUBLICATIONS, Inc., Nashville, TN.

OF WORMS, JELLYFISH, & SPONGES

If animals are simple, it ought to be a simple job for you to describe them—right?
These are five of the simpler invertebrate phyla:

coelenterates • sponges • flatworms • roundworms • segmented worms

Determine to which phylum each pictured invertebrate belongs. Label each one. Then, use the space to write everything you know or can find out about characteristics of animals in that phylum.

1

jellyfish

2

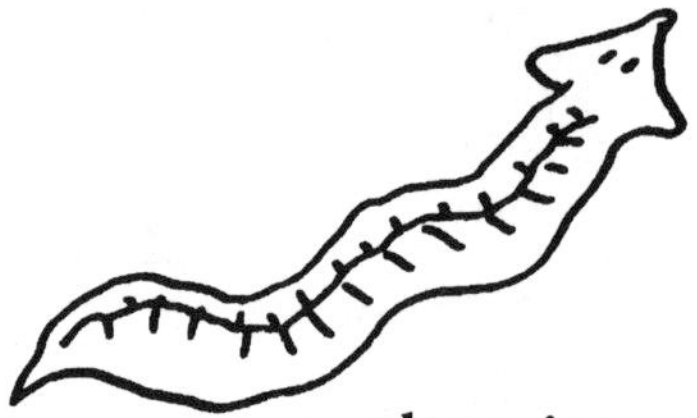

planarian

3

hookworm

4

bristleworm

5

velvet sponge

Name

IT'S HARD TO IGNORE A SQUID

Have you ever have eaten a clam or oyster? Met up with an octopus or squid? Picked up a slug? If so, you've had the honor of knowing a **mollusk.** If you have ever admired a starfish, run into a sea urchin, or collected sand dollars, you've made the acquaintance of an **echinoderm.** Mollusks and echinoderms are animals that many people love to admire, watch, or eat. Some people go so far as to kiss slugs.

I. For each characteristic listed below, write **M** if the characteristic is true of mollusks, **E** if it is true of echinoderms, or **B** if it is true of both.

_____ 1. have a water vascular system for moving and getting food

_____ 2. have bilateral symmetry

_____ 3. have a circulatory system and heart

_____ 4. usually have a hard outer shell

_____ 5. often have tentacles

_____ 6. have a spiny or leathery covering

_____ 7. are invertebrates

_____ 8. all live in salt water

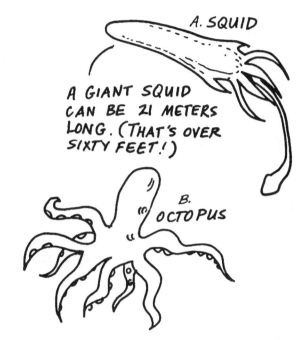

A. SQUID

A GIANT SQUID CAN BE 21 METERS LONG. (THAT'S OVER SIXTY FEET!)

B. OCTOPUS

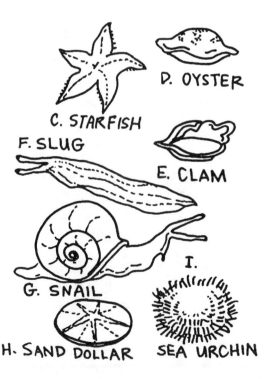

D. OYSTER

C. STARFISH

F. SLUG

E. CLAM

G. SNAIL

I.

H. SAND DOLLAR   SEA URCHIN

_____ 9. (some) live attached to rocks

_____ 10. have radial symmetry

_____ 11. have soft bodies

_____ 12. (some) live on land; some live in water

_____ 13. (some) have a thick, muscular "foot" for movement

_____ 14. have spines extending out of their bodies

_____ 15. (most) move slowly by attaching tube-like feet to things and pulling themselves along

_____ 16. are cold-blooded

II. Label each animal on this page **M** for mollusk or **E** for echinoderm.

Name

     Copyright ©2002 by Incentive Publications, Inc., Nashville, TN.

OUTNUMBERED!

What phylum outnumbers all other kinds of animals put together? What phylum has 1500 different species just in your backyard garden? **Arthropods!** They're everywhere!

Look at the characteristics and animals below. Decide whether each characteristic is true of all arthropods or just of one specific class of arthropods. If the characteristic applies to all arthropods, write its letter in the box that says **ALL.** Otherwise, write its letter in the box for its class. (Some are true of more than one class.) Determine the class in which each animal belongs. Write its letter in the appropriate box.

ALL ARTHROPODS

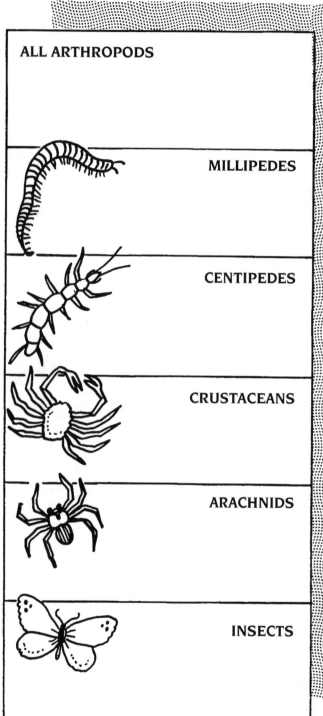

MILLIPEDES

CENTIPEDES

CRUSTACEANS

ARACHNIDS

INSECTS

A. gills

B. 3 pair of legs

C. flat, segmented body

D. 3 body sections

E.

F. jointed legs

G. no antennae

H. exoskeleton

I.

J. 1 pair of legs per segment

K. 1 pair antennae

L. shed exoskeleton periodically by molting

M.

N. 4 pair of legs

O. round, segmented body

P. 2 body sections

Q.

R. 2 pair of antennae

S. bodies divided into sections

T. very hard, flexible exoskeleton

U. 2 pair of legs per segment

V. poison claws on first segment

W. many have 1 or 2 pair of wings

X. mandibles in mouth for chewing

Name

The BASIC/Not Boring Middle Grades Science Book   Copyright ©2002 by Incentive Publications, Inc., Nashville, TN.

CONFUSION IN THE WEB

Some people think that spiders are insects. They are not! They belong to a class of the arthropod phylum called **arachnids.** Some of the animals caught in this web are arachnids, and others aren't. Answer the questions in the boxes to show what you know about arachnids.

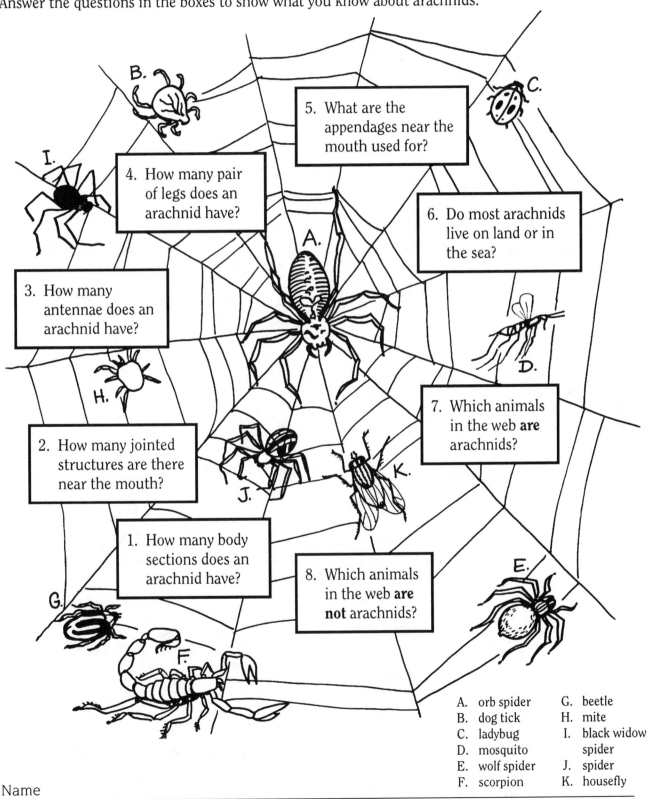

5. What are the appendages near the mouth used for?

4. How many pair of legs does an arachnid have?

6. Do most arachnids live on land or in the sea?

3. How many antennae does an arachnid have?

7. Which animals in the web **are** arachnids?

2. How many jointed structures are there near the mouth?

1. How many body sections does an arachnid have?

8. Which animals in the web **are not** arachnids?

A. orb spider
B. dog tick
C. ladybug
D. mosquito
E. wolf spider
F. scorpion
G. beetle
H. mite
I. black widow spider
J. spider
K. housefly

Name _____

     Copyright ©2002 by Incentive Publications, Inc., Nashville, TN.

BUGS BY THE MILLIONS

Did you know that almost 1 million different species of insects have been given names and descriptions? (How would you like to be the person who has to write down all these?) There are, obviously, far more insects than any other class of animals. How much do you know about these millions of bugs that belong to this exclusive class?

I. Tell whether each statement is true (T) or false (F) about insects.

___ 1. They have 2 body parts.
___ 2. They have 3 pair of legs.
___ 3. They have 1 pair of antennae.
___ 4. All insects are harmful.
___ 5. They have an open circulatory system.
___ 6. They have no antennae.

___ 7. They have 4 pair of legs.
___ 8. They have 2 pair of antennae.
___ 9. Many have 1 or 2 pair of wings.
___ 10. Some are helpful in pollinating flowers.
___ 11. They are the only invertebrates that can fly.
___ 12. Their body sections are: head, thorax, abdomen.
___ 13. Air enters their bodies through spiracles.

II. Tell which creatures in Kate's collection are NOT insects.

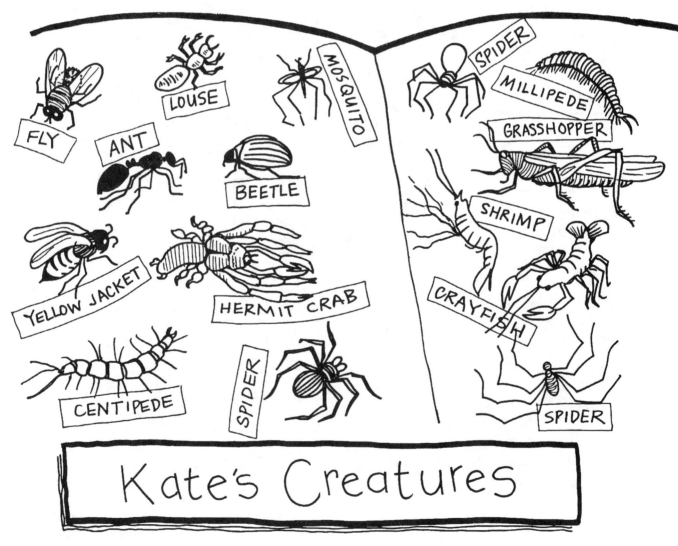

Name

THE MOST AMAZING CHANGES

Imagine starting life as one kind of creature, then changing into something totally different when you become an adult! This is what happens to many insects. An amazing process called **metamorphosis** changes animals from one form into another right before your very eyes. Review what you know about complete metamorphosis and incomplete metamorphosis.

1. Define metamorphosis. _____
   _____

2. Name the 4 stages of development in complete metamorphosis.

   1. _____   3. _____

   2. _____   4. _____

3. Describe the process of incomplete metamorphosis. _____
   _____

4. Name 2 insects that undergo complete metamorphosis. _____
   _____

5. Name 2 insects that undergo incomplete metamorphosis. _____
   _____

6. Describe molting. _____
   _____

7. Which example shows complete metamorphosis? _____

8. Which example shows incomplete metamorphosis? _____

Label the stages of metamorphosis in the butterfly and the grasshopper.

Monarch Butterfly _____

Grasshopper _____

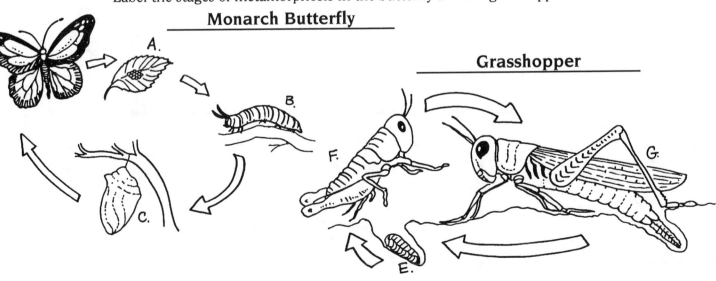

Name _____

BLOOD THAT'S COLD

Besides a skeleton, blood is the major thing that an eel, a turtle, and a toad have in common. Tell what it means to be cold-blooded. Then fill in the missing information about these cold-blooded classes of animals—fish, reptiles, and amphibians.

Explain "cold-blooded." _____

_____

Label each animal pictured as F (fish), R (reptile), or A (amphibian).

_____ 1 are cold-blooded vertebrates which live in _____ 2. They use _____ 3 to get oxygen from water and have 4-chambered hearts. There are _____ 4 different kinds of animals in this class. Those with sucker-like mouths, such as lampreys, are called _____ 5 fish. Sharks are _____ 6 fish because their skeletons are made of cartilage. _____ 7 fish have skeletons made of bones and have hinged jaws and fins. Young fish hatch from _____ 8. Two examples of this class are _____ 9 and _____ 10.

_____ 11 live part of their lives on _____ 12 and part in _____ 13. They return to _____ 14 to reproduce and lay eggs, but as adults, they live mostly on _____ 15. They have _____ 16 skin with no scales. They breathe _____ 17; though some have _____ 18 for breathing in water. Some change appearance as they _____ 19. The young _____ 20 from eggs. Their hearts have _____ 21 chambers. Two examples of this class are _____ 22 and _____ 23.

_____ 24 breathe _____ 25 and live mostly on _____ 26. Most have long bodies and four legs. Their bodies are covered with _____ 27. They have _____ 28 –chambered hearts. The young are hatched from _____ 29. Two examples of this class are _____ 30 and _____ 31.

Name _____

BLOOD THAT'S WARM

You're not the only species with warm blood. Thousands of other animals have warm blood, too. Some of them are not even in your phylum. Tell what it means to be warm-blooded. Then fill in the missing information about the two warm-blooded classes.

Explain "warm-blooded."

_____

_____

_____

_____

_____

_____

_____ are covered with_____. These are lightweight, flexible, strong coverings which protect the animal from _____ and _____. All of these animals have front limbs called _____. Many, but not all, use these structures to fly. The fertilization of eggs takes place _____ the female's body, but eggs are laid to hatch _____. They breathe with _____ and have a _____–chambered heart. Different birds have different kinds of _____ which are adapted to the kinds of food they eat. Two examples of animals in this class are _____ and _____.

Label each animal shown as
B (bird) or
M (mammal).

_____ have hair to help maintain constant body _____. Females produce _____ to feed to their young. Their hearts have _____ chambers. They also have glands that produce _____ to cool them off when their bodies get too hot. The young of this class develop completely _____ the mother's body before they are born, except in a few cases. Two examples of this class of animals are _____ and _____.

Name _____

     Copyright ©2002 by Incentive Publications, Inc., Nashville, TN.

CLASS ASSIGNMENTS

You are in the only group of animals that has to go to school. But, like you, all animals have been assigned to classes. Fill in the chart with information to fit each category for each of the 3 fish classes and the other 4 classes of vertebrates.

Class	Kind of Skeleton	# Heart Chambers	Body Covering	Blood Temp.	Where They Live	Where Young Develop	Special Features
JAWLESS FISH							
CARTILAGE FISH							
BONY FISH							
AMPHIBIANS							
REPTILES							
BIRDS							
MAMMALS							

Name

194   Copyright ©2002 by INCENTIVE PUBLICATIONS, Inc., Nashville, TN.

BACKBONE REQUIRED

You have to have a backbone to be able to solve this puzzle. (And, incidentally, all the words in it have something to do with animals that have a backbone of some kind.) Solve the puzzle.

Across

1. bird covering
3. backbone material that is not bone
6. vertebrate class with hair
8. attaches to brain: spinal _____
10. lives partly in water, partly on land
13. system having spinal cord and brain
14. fish egg fertilization is _____
17. class with 3-chambered heart
18. reptile covering

Down

1. chambers in a bird's heart
2. blood of birds and mammals
3. system with heart and vessels
4. breathe with gills
5. bone system in a vertebrate
7. animal group having backbone
9. system which processes food
11. mammal reproduction is _____
12. phylum having backbones
15. heart chambers in fish
16. has hollow bones

Name

BEHAVING LIKE ANIMALS

Some beetles stand on their heads. Fiddler crabs change color twice a day. Hognose snakes play dead. Flamingos stand on one leg. African grasshoppers blow bubbles. Some daddy frogs hold tadpoles in their mouths. Spiders spin webs. And Arctic terns fly 11,000 miles for their summer vacation. These are just some of the strange activities that are a part of animal behavior.

Match the behavior-related terms below (A-P) with their descriptions on the right. (If you have some extra time, try to find out why the 8 animals described above do those strange things!)

A. behavior
B. migration
C. territoriality
D. reflex
E. instinct
F. inborn behavior
G. courtship behavior
H. defensive behavior
I. response
J. stimulus
K. trial and error
L. conditioning
M. hibernation
N. camouflage
O. adaptation
P. acquired behavior

_____ 1. an inborn behavior that involves a response to a stimulus

_____ 2. the way an animal acts

_____ 3. behavior learned during life

_____ 4. an action resulting from a stimulus

_____ 5. behavior an animal inherits

_____ 6. quick action not involving the brain

_____ 7. travel to another place to reproduce, avoid cold, find food, or raise young

_____ 8. behavior where animal defends an area

_____ 9. males and females act in certain ways to attract one another for mating

_____ 10. training to cause a certain response to a specific stimulus

_____ 11. an adaptation for winter survival

_____ 12. a change that helps an animal survive in its environment

_____ 13. something that causes a behavior

_____ 14. behavior an animal does to defend itself

_____ 15. changing body coloring that protects an animal

_____ 16. behavior learned based on avoiding mistakes

Name

SCALES FOR A CROCODILE?

Why does a crocodile have scales, anyway? Answer these questions to show that you know these animal-related terms.

1. If a crocodile's **scales** are not for weighing, what are they for? _____
   _____

2. An **exoskeleton** is not a group of exercising bones. What is it?_____
   _____

3. Is a **symmetry** a kind of tree? _____What is it?

4. Is a **spinal cord** anything like a musical chord? _____ Why, or why not?_____
   _____

5. Does a radial tire have **radial symmetry**? _____
   _____

6. Is a jellyfish really a **fish**? _____
   _____

7. If someone has **arachnophobia**, exactly what are they afraid of?_____

8. Is **molt** a kind of **mold**? __ If not, what is it? _____

9. How is a **flagella** like a flag? _____
   _____

10. **Tentacles** have nothing to do with camping. What are they? _____
    _____

11. What would you find in a cart full of **cartilage**? _____

12. Which is simpler, a **protist** or a **sponge**?_____

13. Is a **cold-blooded** animal more cruel than a **warm-blooded** one? _____

14. Could you fit a **phylum** into a file? _____ Why or why not?_____

15. Does an animal need a generator for **regeneration**?_____

16. Why might someone scream, "Eeek! An **echinoderm**!" ____

17. Would you rather hold a handful of **larvae** or **pupae**? Why?

18. Could you chop wood with a **thorax**? Why or why not? ____

19. What is "pseudo" (fake) about **pseudopods**? _____
    _____

Name _____

 Copyright ©2002 by Incentive Publications, Inc., Nashville, TN.

THE HABITAT HABIT

You wouldn't get along too well living in the mud at the bottom of a pond . . . or under the bark of a tree . . . or on the back of a rhinoceros. All living things have this habit of living in a habitat that makes it possible for us to survive. Remember that a habitat is the place in an ecosystem where an organism (and others like it) live and grow.

Describe a habitat which would be suitable for each organism. (Note: Some organisms may be found in more than one habitat. Describe just one.)

1. mosquito _____

2. mushroom _____

3. rattlesnake _____

4. earthworm _____

5. lichen _____

6. ants _____

7. squid _____

8. tree frog _____

9. rhinoceros _____

10. sea cucumber _____

11. roundworm _____

12. mold _____

13. moose _____

14. walrus _____

15. cactus _____

16. trout _____

17. leopard _____

18. antelope _____

19. prairie dog _____

20. alligators _____

21. armadillo _____

22. lizard _____

23. louse _____

24. dog tick _____

25. robin egg _____

26. tapeworm _____

27. mole _____

28. tulip bulb _____

29. fern _____

30. orchid _____

31. hookworm _____

32. brain coral _____

33. fiddler crab _____

Name _____

SOMETHING'S WRONG HERE

The pictures show organisms mixed up about their habitats. Tell what is wrong with each picture, and write a description of what the proper habitat would be for each organism below.

C. _____
_____
_____

A. _____
_____
_____
_____
_____
_____

B. _____
_____
_____

D. _____
_____

F. _____
_____
_____

E. _____
_____

Name _____

HOME, HOME ON THE BIOME

You probably don't think much about your biome, do you? Maybe if you were a lizard or a coral or a polar bear, you'd be more aware of it. Or, then again, maybe you'd still take your biome for granted.

A **biome** is a region with a distinct climate, a dominant type of plant, and specific organisms which are characteristic to that region. There are 6 major land biomes and 2 major water biomes on the earth.

Use the information in the boxes at the bottom of pages 200 and 201 to complete the following tasks. Write your answers in the box for each corresponding biome.

    I. Label the name of each biome.

    II. Write characteristics of each biome.

    III. List some organisms that would be found in that biome.

A.

_____

_____

_____

B.

_____

_____

_____

Biomes	Organisms			
tropical rain forest	leopards	crayfish	moose	lichens &
temperate deciduous forest	deer	sharks	corals	mosses
grassland	parrot	caribou	cacti	armadillos
desert	vines	squirrels	trout	bears
taiga	sagebrush	prairie dogs	plankton	sponges
tundra	monkeys	antelope	armadillos	whales
salt water	snakes	polar bears	orchids	alligators
fresh water	ferns	woodpecker	water lilies	tadpoles
	fir trees	palm trees	birch trees	cougars
	walrus	grasses	pine trees	penguins
	algae	pondweed	maple trees	
	foxes	lizards	lions	

Use with page 201.

Name

 Copyright ©2002 by Incentive Publications, Inc., Nashville, TN.

Use with page 200.

C.

_____
_____
_____

D.

_____
_____
_____

E.

_____
_____
_____

F.

_____
_____
_____

G.

_____
_____
_____

H.

_____
_____
_____

Characteristics of Biomes

salt water	ponds	permafrost	plentiful rainfall
no trees	fleshy plants	grazing animals	very hot temperatures
little rain	rivers	swamps	large, juicy fruit
streams	sparse plant life	trees lose leaves	irregular precipitation
coniferous forests	marshes	cold desert	plants that store water

Name _____

EVERYBODY'S IN A CHAIN

Who's eating whom (or what)? That's the big question in a food chain. A **food chain** is a pathway of food and energy through an ecosystem. Each species in the chain depends on the other species in some way. And each species has a role as **producer** (one who makes food) or **consumer** (one who eats food).

    I. Label the role of each organism in these food chains—**producer, primary consumer,** or **secondary consumer.**

A.

B.

C.

D.

    II. Label each organism here **producer** (P) or **consumer** (C).

Name

WHAT'S WHAT IN THE ECOSYSTEM?

A drop of pond water is one. A whole ocean is one. So is a rotten log in the forest. So is a coral reef and the bark of a tree. **One what?** An **ecosystem!** You might think of an ecosystem as being something huge. But, actually, it can be any size. It is any spot where living organisms are interacting with each other and their nonliving environment. Show how much you know about ecosystems by answering the following questions.

1. What is the difference between a **biosphere** and a **community?** _____
   _____

2. Is there only one **population** in a **community?** _____
   _____

3. What is a **niche** in a community? _____
   _____

4. If you study **ecology**, what are you studying? _____
   _____

5. What is the difference between an **environment** and an **ecosystem?** _____
   _____

6. When organisms in a community have a **contest** against each other for the life requirements, what are they doing? _____
   _____

7. When a raccoon eats a frog, which animal is the **prey?** _____
   _____

8. In a relationship of **commensalism**, is either of the two organisms harmed? _____
   _____

9. In a **parasitic** relationship, is either of the two organisms harmed? _____
   _____

10. What do **decomposers** and **scavengers** have in common? _____
    _____

11. What is the first link in every **food chain?** _____
    _____

12. What is the difference between a **food web** and a **food chain?** _____

I'M STILL LOOKING FOR MY NICHE

Name _____

RELATIONSHIPS IN THE ECOSYSTEM

It may look as if this bear is simply eating this fish. But it is far from simple. These two animals are in a relationship! Not a very comfortable one for the fish, of course, but an important one in the ecosystem nonetheless!

Use one of the terms at the bottom of the page to label each example described.

1. Vultures gather around a dead deer._____

2. Camels, cacti, sagebrush, lizards, snakes, and insects all live together in a section of desert._____

3. A tick feeds on your dog._____

4. Beetles and termites want to break down the dead material in the same spot on the same dead tree._____

5. Mice feed on acorns; owls feed on mice. _____

6. A pond frog catches a nice fly on his sticky tongue. _____

7. The dandelions seem to be taking over your lawn. _____

8. Mule deer live in the forest behind my house._____

9. A bacteria causes your throat to be sore. _____

10. An orchid attaches itself to a tree branch without doing the tree any harm. _____

11. A poisonous sea anemone gives protection to a fish, but feeds on the predators that come after it. _____

12. A mountain lion stalks a young deer._____

13. A fungus grows on a rotting log. _____

14. Ants crawl all over a dead worm. _____

15. Some bacteria live and get their nourishment inside your intestines, and help to keep them healthy. _____

16. Weeds choke out the young corn plants in your garden. _____

17. A spider traps a fat fly in her web. _____

commensalism
scavengers
community
competition
food chain
mutualism
population
predator-prey
dominant species
decomposer
parasitism
scavenger

Name

Copyright ©2002 by Incentive Publications, Inc., Nashville, TN.

CYCLE CIRCLES

Some major cycles are going on all the time in the ecosystem—affecting the lives of living things. You may not be aware of them, but they just keep going on anyway. The three circles illustrate three major life cycles:

NITROGEN CYCLE   **CARBON DIOXIDE–OXYGEN CYCLE**   **WATER CYCLE**

    I. Label each circle with the name of the cycle.

   II. Label each arrow within each circle.

  III. Beneath each circle, write an explanation of the cycle.

A. _____ CYCLE

B. _____ CYCLE

C. _____ CYCLE

A. _____

_____

_____

_____

B. _____

_____

_____

C. _____

_____

Name _____

ECO-TALK

This backwards puzzle is loaded with ecology vocabulary. It's "backwards" because the puzzle is already solved. So, instead of solving it, your job is to make up the clues and write them in the appropriate places.

Across

2. _____

4. _____

6. _____

8. _____

10. _____

12. _____

13. _____

14. _____

15. _____

16. _____

17. _____

Down

1. _____

3. _____

5. _____

7. _____

9. _____

10. _____

11. _____

Name _____

     Copyright ©2002 by Incentive Publications, Inc., Nashville, TN.

HOW RESOURCEFUL ARE YOU?

This animal is rather resourceful in dealing with a particular problem with its air quality. Are you as resourceful in matching the meanings with these terms about resources? Tell if each of these words is correctly matched with its meaning by writing **yes** or **no**. If your answer is **no**, give the correct letter for the answer.

yes/no

B ____ 1. acid rain

Q ____ 2. biodegradable

N ____ 3. conservation

P ____ 4. endangered species

D ____ 5. erosion

J ____ 6. extinction

E ____ 7. fossil fuel

L ____ 8. noise pollution

G ____ 9. renewable resources

yes/no

A ____ 10. nonrenewable resources

K ____ 11. pollution

I ____ 12. recycling

M ____ 13. smog

O ____ 14. reforestation

R ____ 15. wildlife preservation

C ____ 16. thermal pollution

F ____ 17. geothermal energy

H ____ 18. sewage

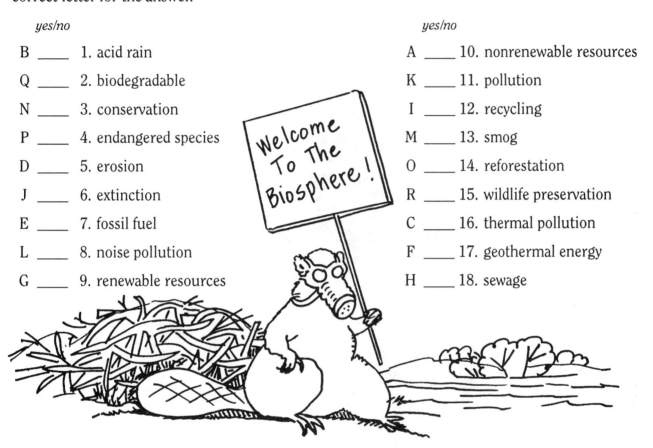

A. resources that can be replaced by nature

B. nonrenewable fuels formed by millions of years of decay of layers of organisms below the earth's surface

C. pollution where hot water raises the temperature of water in a waterway

D. polluted fog

E. energy obtained from hot spots on or in the earth

F. removal of soil by wind, ice, water, or gravity

G. resources that take hundreds or millions of years to form

H. human waste material

I. renewing a forest by seeding or planting trees

J. adding of impurities to the environment

K. wastes are decomposed by bacteria into materials that do not harm the environment

L. loud or unpleasant sounds

M. water vapor combined with sulfur dioxide in the air

N. wise and careful use of resources

O. no members of a species are left alive

P. only a small number of a species are left

Q. using something over again

R. maintaining living species to protect from extinction

Name

  Copyright ©2002 by Incentive Publications, Inc., Nashville, TN.

UNDER THE MICROSCOPE

You never know what you'll find under the microscope! But to find anything, you need to know how to use one. Label the parts of this light microscope and answer the questions about how it works.

eyepiece

body tube

arm

nosepiece

high power
   objective

low power
   objective

coarse
   adjustment

fine
   adjustment

stage clips

stage

diaphragm

mirror

base

slide

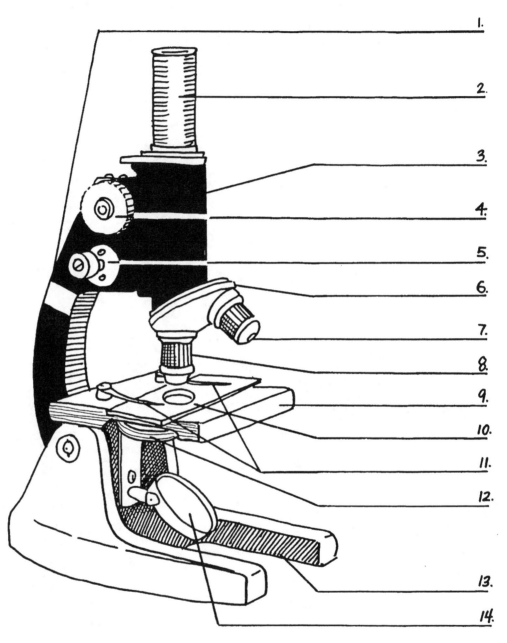

1. _____

2. _____

3. _____

4. _____

5. _____

6. _____

7. _____

8. _____

9. _____

10. _____

11. _____

12. _____

13. _____

14. _____

15. What provides slight focusing to sharpen the image? _____

16. What provides the least magnification? _____

17. What reflects light upwards? _____

18. What regulates the amount of light that enters the body tube? _____

19. What moves the body tube in large movements up and down? _____

20. What holds the microscope slide in place? _____

Name _____

LIFE SCIENCE
ASSESSMENT AND ANSWER KEYS

LIFE SCIENCE
SKILLS TEST

Write the correct answer to each question in its corresponding blank.

_____ 1. Which is **not** a characteristic of all living organisms?
      a. ability to move   b. needs water   c. gives off waste   d. is made of cells

_____ 2. What part of the cell controls movement of materials in and out of the cell?

_____ 3. In what cell structure are proteins made?
      a. mitochondria   b. Golgi bodies   c. ribosomes   d. nucleus

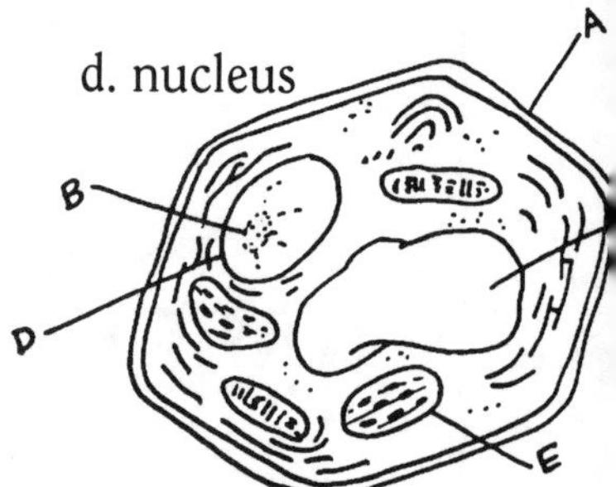

_____ 4. What structure in a plant cell contains chlorophyll?

_____ 5. What kind of a cell is pictured here: plant or animal?

_____ 6. Which part of the pictured cell regulates the movement of materials in and out of the nucleus?

_____ 7. Which part of the pictured cell stores water and dissolved materials?

_____ 8. What process is happening when a cell's cytoplasm shrinks due to water loss?
      a. metabolism   b. active transport   c. mitosis   d. plasmolysis

_____ 9. During what process do plants release energy from stored food?
      a. feedback   b. photosynthesis   c. respiration   d. diffusion

_____ 10. What process is the tendency of an organism to adjust itself to maintain a balanced state?

_____ 11. What is the basic unit of structure and function in all organisms?

_____ 12. A(n) _____ is a trait whereby an organism changes to survive changes in its environment.

_____ 13. What is the smallest division of a kingdom for classification of living things?

_____ 14. Water passes through a cell membrane by
      a. photosynthesis   b. respiration   c. adaptation   d. osmosis

_____ 15. The part of a compound microscope that moves the body tube up and down for focusing is the _____ .

_____ 16. The part of a compound microscope that holds a slide in place is the _____ .

_____ 17. What kingdom is represented by E (pictured at the right)?

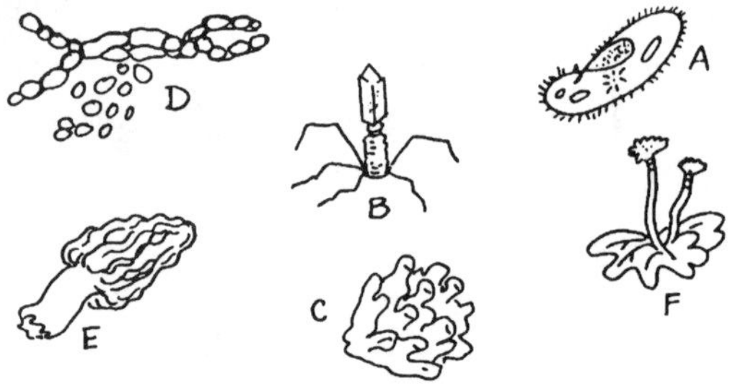

_____ 18. Which organism pictured belongs to the protist kingdom?

_____ 19. Which organism pictured belongs to the animal kingdom?

_____ 20. What short, hairlike structures help some protists move?

_____ 21. Which of these have properties of both living and nonliving things?
      a. bacteria   b. viruses   c. fungi   d. protists

_____ 22. Which of the simple organisms pictured below are **neither** fungi **nor** protists?

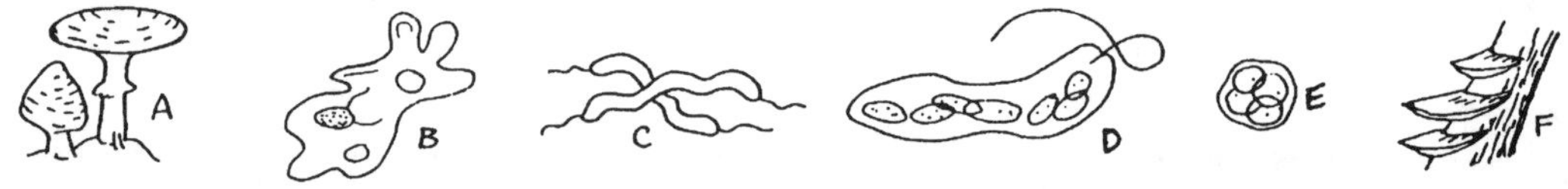

Name _____

The BASIC/Not Boring Middle Grades Science Book   Copyright ©2002 by Incentive Publications, Inc., Nashville, TN.

_____ 23. What is added to the atmosphere during respiration?
_____ 24. A plant that has tubelike structures to carry water and nutrients is a(n) ___ plant.
_____ 25. A plant that grows, reproduces, and dies within one season is a(n) _____ plant.
_____ 26. During the process of _____ , water is lost through the stomata in plant leaves.
_____ 27. A(n) _____ is a young plant growing within a seed.
_____ 28. Fir, pine, spruce, and redwood trees are
       a. angiosperms   b. gymnosperms   c. nonvascular plants   d. deciduous
_____ 29. Plants get the nitrogen they need from _____ .
_____ 30. The part of the flower that produces pollen is the _____ .
_____ 31. The _____ is the female reproductive organ of a flowering plant.
_____ 32. Most of the oxygen in the atmosphere comes from
       a. evaporation   b. diffusion   c. transpiration   d. photosynthesis
_____ 33. The ____ is the part of the plant that traps light energy for use in photosynthesis.
_____ 34. In the flower pictured at right, A is the _____ . 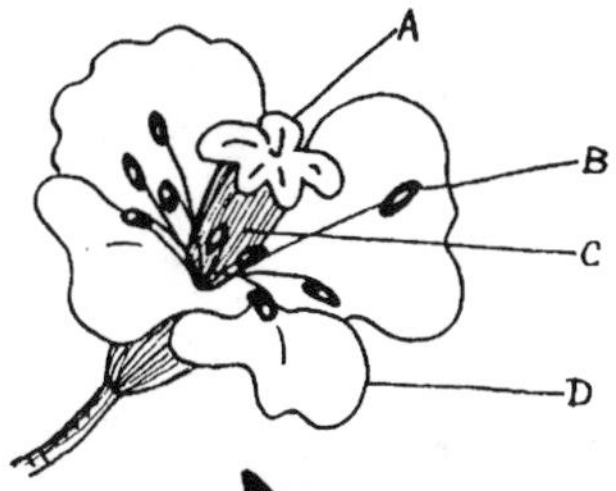
_____ 35. Which letter labels the flower part that will develop into a fruit?
_____ 36. Which letter labels the male reproductive organ?
_____ 37. Animals with backbones belong to what phylum?
_____ 38. Which animals pictured below are invertebrates?

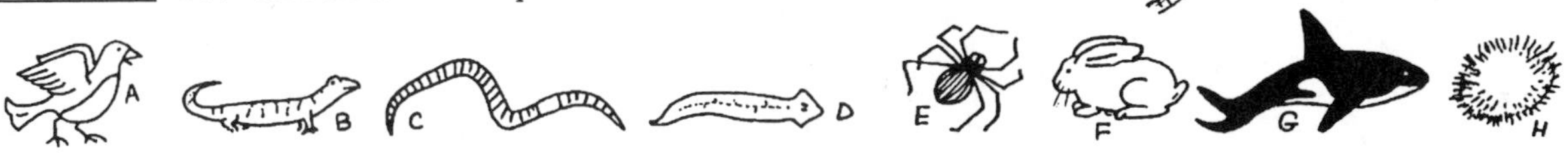

_____ 39. Starfish and sand dollars belong to the _____ phylum.
_____ 40. Jellyfish and coral belong to the same phylum as
       a. snails   b. sponges   c. sea anemones   d. fish
_____ 41. An animal belonging to the phylum arthropoda is a
       a. tapeworm   b. lobster   c. squid   d. slug
_____ 42. An animal that is **not** a mollusk is a
       a. clam   c. slug
       b. octopus   d. sea cucumber
_____ 43. Which organism(s) pictured at right has(ve) **no** symmetry? 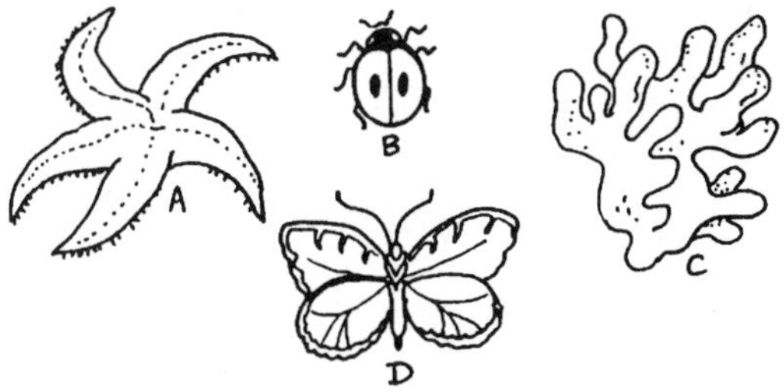
_____ 44. Which organism(s) pictured at right has(ve) **radial** symmetry?
_____ 45. Which organism(s) pictured above has(ve) **bilateral** symmetry?
_____ 46. _____ animals keep a constant body temperature.
_____ 47. _____ are structures that help fish get oxygen from water.
_____ 48. The number of body segments that insects have is _____ .
_____ 49. _____ is the process where insects shed their exoskeletons as they grow.
_____ 50. The bodies of mammals are covered with _____ .
_____ 51. Animals in the _____ phylum have jointed legs.
_____ 52. _____ is the class of arthropods which have 8 legs. 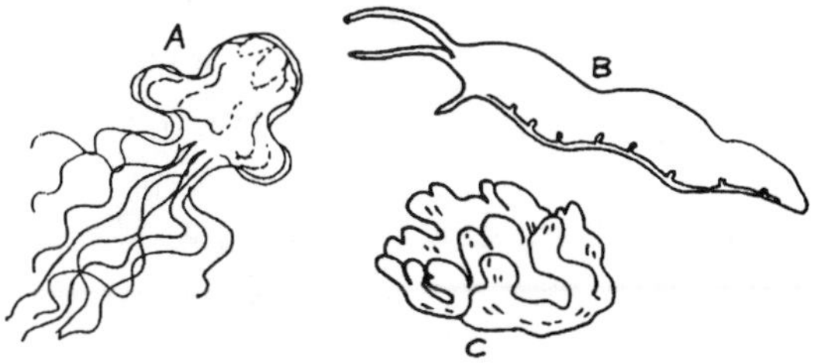
_____ 53. Which animal (at right) is a coelenterate?
_____ 54. Which animal (at right) is a sponge?

Name _____

_____ 55. In the examples shown below, to what phylum does B belong?

        a. segmented worm   b. roundworm   c. flatworm   d. echinoderm

_____ 56. In the examples below, which animal has bilateral symmetry?

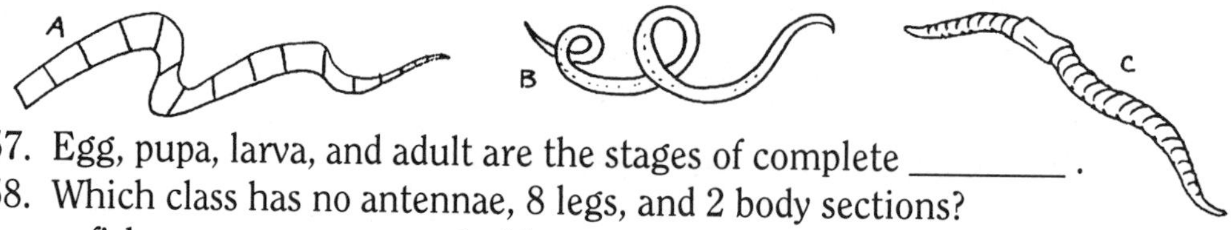

_____ 57. Egg, pupa, larva, and adult are the stages of complete _____ .

_____ 58. Which class has no antennae, 8 legs, and 2 body sections?

        a. fish   c. arachnids

        b. crustaceans   d. insects

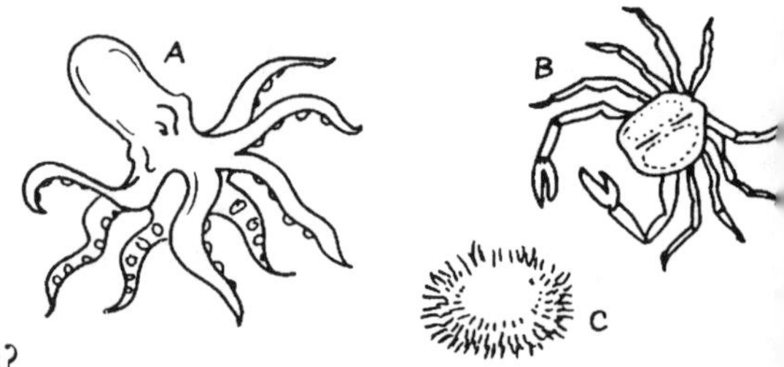

_____ 59. Which animal (at right) is an arthropod?

_____ 60. Which animal (at right) is a mollusk?

_____ 61. Which animal (at right) has radial symmetry?

_____ 62. Which is **not** a characteristic of mammals?

        a. hair covering   b. 3-chambered heart   c. produce milk   d. produce sweat

_____ 63. Which is **not** a characteristic of birds?

        a. 4-chambered heart   b. hollow bones   c. cold-blooded   d. lungs

_____ 64. Which is **not** a characteristic of reptiles?

        a. exoskeleton   b. backbone   c. scale covering   d. cold-blooded

_____ 65. Which organism undergoes complete metamorphosis?

        a. fish   b. frog   c. grasshopper   d. moth

_____ 66. What class of arthropods has 2 pair of antennae, gills, and a flexible exoskeleton?

_____ 67. Which animal pictured below is a millipede?

_____ 68. Which animal pictured below is a crustacean?

_____ 69. E (pictured below) belongs to what class of arthropod?

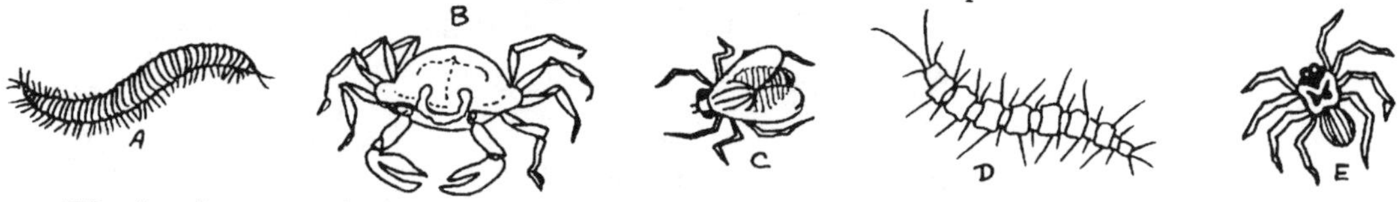

_____ 70. In the row of animals below, to what class does A belong?

_____ 71. Which animals below are **not** warm-blooded?

_____ 72. Which animal pictured below has gills and lungs?

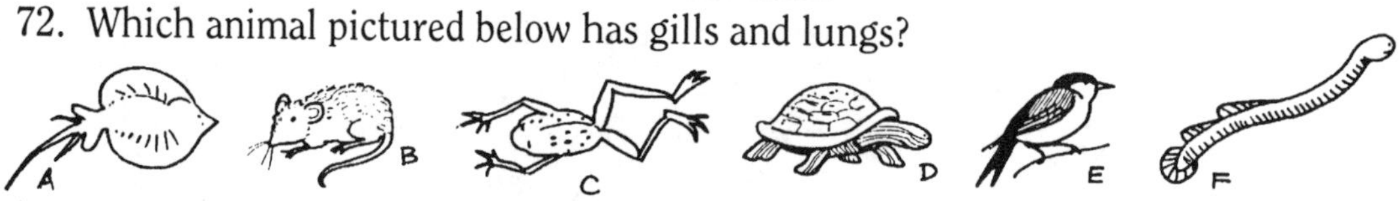

_____ 73. A _____ is a place in the ecosystem where populations of organisms live and grow.

_____ 74. Organisms that remove and eat dead organisms are called _____ .

_____ 75. A _____ is all the organisms of one species in a community.

_____ 76. Which of these represents an ecosystem?

        a. a dead tree   c. a coral reef

        b. a drop of pond water   d. all of these

_____ 77. The picture on the right represents which biome?

        a. taiga   c. desert

        b. tundra   d. temperate forest

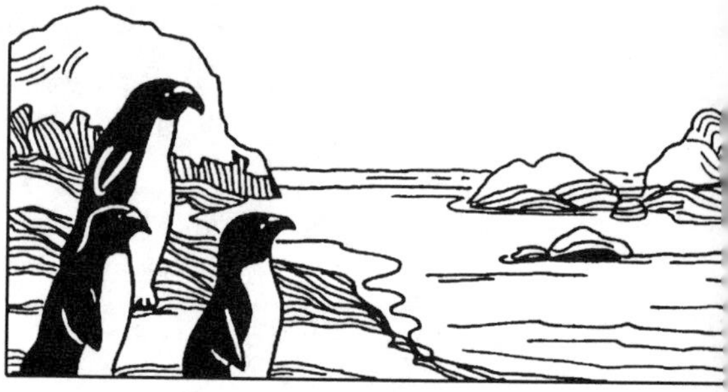

Name

_____ 78. A _____ is the role an organism plays in a community.
_____ 79. The first link in a food chain is always
    a. grass   b. a producer   c. a primary consumer   d. a secondary consumer
_____ 80. The part of the biosphere that surrounds an organism is its _____ .
_____ 81. What kind of resources are coal, petroleum, and natural gas?
_____ 82. If a species is _____ , its organisms are found in very small numbers.
_____ 83. A complex network of food relationships is called a _____ .
_____ 84. A biome that supports large herds of animals is _____ .
_____ 85. Which would **not** be found in a temperate deciduous forest?
    a. coral   b. maple trees   c. deer   d. insects
_____ 86. Which would **not** be found in a taiga biome?
    a. pine trees   c. fir trees
    b. permafrost   d. moose and bears
_____ 87. Which organisms in these food chains (at right) are primary consumers?
_____ 88. Which organisms in these food chains are producers?
_____ 89. Which organisms in these food chains are secondary consumers?
_____ 90. An orchid lives on a tree without causing the tree harm. This is _____ .
    a. predatorism   b. parasitism   c. commensalism   d. pollination
_____ 91. A fungus causes the decay of a dead log. The fungus is a _____ .
    a. decomposer   b. scavenger   c. competitor   d. predator
_____ 92. Some fish and sea anemone live together in a relationship that benefits both. This is called _____ .
    a. parasitism   b. mutualism   c. commensalism   d. competition
_____ 93. Sulfur dioxide combines with water vapor in the air to produce a pollutant called _____ .
_____ 94. Animals and crops raised for food and trees are examples of _____ resources.
_____ 95. Which organisms pictured above are consumers?
_____ 96. Ash, dust, smog, acid rain, noise, and auto exhaust are all examples of _____ .
_____ 97. _____ is the renewing of a forest by planting new trees or seeds.
_____ 98. _____ substances are organic wastes that are **not** harmful to the environment when decomposed.
_____ 99. Are wood and coal both fossil fuels?
_____ 100. _____ pollution raises the temperature of water in waterways.

SCORE: Total Points _____ out of a possible 100 points

Name _____

  Copyright ©2002 by Incentive Publications, Inc., Nashville, TN.

LIFE SCIENCE
SKILLS TEST ANSWER KEY

1. a
2. cell membrane
3. c
4. chloroplast
5. plant
6. D
7. C
8. d
9. c
10. homeostasis
11. cell
12. adaptation
13. species
14. d
15. coarse adjustment
16. stage clips
17. fungus
18. A
19. C
20. cilia
21. b
22. C and D
23. carbon dioxide
24. vascular
25. annual
26. transpiration
27. embryo
28. b
29. soil
30. anther
31. pistil
32. d
33. leaf (or chlorophyll)
34. stigma

35. C
36. B
37. chordata
38. C, D, E, H
39. echinodermata
40. c
41. b
42. d
43. C
44. A
45. B and D
46. warm-blooded
47. gills
48. three
49. molting
50. hair
51. arthropod
52. arachnid
53. A
54. C
55. b
56. A
57. metamorphosis
58. c
59. B
60. A
61. A
62. b
63. c
64. a
65. d
66. crustaceans
67. A
68. B

69. arachnid
70. fish
71. A, C, D, F
72. C
73. community
74. scavengers
75. population
76. d
77. b
78. niche
79. b
80. environment
81. nonrenewable
82. endangered
83. food web
84. grassland
85. a
86. b
87. mouse and small fish
88. acorn and sea plants
89. owl, big fish, person
90. c
91. a
92. b
93. acid rain (or snow)
94. renewable
95. B and D
96. pollution
97. reforestation
98. biodegradable
99. no
100. thermal

Copyright ©2002 by Incentive Publications, Inc., Nashville, TN.

ANSWERS

1. diffusion
2. plasmolysis
3. mitosis
4. osmosis
5. metabolism
6. cell division
7. respiration
8. homeostasis
9. active transport
10. homeostasis
11. diffusion
12. mitosis
13. metabolism

Page 174
1. animal kingdom
2. plant kingdom
3. fungus kingdom
4. protist kingdom
5. moneran kingdom
6. protist
7. plant, fungus, moneran
8. animal
9. protist, animal
10. moneran
11. plant, fungus
12. moneran
13. plant
14. animal, fungus
15. protist, moneran
16. phylum, class, order, family, genus, species

Page 175
1. no	11. no
2. no	12. yes
3. an organism	13. moneran
4. microscope	14. saprophyte
5. yes	15. yes
6. (vary) insects, air, water, food	16. no
	17. yes
7. no	18. no
8. both	19. pasteurization
9. interferon	20. spirilla
10. (vary) some are polio, rubella, yellow fever, smallpox, influenza	21. bocci
	22. bacilli
	23. mutualism
	24. parasitism

Page 176
1. T	5. F	9. F	13. F
2. T	6. F	10. T	14. F
3. F	7. F	11. T	15. T
4. T	8. F	12. T	16. F

Page 177

1. plant organ that traps light and makes food for the plant
2. plant tissue that transports water around the plant
3. system where food is stored in a thick, long, main root
4. thin layer of brick-shaped cells that cover and protect the surface of the leaf
5. waxy covering of the leaf epidermis
6. plant tissue that transports food from leaves to other plant parts
7. tubelike structures that transport water and nutrients around the plant
8. plant growth tissue that makes new xylem and phloem cells
9. part of the leaf that traps sunlight
10. tiny openings in epidermis of leaf that let things pass in & out
11. leaf stalk that attaches leaf to stem in many plants
12. root system with many branches
13. threadlike cells that bring water and nutrients into root
14. structures that anchor plants into the ground and take in water and nutrients
15. B
16. A

Page 178
(Answers will vary somewhat.)

PHOTOSYNTHESIS

Green plants trap and use energy from light to make food. The chlorophyll in the green plant cells are what traps the light. The plant combines carbon dioxide and water to produce sugar and oxygen. Energy is stored in the food (sugar); some oxygen is released into the air. This is the opposite of respiration.

RESPIRATION

Respiration is opposite from photosynthesis. In respiration, energy is released from food. The plant uses oxygen to breakdown sugar so the plant can use the energy for its life processes. Water and carbon dioxide are released as this process takes place.

GAS EXCHANGE

Tiny openings in the leaf epidermis, called stomata, allow gases to pass in and out of the leaf by diffusion. The gases that move in and out are carbon dioxide, oxygen, and water vapor. The stomata are usually open during the day and closed at night.

TRANSPIRATION

Plants lose water vapor through the stomata in the leaves. A plant takes in water through its roots and loses a substantial amount of water through transpiration each day.

Page 179
Corrected version of story:

I'm the really important part of the whole plan! I carry pollen grains from the anthers on top of the filaments of the stamen on one flower and leave them on the sticky stigma (which is part of the pistil) of another.

After I leave this stuff on the sticky stigma, a sepal grows down through the petal toward the ovule. The sperm passes out of the pollen tube into the egg and fertilizes it.

The fertilized seed develops into an embryo, and the wall of the surrounding ovary develops into a fruit. When the fruit bursts open or is thrown on the ground, the seeds fall into the ground and start new plants.

1. stigma	7. ovule
2. style	8. ovary
3. pistil	9. filament
4. petal	10. anther
5. embryo	11. stamen
6. sepal	12. pollen

Pages 180–181
A. 9	K. 11	U. 27
B. 1	L. 24	V. 29
C. 12	M. 23	W. 22
D. 16	N. 28	X. 25
E. 20	O. 19	Y. 17
F. 30	P. 8	Z. 14
G. 26	Q. 5	AA. 6
H. 13	R. 2	BB. 10
I. 3	S. 15	XX. 4
J. 18	T. 21	ZZ. 7

Page 182
BONES:
1, 3, 4, 7, 8, 10, 11, 14, 19, 20, 21, 22, 23, 26, 27, 28, 29, 31, 32
NO BONES:
2, 5, 6, 9, 12, 13, 15, 16, 17, 18, 24, 25, 30

Page 183
1. B	6. R	11. B	16. R
2. B	7. B	12. R	17. R
3. B	8. N	13. R	18. B
4. B	9. R	14. R	19. B
5. R	10. B	15. R	20. N

His body has bilateral symmetry.

Page 184
PORIFERA: elephant ear sponge ..(A)
PLATYHELMINTHES: tapeworm ..(H)
COELENTERATA: jellyfish ....(D)
NEMOTODA: hookworm................(I)
MOLLUSCA: octopus, clam ....(B)
ANNELIDA: bristleworm, earthworm ....(G)
ECHINODERMATA: sea urchin .....(C)
ARTHROPODA: ant, bee, shrimp ..(E)
CHORDATA: hawk, gull, frog, ray .(F)

Page 186
Descriptions will vary.

1. coelenterates—live in water, some float, some are attached; have a central cavity and a mouth; most have tentacles
2. flatworms—live in water or attached to other organism as a parasite; have flattened body
3. roundworms—live in water or on land or attached to other organism as a parasite; have round body
4. segmented worms—live in water or on land; body is divided into segments; body segments have bristles
5. sponges—live in water, stay attached to one place; are made of a thick sack of cells with canals, chambers, or pores

Page 187
I.	1. E	5. M	9. M	13. M
	2. M	6. E	10. E	14. E
	3. M	7. B	11. M	15. M
	4. M	8. E	12. M	16. B
II.	A. M	D. M	G. M	
	B. M	E. M	H. E	
	C. E	F. M	I. E	

Page 188
ALL ARTHROPODS: .... f, h, s
MILLIPEDES: .... k, o, u
CENTIPEDES: .... c, j, k, v
CRUSTACEANS:... a, i, l, p, r, t, x
ARACHNIDS: .... g, p, q, n
INSECTS: .... b, d, e, k, m, w

Page 189

1. 2	4. 4	6. land
2. 2	5. biting and	7. a, b, e, f, h, i, j
3. 0	chewing	8. c, d, g, k

Page 190

I.
1. F	5. T	9. T	13. T
2. T	6. F	10. T	
3. T	7. F	11. T	
4. F	8. F	12. T	

II.
hermit crab	spider	millipede	crayfish
centipede	spider	shrimp	spider

Page 191

1. set of stages that occur as some organisms grow into adults

2. 1) egg   2) larva   3) pupa   4) adult

3. the egg grows into a nymph that looks like a miniature adult; as the nymph grows, it molts several times and grows larger, and sometimes adds wings. At the end of all the molting stages, it becomes an adult.

4. (vary) bees, ants, flies, fleas, moths, etc.

5. (vary) grasshopper, termite, cockroach, dragonfly, etc.

6. the animal sheds its exoskeleton

7. A. the monarch

8. B. the grasshopper

butterfly: A. eggs   B. larva   C. pupa   D. adult
grasshopper: E. eggs   F. nymph   G. adult

Page 192

A cold-blooded animal has a body temperature that changes with the temperature of the environment.

1. fish	18. gills
2. water	19. develop or grow
3. gills	20. hatch
4. three	21. three
5. jawless	22-23. Answers will vary.
6. cartilage	24. reptiles
7. bony	25. air
8. eggs	26. land
9-10. Answers will vary.	27. scales
11. amphibians	28. three
12-13. land, water	29. eggs
14. water	30-31. Answers will vary.
15. land	F—fish;
16. moist	A—frog;
17. air	R—turtle, snake

Page 193

A warm-blooded animal maintains a nearly constant body temperature despite its surroundings.

1. birds	13. mammals
2. feathers	14. temperature
3-4. hot, cold	15. milk
5. wings	16. four
6. inside	17. sweat
7. outside	18. inside
8. lungs	19-20. Answers
9. four	will vary.
10. beaks	B—all birds shown;
11-12. Answers will vary.	M—monkey, bat

Page 194

CLASS	Kind of Skeleton	# Heart Chmbrs.	Body Covering	Blood Temp.	Where They Live	Where Young Develop	Special Features
JAWLESS FISH	cartilage	2	scales	cold	fresh or salt water	external in eggs	gills, sucker-mouths
CARTILAGE FISH	cartilage	2	scales	cold	mostly salt water	external in eggs	gills, hinged jaws
BONY FISH	bones	2	scales	cold	fresh or salt water	external in eggs	gills, fins, hinged jaws
AMPHIBIANS	bones	3	moist skin	cold	land or water	external in eggs	can breathe in water or on land
REPTILES	bones	3	scales	cold	mainly on land	external in eggs	
BIRDS	bones	4	feathers	warm	land, water, air	external in eggs	hollow bones, wings
MAMMALS	bones	4	hair	warm	mostly land	mostly internal	produce milk, sweat

Page 195

Page 196

1. E	3. P	5. F	7. B	9. G	11. M	13. J	15. N
2. A	4. I	6. D	8. C	10. L	12. O	14. H	16. K

Page 197

1. prevent loss of water from body

2. a hard outer covering that protects the inside parts of an arthropod

3. no; similarity or likeness of parts

4. Answers will vary.

5. yes

6. no; it is in a different phylum—coelenterate

7. creatures with 2 body parts, 8 legs, no antennae—a kind of arthropod

8. no; the process of shedding the exoskeleton

9. it is long and skinny and waves around

0. ropelike tissue on some animals; used to obtain food
1. tough, flexible tissue found in joints; not as stiff as bone
2. protist
3. not necessarily
4. no; a phylum is a large group of animals
5. no; they just do it on their own
6. maybe because of the spines sticking out, or the weird looks
7. pupae; larvae are too squirmy (answers may vary)
8. no; it is not an axe, it is the middle section of a body
9. they are not real feet, they just work like feet

Page 198

Answers will vary. Accept any reasonable answer.

Page 199

Accept reasonable answers and explanations about what is wrong with each example.

Pages 200–201

A. fresh water biome: algae, trout, tadpoles, streams, ponds, rivers, water lilies, marsh, swamp, crayfish, alligators, snakes, pondweeds

B. salt water biome: corals, whales, sponges, sharks, plankton

C. tropical rainforest biome: vines, palm trees, ferns, parrots, monkeys, orchids, plentiful rainfall, large juicy fruit, very hot temperatures, snakes, leopards

D. taiga biome: deer, fir trees, foxes, squirrels, woodpecker, moose, pine trees, bears, coniferous forests

E. temperate deciduous forest biome: deer, bears, foxes, squirrels, woodpeckers, birch trees, maple trees, trees that lose leaves

F. tundra biome: grasses, lichens and mosses, polar bears, permafrost, caribou, walrus, no trees, cold desert, penguins, sparse plant life, swamps

G. grassland biome: antelope, prairie dogs, grasses, grazing animals, cougars, lions, irregular precipitation

H. desert biome: lizards, snakes, cacti, sagebrush, armadillos, little rain, fleshy plants, plants that store water

Page 202

I. A. owl—secondary consumer; mouse—primary consumer; acorns—producer
   B. pelican—secondary consumer; fish—primary consumer; plants—producer
   C. fox—secondary consumer; rabbit—primary consumer; plants—producer
   D. people—secondary consumer; sheep—primary consumer; grass—producer

II. 1. C 4. P 7. P 10. C
    2. C 5. C 8. C
    3. C 6. P 9. P

Page 203

1. biosphere is the space around the earth where organisms can live; a community is all the organisms that live in a certain area
2. usually there are many populations
3. the role of an organism in a community
4. interactions between organisms and their environment
5. ecosystem has to do with the interactions between organisms; environment is the surroundings of an organism
6. competing
7. frog
8. no
9. yes
10. they both hang around dead organisms
11. a producer
12. a food chain is a pathway of food and energy; a food web is a complex network of food relationships which includes many food chains

Page 204

1. scavengers
2. community
3. parasitism
4. competition
5. food chain; predator-prey
6. predator-prey
7. dominant species
8. population
9. parasitism
10. commensalism
11. mutualism
12. predator-prey
13. decomposer
14. scavengers

15. mutualism
16. competition
17. predator-prey

Page 205

(Explanations and labels may vary slightly.)

A. WATER CYCLE
   Labels:
   up arrow—evaporation; down arrow: precipitation.

All organisms need water. There is a constant cycle of water in the environment. Water evaporates from the surfaces of rivers, lakes, oceans, and soil. Plants give off water during transpiration. Water vapor in the air forms clouds and returns to the earth as rain, snow, or other precipitation.

B. NITROGEN CYCLE
   Labels: down arrow: soil bacteria remove nitrogen from air; up arrow: nitrogen returned to air by dying organisms.

Bacteria in the soil remove nitrogen from the air and combine it with oxygen to make nitrates. Plants can absorb these nitrates and use them to make compounds that animals need. Animals take in the nitrates through these compounds (such as proteins). When plants and animals die, they decompose and return these nitrates to the soil. Bacteria in the soil break them down and return nitrogen to the air.

C. CARBON DIOXIDE–OXYGEN CYCLE
   top arrow: oxygen from plants; bottom arrow: carbon dioxide from animals.

Plants and animals need carbon dioxide and oxygen. Plants and animals take in oxygen and give off carbon dioxide as they breathe. Plants remove carbon dioxide during photosynthesis and return oxygen to the air. Plants and animals are continuously exchanging the oxygen and carbon dioxide that they need.

Page 206

Across
2. eats other organisms
4. contest among organisms
6. gradual change in a community over time
8. one organism lives off another

without harm
10. narrow zone on Earth that supports life
12. pathway of food through ecosystem: food _____
13. removes and eats dead animals
14. most prevalent species in an area
15. all organisms living together in an area
16. study of interactions between organisms and environment
17. any source of raw material

Down
1. smallest category of classification of living things
3. two organisms live together for mutual benefit
5. role of an organism in the community
7. system where living and nonliving things interact
9. place in ecosystem where population lives
10. region with a distinct climate, dominant plant type, and distinctive organisms
11. contains chlorophyll to make food for itself and other organisms

Page 207

1. no—M   10. no—G
2. no—K   11. no—J
3. yes—N   12. no—Q
4. yes—P   13. no—D
5. no—F   14. no—I
6. no—O   15. yes—R
7. no—B   16. yes—C
8. yes—L   17. no—E
9. no—A   18. yes—H

Page 208

1. arm
2. eyepiece
3. body tube
4. coarse adjustment
5. fine adjustment
6. nosepiece
7. low power objective
8. high power objective
9. stage
10. slide
11. stage clips
12. diaphragm
13. base
14. mirror
15. fine adjustment
16. low power objective
17. mirror
18. diaphragm
19. coarse adjustment
20. stage clips

HUMAN BODY & HEALTH

Skills Exercises

Entering CITY MEDICAL CENTER

SKILLS CHECKLIST FOR HUMAN BODY & HEALTH

✔	SKILL	PAGE(S)
	Identify different body processes, body activities, and body parts	220–223
	Identify some parts of the human cell and their functions	224
	Identify different types of cells	225
	Distinguish between cells, tissue, organs and systems; name different kinds of tissue, organs, and systems	225
	Identify functions of different body systems; distinguish among systems	226, 227
	Identify specific organs within systems	227
	Identify bones in the skeletal system and functioning of the skeletal system	228–231
	Identify joints, ligaments, cartilage, and their functions	230
	Identify muscles and understand functioning of the muscular system	231
	Identify parts of the nervous system and understand functioning of the system	232, 233
	Identify different parts of the brain and their functions	232, 233
	Show understanding of the function of sensory organs	234–237
	Identify the parts of the eye and the way the eye sees objects	234
	Identify parts of the ear and the way they help in hearing	235
	Show understanding of the way the nose and tongue work to enable the sensations of taste and smell	236
	Identify parts of the skin and show understanding of the functions of the skin	237
	Identify parts of the circulatory system and understand functioning of the system	238, 239
	Show understanding of the workings of the heart	239
	Identify parts of the respiratory system and understand functioning of the system	240, 241
	Identify parts of the digestive system and understand functioning of the system	242, 243
	Identify glands of the endocrine system and understand their functions	244
	Identify organs that are part of the excretory system and understand their functions	245
	Identify parts of the male and female reproductive systems and understand functioning of the systems	246
	Show understanding of the process of fertilization and of the process by which a fertilized egg develops into a human offspring	246, 247
	Show a basic understanding of some concepts of genetics and heredity	248, 249
	Identify different diseases and disorders and their symptoms and causes	250, 251
	Identify the ways bodies can defend against disease, including natural defenses and other interventions	252, 253
	Show understanding of the ways exercise is beneficial to health	254, 255
	Show understanding of nutrition concepts and components of a healthy diet	256, 257
	Show ability to apply fitness and health concepts to personal life	258

BODY MYSTERIES

Students at the Body-Wise Medical Center learn about mysteries of the human body. These 22 mysteries are part of a study guide they are using to prepare for a test. Use your clever thinking, good resources, and knowledge of the human body to track down the solutions to these mysteries.

5. A liquid is always flowing through the kidneys, being filtered by a million tiny filtering units called nephrons. What is the flowing substance?

2. A green substance is lurking in the gallbladder. What is this substance?

3. Several small white structures are lodged in sockets in the maxillae and the mandible. What are these structures?

6. A mysterious substance is frequently coming out of the Islets of Langerhans. What is this substance?

1. Dr. Neuron is standing on her head. Amazingly, when she eats a cookie, it goes through her esophagus into her stomach. What process keeps the food from sliding back up into her mouth as she stands on her head?

4. Some reactions are having a great time leaping across synapses. What are these reactions?

7. A substance is getting smashed into tiny pieces in the liver during digestion. What is this substance?

8. Red blood cells are busy carrying heavy loads of a substance. What is it?

9. A strange reaction is happening inside a body. The diaphragm muscle and muscles in the abdominal wall are strongly contracting. Partly digested food is being forced up out of the stomach. What is happening?

10. Dr. Neuron's wrist rotates when she does her jump rope workout. What allows her wrist to rotate?

Use with page 221.

Name

11. A fluid called perilymph sloshes around in a coiled tube. What is this tube and where is it located?

_____

_____

12. Two substances are mixing together with food in the duodenum. What are these substances?

_____

_____

13. A body detective has come across a bunch of cones. What organ is she exploring?

_____

14. Tiny structures with great potential make their home in the ovaries. Every month one of them matures and leaves its home. What are these structures?

_____

15. A slippery fluid is in the nose. It traps dust particles. What is this fluid?

16. A body detective searches for clues in a layer of dentine under a crown. What structure is he exploring?

_____

17. A great deal of liquid is passing into the blood through the walls of the colon (the first part of the large intestine). What is this liquid?

_____

18. Plasma is busily flowing around the body as a part of the blood. What is plasma carrying?

_____

19. Bodies have parts attached to them that have grown out of roots. The visible part is composed of dead cells made hard by a substance called keratin. What are these parts?

_____

20. When Dr. Neuron is startled by a terrible crash, her heart pounds. What makes that sound coming from her heart?

_____

21. A substance pours into the professor's blood when she hears the crash. This substance prepares her for emergency action such as running away or fighting to protect herself. What is this substance?

_____

22. Professor Neuron was so frightened by the noise that she broke the test tube in her hand and sliced two fingers. Amazingly, after a few minutes, the blood clotted and the bleeding stopped. What body structures made this happen?

_____

Use with page 220.

Name _____

 Copyright ©2002 by Incentive Publications, Inc., Nashville, TN.

HOT JOBS FOR BODY PARTS

There are plenty of job opportunities for hard-working body parts. Several of the jobs are described here (pages 222 and 223). But which parts are qualified to apply?

Read each job description from the newspaper. Write the name of at least one body part that is qualified and able to do the job. (See the list of possible applicants on page 223.)

JOBS AVAILABLE

1. CARRIERS NEEDED

Carry repeated loads of oxygen-rich blood away from the heart.

_____

2. HELP WANTED

Workers needed to separate unwanted substances out of the blood. Please apply in pairs.

_____

3. WANTED

Strong applicants to protect human bones. Must have extensive experience in the task of multiplying to grow and repair broken bones.

_____

4. APPLY TODAY

Sit a-top the trachea and move muscles to change the shape of vocal cords.

_____

5. HELP WANTED

Suck in air and pass it down into the bronchi.

_____

6. AVAILABLE

Keep pressure equal on both sides of the eardrum. Must be able to open and close to let air in and out. Please apply in pairs.

_____

7. WANTED

Need workers to bend and straighten knees.

_____

8. APPLY TODAY

Work with others to raise and lower the forearm.

_____

9. APPLICANTS NEEDED

Applicants needed for group work to insulate nerve fibers through an entire body.

_____

10. WANTED IMMEDIATELY

Efficient organ needed to produce insulin.

_____

11. NEEDED

Tubes needed to carry urine from kidneys to bladder.

_____

12. COODINATOR

Experienced worker is needed to balance and coordinate all the body's movements.

_____

13. WANTED

Need muscular worker able to move up and down for moving air in and out of the lungs.

_____

14. JOB OPEN

Produce hormone to regulate the balance of calcium in the blood and bones.

_____

15. HIRING NOW

Workers needed to wrap around harmful bacteria and produce antibodies to combat diseases.

_____

Use with page 223.

Name

APPLICANTS

alveoli	cerebrum	gall bladder	ovaries	retina	thymus
aorta	cerebellum	humerus	pancreas	sacrum	thyroid
arteries	coccyx	incisors	parathyroid gland	scapula	tongue
appendix	cochlea	iris	patella	semicircular canal	trachea
adrenal glands	cornea	kidneys	periosteum	small intestine	triceps
atrium	dendrites	larynx	pharynx	spinal cord	ureters
biceps	diaphragm	liver	pituitary gland	sternum	urethra
bicuspids	epidermis	marrow	plasma	stomach	uterus
bronchial tubes	epiglottis	medulla	platelets	tear duct	veins
bronchiole	esophagus	molars	pulp	teeth	ventricle
cartilage	Eustachian tube	myelin	quadriceps	tendon	villi
capillaries	Fallopian tube	optic nerve	rectum	testes	white blood cells

JOBS AVAILABLE

16. GATEKEEPERS
Absorb food and pass it into blood vessels from the ileum.

_____

17. OPPORTUNITY
Keep many bones from grinding against each other when they move. Rubbery applicants only, please.

_____

18. APPLY TODAY
Force food back into pharynx so that it can glide easily down the esophagus.

_____

19. OPENING
Light-sensitive worker needed to receive visual images and transmit impulses to the brain.

_____

20. WANTED
Worker to help immune system recognize germs and reject them.

_____

21. JOB AVAILABLE
Join muscles to bone. Several positions available.

I've got to 'bone up' on my body parts!

22. WORKER NEEDED
Make bile to break up fats during digestion.

23. APPLY NOW
Worker needed to produce eleven hormones that control the actions of other endocrine glands.

24. OPENING
Regulate heart rate and breathing, swallowing, sneezing, and coughing.

_____

25. POSITION AVAILABLE
Take up residence at the end of the vertebrae column. Little activity required for the job.

_____

26. JOB OPEN
Keep trachea covered during swallowing.

_____

27. HELP WANTED
Workers needed to make blood cells.

_____

28. WANTED
Strong workers needed to crush and grind food.

_____

29. WANTED NOW
Pair of workers needed to produce estrogen.

_____

30. OPENINGS
Workers needed to pass oxygen from lungs into blood vessels and welcome carbon dioxide into the lungs.

_____

Use with page 222.

Name _____

STARTING OUT SIMPLE

Professor Gertrude Golgi is lecturing her
students on the basics of human physiology.
Finish her chart by writing the name of each
cell part that is pictured and described.

I celebrate the cell.

The cell is the body's
basic unit of life.
Although there are different kinds of cells,
most of them have a similar structure.

1. _____

This fine layer holds the
cell together and keeps it
separate from other cells.
It allows certain
substances to pass in and
out of the cell. It keeps
other substances out.

2. _____

This is the "brain" of the
cell, which controls all cell
activities. It also houses
special threads called
chromosomes that are the
coded instructions. These
tell the cells what to do.

3. _____

This is the power station
of the cell. Here oxygen
and food react to produce
energy for the cell.

4. _____

This is a jelly-like
substance that makes up
the material of the cell.
It is mostly
water and protein.

5. _____

These are the
protein-manufacturing
factories of the cell.

6. _____

These act as storage
sheds, storing and
releasing chemicals
for cell use.

7. _____

This is a network of tubes
that hold the ribosomes
(where cell substances
are produced).

Use with page 225.

Name

GETTING COMPLICATED

The structures that make up human bodies start out simple and get complicated quickly. Identify these different cell types. Label each with one of these: bone, blood, nerve, sperm, muscle.

Every body has more than 50 billion **cells**.

1

Cells group together to form **tissues**.

2

Different kinds of tissues group together to form **organs**. Each organ has a special job in the body.

3

Organs that have closely-related jobs work together in **systems**.

4

1._____

2._____   3._____

4._____   5._____

Name the 4 kinds of tissue in the human body.

6. _____   8. _____

7. _____   9. _____

Name 10 organs in the human body.

10. _____   15. _____

11. _____   16. _____

12. _____   17. _____

13. _____   18. _____

14. _____   19. _____

Name 5 different body systems.

20. _____   22. _____

21. _____   23. _____

24. _____

Use with page 224.

Name _____

SORTING OUT SYSTEMS

Dr. Scapula works in the research section of the hospital where different body systems are studied. Each system is studied on a different floor of the building. The elevator will take the doctor to the floor of his choice. Write the number of the correct floor for each of the questions. (There may be more than one correct answer to some questions, and a floor may be used more than once as an answer.)

Which floor will Professor Scapula visit to investigate . . .

_____ A. ways that the body changes food to a form that is usable by all its cells?

_____ B. organs and structures that cover and protect the body?

_____ C. ways the body gets rid of its waste products?

_____ D. a system that gives shape and strength to the body?

_____ E. a system that enables the body to move?

_____ F. a system that enables people to produce offspring?

_____ G. how the body transports blood, nutrients, and other materials through a system of vessels?

_____ H. the system designed to carry messages between the brain and the rest of the body?

_____ I. how the body produces the hormones and chemicals that control many of its functions?

_____ J. a system that supplies oxygen to the cells and removes carbon dioxide from the blood?

_____ K. the system that controls muscles and regulates body activities?

_____ L. the system that supports and shapes the body and protects its internal organs?

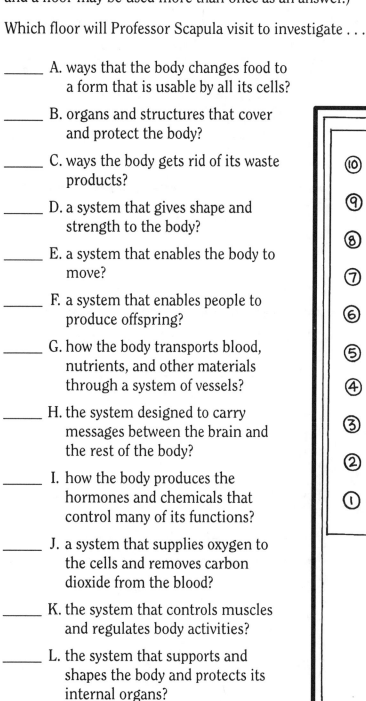

⑩ endocrine

⑨ nervous

⑧ digestive

⑦ integumentary

⑥ respiratory

⑤ reproductive

④ excretory

③ muscular

② skeletal

① circulatory

Going up?

Use with page 227.

Name

GET ORGAN-IZED!

Nurse Constance Kare is escorting a patient for a treatment. She needs to understand the different body systems in order to get the patient to the right department in the hospital. Help her understand which organs belong to which systems. (Circle one answer for each question.)

Where would you find . . .

1. a **thyroid gland**?
   a. in the digestive system
   b. in the integumentary system
   c. in the endocrine system
   d. in the circulatory system

2. **phalanges**?
   a. in the reproductive system
   b. in the respiratory system
   c. in the excretory system
   d. in the skeletal system

3. a **gall bladder**?
   a. in the nervous system
   b. in the integumentary system
   c. in the digestive system
   d. in the circulatory system

4. an **axon**?
   a. in the respiratory system
   b. in the reproductive system
   c. in the circulatory system
   d. in the nervous system

5. a **ventricle**?
   a. in integumentary system
   b. in the circulatory system
   c. in the excretory system
   d. in the endocrine system

6. a **Fallopian tube**?
   a. in the reproductive system
   b. in the muscular system
   c. in the skeletal system
   d. in the digestive system

7. a **duodenum**?
   a. in the digestive system
   b. in the nervous system
   c. in the reproductive system
   d. in the circulatory system

Which is NOT in . . .

8. the **endocrine system**?
   a. diaphragm   c. adrenal gland
   b. parathyroid   d. pineal gland

9. the **digestive system**?
   a. liver   c. small intestine
   b. esophagus   d. Eustachian tube

10. the **respiratory system**?
    a. bronchiole   c. trachea
    b. stirrup   d. lungs

11. the **skeletal system**?
    a. ulna   c. patella
    b. testes   d. clavicle

12. the **circulatory system**?
    a. platelets   c. pancreas
    b. vena cava   d. atrium

13. the **integumentary system**?
    a. blood cells   c. hair
    b. skin   d. fingernails

14. the **nervous system**?
    a. dendrites   c. radius
    b. ganglia   d. spinal cord

15. the **excretory system**?
    a. kidneys   c. urethra
    b. skin   d. ligaments

16. the **muscle system**?
    a. deltoids   c. quadriceps
    b. pelvis   d. triceps

17. a **reproductive system**?
    a. uterus   c. urethra
    b. cervix   d. bladder

Use with page 226.

Name

      Copyright ©2002 by Incentive Publications, Inc., Nashville, TN.

KNOW YOUR BONES

Do you know these bones? Students of medicine need to know these and the many other bones in the body. They study a model and ask questions to learn about bones. Answer these questions. Then use the skeleton to help you complete the chart for the Broken Bones Clinic on the next page (page 229).

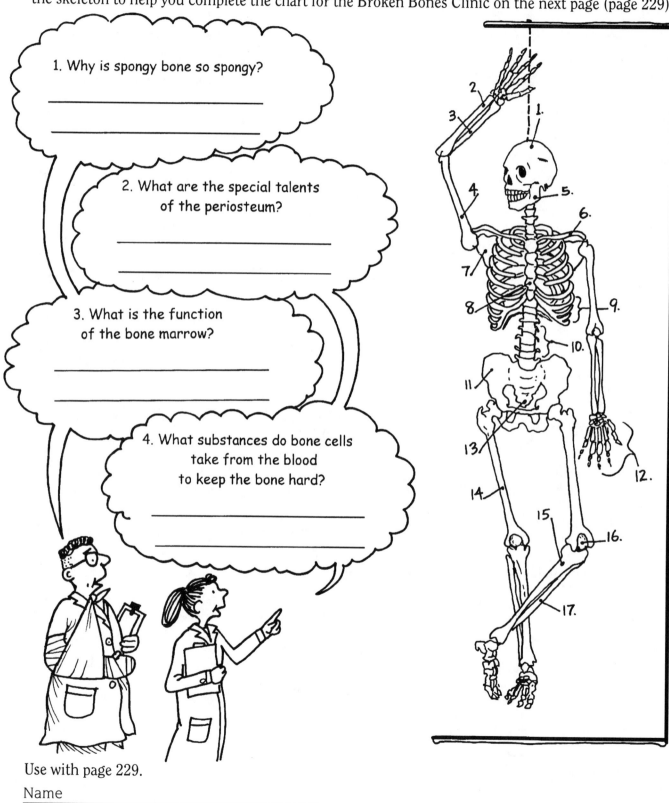

1. Why is spongy bone so spongy?

_____

_____

2. What are the special talents of the periosteum?

_____

_____

3. What is the function of the bone marrow?

_____

_____

4. What substances do bone cells take from the blood to keep the bone hard?

_____

_____

Use with page 229.

Name

The doctors at the Broken Bones Clinic see every kind of broken bone. They keep track of which bones each patient has broken. Finish this week's chart. Write the name of the bone for each description. Then write the number of that bone as shown on the diagram on page 228.

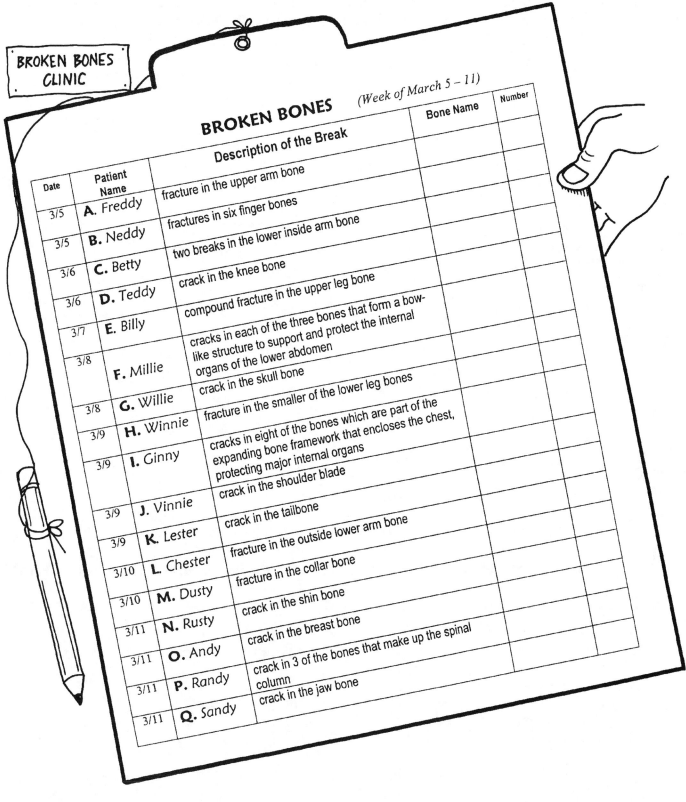

BROKEN BONES CLINIC

BROKEN BONES *(Week of March 5 – 11)*

Date	Patient Name	Description of the Break	Bone Name	Number
3/5	A. Freddy	fracture in the upper arm bone		
3/5	B. Neddy	fractures in six finger bones		
3/6	C. Betty	two breaks in the lower inside arm bone		
3/6	D. Teddy	crack in the knee bone		
3/7	E. Billy	compound fracture in the upper leg bone		
3/8	F. Millie	cracks in each of the three bones that form a bow-like structure to support and protect the internal organs of the lower abdomen		
3/8	G. Willie	crack in the skull bone		
3/9	H. Winnie	fracture in the smaller of the lower leg bones		
3/9	I. Ginny	cracks in eight of the bones which are part of the expanding bone framework that encloses the chest, protecting major internal organs		
3/9	J. Vinnie	crack in the shoulder blade		
3/9	K. Lester	crack in the tailbone		
3/10	L. Chester	fracture in the outside lower arm bone		
3/10	M. Dusty	fracture in the collar bone		
3/11	N. Rusty	crack in the shin bone		
3/11	O. Andy	crack in the breast bone		
3/11	P. Randy	crack in 3 of the bones that make up the spinal column		
3/11	Q. Sandy	crack in the jaw bone		

Use with page 228.

Name

A MATTER OF MOVEMENT

Dr. Sara Bellum begins her day in the hospital gym doing a morning workout. She could not do these exercises if her body could not bend. This bending is made possible by certain body structures. Answer these questions about some of the movements that are a part of her workout.

1. What structures allow Dr. Bellum's body to bend at places such as the knees, spine, elbows, and neck?

   _____

2. What strong, flexible fibers hold her bones together and stretch to allow bending?

   _____

3. Pads of rubbery protein cushion the movable joints at the ends of many of her bones. What are these pads?

   _____

4. What kind of joint allows Sara to bend her knees while she does knee bends? _____

5. What kind of joint allows Sara to do head circles? _____

6. What kind of joint allows her to do arm circles? _____

7. What kind of joint allows her spine to bend as she stretches toward the floor? _____

8. Last year Sara stretched an ankle ligament beyond its limit while exercising. This caused an injury to her ankle. What is this kind of injury called? _____

Look at the examples of the different kinds of joints.
Name the kind of joint shown: *fixed, sliding, ball & socket, pivot,* or *hinge*

9. _____
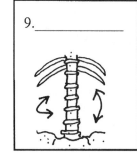

10. _____
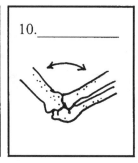

11. _____
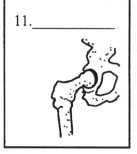

12. _____
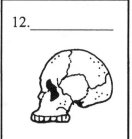

13. _____
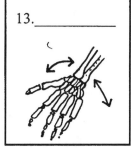

Name _____

A MATTER OF MUSCLE

Reginald is recovering from a bad accident. After lying in bed for weeks, his muscles have become weak. He needs regular physical therapy and exercise to rebuild his strength. Answer these questions about his body's activities during his physical therapy session.

1. When Reginald starts doing the pull-ups (using his arms to pull his chin up to a bar), which muscle group is LEAST likely to be strengthened?
   - a. trapezius
   - b. pectorals
   - c. triceps
   - d. quadriceps
   - e. biceps
   - f. deltoids

2. When his arms bend to pull his body up, which muscle group will contract?
   - a. the biceps
   - b. the triceps

3. When Reginald bends his arm to lift a heavy barbell toward his chest, which muscle group will relax?
   - a. the biceps
   - b. the triceps

4. While he exercises his lower body on the stair-stepper, what muscles is Reginald using?
   - a. gastrocnemius
   - b. deltoids
   - c. hamstrings
   - d. quadriceps
   - e. satori
   - f. gluteus maximus

5. When Reginald bends his knee to push on the step, which muscle group will relax?
   - a. the hamstrings
   - b. the quadriceps

6. When his quadriceps bulge out, are these muscles contracting or relaxing?

7. What joins his muscles to his bones? _____

Name the three different kinds of muscles:

8. _____ muscle, found in arteries and walls of the digestive system, moves in slow, automatic contractions.

9. _____ muscle, found only in the heart, moves with strong automatic contractions.

10. _____ muscle, using powerful contractions, performs body movements.

Name _____

The BASIC/Not Boring Middle Grades Science Book   Copyright ©2002 by Incentive Publications, Inc., Nashville, TN.

A BRAINY PUZZLER

Neurologist, Dr. Nellie Neuron, has designed a puzzle to sharpen her students' knowledge about the nervous system. Use your brain cells and your understanding of the nervous system to solve her puzzle. The clues for the puzzle are found on the next page (page 233).

Use with page 233.

Name

      Copyright ©2002 by Incentive Publications, Inc., Nashville, TN.

Use the clues below to solve the "brainy puzzle" on page 232.

CLUES

Across

2. the nervous system made up of nerves outside the brain and spinal cord

4. a long nerve fiber that carries impulses from one nerve cell to the next

5. the space between neurons

7. the branch of a nerve cell that receives stimuli

10. part of the brain that controls balance

12. the largest part of the brain; controls thinking and memory

13. neurons that carry impulses from receptors to the central nervous system

14. neurons that carry impulses away from the central nervous system to the body parts that react (such as muscles)

16. small groups of nerves outside the brain and spinal cord

18. the system of nerves that work automatically

Down

1. thick cord of nerves that runs from the brain down through the column of vertebrae

3. connecting nerve cells

6. response to a stimulus that does not involve the brain

8. a nerve message

9. a nerve cell

11. part of the brain at the base of the skull; controls breathing, heartbeat, and reflexes

12. the nervous system made up of the brain and the spinal cord

14. fatty layer that encloses some axons, helping to speed up the passage of messages along the nerve

15. the side of the brain responsible for imagination

17. the side of the brain responsible for logical thinking

During Dr. Neuron's class, one of the students was stung by a yellow jacket. Briefly explain the nerve activities that led the student to respond by brushing away the bee from her arm.

Use with page 232.

Name

THE EYES HAVE IT

In the Eye Clinic, Nurse Victor V. Ishun gives an eye exam to 5-year old Sam.
Finish the description of the way Sam's eyes see the elephant on the chart.

Like everything else Sam sees, the elephant picture reflects rays of light. The light rays bounce off the picture and travel to Sam's eyes. The light enters each eye by first traveling through the thin, transparent protective layer over the eye. This layer is the [1]_____. Next, the light passes through a tougher outer protective layer called the [2] _____. Although it is transparent at the front of the eye, this is part of the whole layer that Sam thinks of as the "whites" of his eye. The proper name for the "whites" of the eye is the [3] _____. Next, the light rays enter further into the eye through the [4] _____, a small hole at the center. The colored part of the eye, the [5] _____, is muscular and can change the size of the hole to let more or less light inside.

Next, the light carrying the image passes through the [6] _____, a transparent disc which helps to focus the image by bending the light just the right amount. The light goes on through the center of the eye, passing through clear fluids called [7] _____. The image is projected onto the [8] _____, a layer in the back of the eye which is made up of millions of light-sensitive receptors. By the time the light gets to this area, it has been bent so that the image is upside down. The [9] _____ carries this image, in the form of impulses, along to the brain. The brain is able to interpret the image right side up.

Sam's eye has some other important features. The [10] _____ can close to cover and protect his eyes. Every time they close, they wash [11] _____ over the eyes to keep them clean. Sam's [12] _____ keep specks of dust and dirt out of his eyes. Six [13] _____ attached to each eye control and coordinate the movements of the eye. Many blood cells bring food and oxygen to his eyes in a layer called the [14] _____.

EYE CHART

Name _____

     Copyright ©2002 by Incentive Publications, Inc., Nashville, TN.

MUSIC TO THE EARS

At night, Patricia Pitch mops the floors in the hospital halls. Tonight she is listening to some great jazz music on her CD player as she works.

Identify the parts of her ear that make it possible for her to hear this music. Write the letter from the diagram for each structure. Then write the name of the structure.

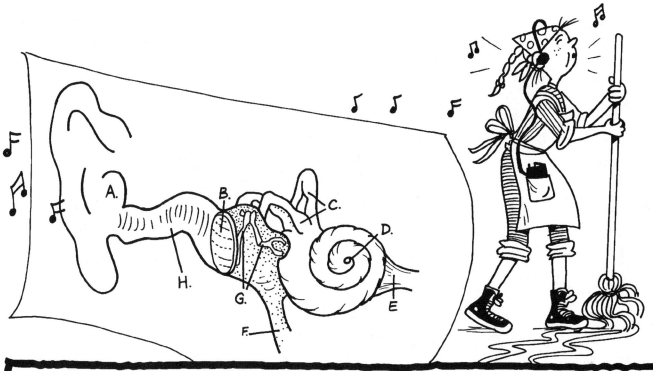

Ear Structure	Name	Letter
This tightly-stretched membrane separates Patricia's outer ear from the inner ear. It vibrates when sound hits it.	1.	
This fluid-filled, coiled tube contains nerve endings that pick up vibrations from the sound. The fluid vibrates hair cells, which pass a signal to the nerve that carries the impulses on to the brain.	2.	
This carries the impulses from the receptor cells in the cochlea to her brain.	3.	
This funnel-shaped structure directs the sound into Patricia's ear.	4.	
This passageway from the back of the nose allows air to pass into her middle ear. This is important, because it allows the air pressure on both sides of her eardrum to remain equal.	5.	
These canals contain fluid and nerve cells. The nerve cells are very sensitive to movement, and help Patricia keep her balance.	6.	
This tube is lined with hairs and produces wax. The sound waves carrying the music pass through this tube toward the ear drum.	7.	
These tiny bones pass the music vibrations from the eardrum on to Patricia's inner ear. *(Name all three.)*	8.	

Name

Copyright ©2002 by Incentive Publications, Inc., Nashville, TN.

ABOUT THAT HOSPITAL FOOD . . .

The patients on Floor 12 spend a lot of time discussing the hospital food. They have strong opinions about its taste, smell, and appearance. Bud deSalva, a patient on this floor, can smell the food even before it arrives by his bedside. His mouth starts salivating when he hears the food cart in the hall!

Today, the patients have been asked to complete a questionnaire about the hospital food. Bud has answered the easy questions. Answer the questions he has not finished. These may take some research.

FOOD QUESTIONNAIRE- Body-Wise Medical Center

Date: 7/5   Name Bud de Salva   Room # 1223

1. How would you rate the taste of the meals you've been served at the medical center?
   a. superb   b. very good   c. just okay   d. not great   e. inedible

2. How would you rate the smell of the food?
   a. extremely appealing   b. average   c. worse than average   d. terrible

3. How would you rate the food's preparation and appearance?
   a. appealing   b. somewhat appealing   c. average   d. poor   e. very unappealing

4. What suggestions do you have for the food? more milkshakes and pizza

5. What special cells allow you to smell the hospital food? _____

6. How do these cells work to make smell possible? _____

7. How do taste buds make it possible for you to taste your food? _____

8. About how many taste buds do you have? _____

9. How does saliva play a part in tasting food? _____

10. What part of the tongue tastes the sweet jello? _____

11. What part of the tongue tastes the salty ham? _____

12. What part of the tongue tastes the bitter black tea? _____

13. What part of the tongue tastes the sour pickles? _____

14. What area of the brain interprets smells? _____

Name _____

A TOUCHING EXPERIENCE

The sensitivity of skin is something that Lester Lesion knows all too well these days. Lester spent a week on a difficult mountain bike adventure. It was so bad that he ended up with terrible, blistering sunburn. But worse, Lester took a monumental spill on his bike and slid several feet on a gravel road. The doctor is explaining some things to Lester about his skin.

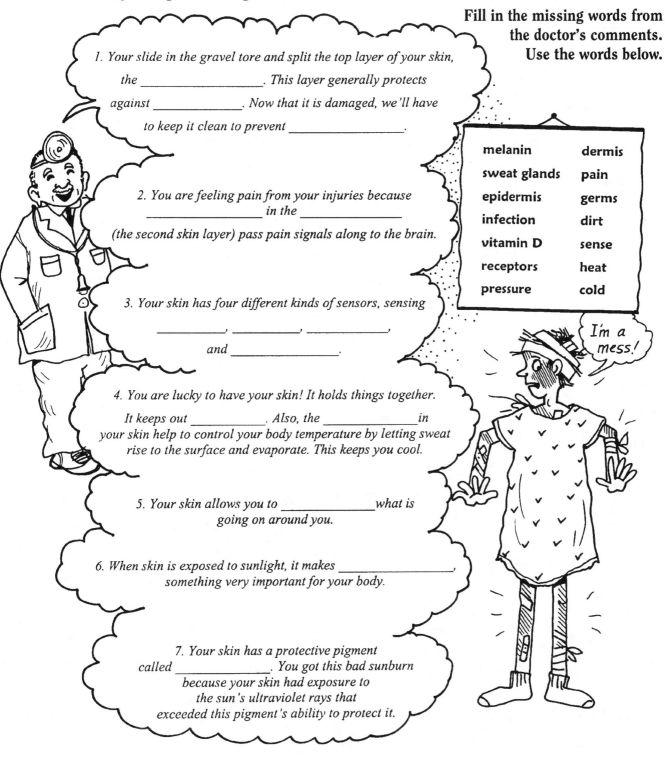

Fill in the missing words from the doctor's comments. Use the words below.

1. Your slide in the gravel tore and split the top layer of your skin, the _____. This layer generally protects against _____. Now that it is damaged, we'll have to keep it clean to prevent _____.

melanin	dermis
sweat glands	pain
epidermis	germs
infection	dirt
vitamin D	sense
receptors	heat
pressure	cold

2. You are feeling pain from your injuries because _____ in the _____ (the second skin layer) pass pain signals along to the brain.

3. Your skin has four different kinds of sensors, sensing _____, _____, _____, and _____.

4. You are lucky to have your skin! It holds things together. It keeps out _____. Also, the _____ in your skin help to control your body temperature by letting sweat rise to the surface and evaporate. This keeps you cool.

5. Your skin allows you to _____ what is going on around you.

6. When skin is exposed to sunlight, it makes _____, something very important for your body.

7. Your skin has a protective pigment called _____. You got this bad sunburn because your skin had exposure to the sun's ultraviolet rays that exceeded this pigment's ability to protect it.

I'm a mess!

Name _____

BLOOD REALLY GETS AROUND

Herman Globin has stopped in at the clinic to donate blood. While waiting for his blood to be taken, he talks loudly to the donor next to him. Herman is sure he knows all the facts about blood and circulation.

BLOOD BANK
WAITING ROOM

I know everything. Let me tell you...

How much does he really know? Read his statements. Circle the number if the statement is correct. If it is wrong, cross out the wrong words and write words to make the statement correct.

1. A person with type B blood can safely receive blood only from a type AB or a type B.

2. White blood cells can pass through the walls of your blood vessels into other tissues.

3. Plasma is a part of blood that carries digested food substances and waste products.

4. A donor with blood type AB can give blood to someone with any other blood type.

5. The disease fighters in your blood that make antibodies are white blood cells.

6. Your veins are red because they have hemoglobin, which carries oxygen.

7. There are many more white blood cells than red blood cells in your body.

8. The tiny pieces of cells that help your blood clot are called platelets.

9. Your arteries have valves to prevent the blood from flowing backwards.

10. Your arteries are blue, because they carry blood with wastes.

11. The blood flows at a higher pressure in veins than in arteries.

12. You have thousands of miles of blood vessels in your body.

13. The walls in arteries are thicker than the walls in veins.

14. Blood travels around your body in tubes called vessels.

15. Blood is made up of different cells floating in plasma.

16. The main artery in the body is the carotid artery.

17. The main vein in your body is the vena cava.

18. All your blood cells are made in your liver.

19. The walls of capillaries are one cell thick.

20. The aorta carries blood to the brain.

No one told me that there would be a needle involved!

Name

A "HEART"-Y INVESTIGATION

At the end of her workout, Nurse Paula Monnary stops to check her pulse. She finds that her heart rate is 138. Do some "hearty" research to find out some facts about Paula's heart structure and functions.

1. What causes Paula to have a pulse?

   _____

2. What is a heart rate?

   _____

3. What causes the sound of Paula's heartbeat?

   _____

4. Give a general explanation of the way Paula's heart works to circulate blood around her body. Use the diagram, the letters from the diagram, and these words as a part of your explanation.

pulmonary artery	*left ventricle*	*left atrium*
right ventricle	*valve*	*chamber*
pulmonary veins	*carbon dioxide*	*muscle*
atrium	*aorta*	*lungs*
vena cava	*right atrium*	*oxygen*

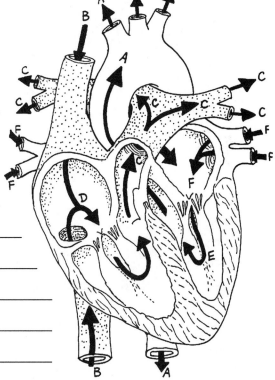

_____

_____

_____

_____

_____

_____

_____

_____

_____

_____

_____

Name _____

Copyright ©2002 by Incentive Publications, Inc., Nashville, TN.

EASY BREATHING

The entire staff in the obstetrical unit is celebrating the birth of triplets. They are blowing up balloons to decorate the nursery. It's a good thing there are some healthy respiratory systems in the group!

Since they've got 100 balloons, they'll need to do a lot of breathing in and out for this task.

Label the body structures that are used in the breathing process.

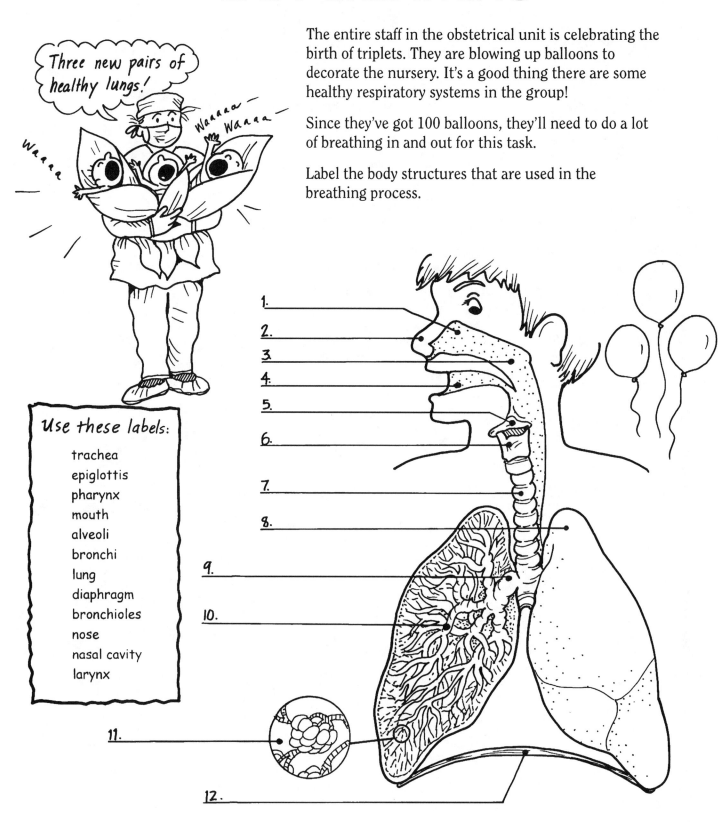

Three new pairs of healthy lungs!

Waaaa Waaaa Waaaa

Use these labels:

trachea
epiglottis
pharynx
mouth
alveoli
bronchi
lung
diaphragm
bronchioles
nose
nasal cavity
larynx

1. _____
2. _____
3. _____
4. _____
5. _____
6. _____
7. _____
8. _____
9. _____
10. _____
11. _____
12. _____

Use with page 241.

Name _____

The BASIC/Not Boring Middle Grades Science Book   Copyright ©2002 by Incentive Publications, Inc., Nashville, TN.

Answer the questions to describe how the respiratory system of Nurse Rex Hale is functioning as he breathes in and out to blow up balloons.

═ BREATHING IN ═

1. What do the hairs in his nose and the mucus in his nose and throat accomplish when he inhales?

   _____

2. Where does air travel after it is taken into his mouth? _____

3. What happens to his ribs when he inhales? _____

4. What does his diaphragm do when he inhales? _____

5. What happens to the volume of his chest cavity when he inhales? _____

6. How does oxygen that he breathes in with the air get into his blood? _____

7. What does his epiglottis do when he inhales? _____

═ BREATHING OUT ═

8. How does the carbon dioxide get out of the bloodstream back into his lungs to be breathed out?

   _____

9. What path does the air with wastes follow to leave his body? _____

   _____

10. What happens to his ribs when he exhales? _____

11. What does his diaphragm do when he exhales? _____

12. What happens to the volume of his chest cavity when he inhales? _____

Use with page 240.

Name _____

ONCE UPON A SWALLOW

When Bertha Byal took a huge bite of a delicious burrito, she had no idea that she was eating something other than the soft gooey cheese, beans, and tortilla. A large safety pin had fallen off the cook's apron and was wrapped up in her burrito. When she realized her predicament, she rushed to the hospital with the pin stuck somewhere in her digestive system.

Where was the pin? At the hospital, doctors probed, poked, and X-rayed the organs and structures that are part of her digestive system looking for the pin.

First, label the parts of the digestive system shown on the doctor's chart. Then, follow along with the doctors as they hunt for the pin. As each place they search is described (on page 33), write the name of the organ or structure.

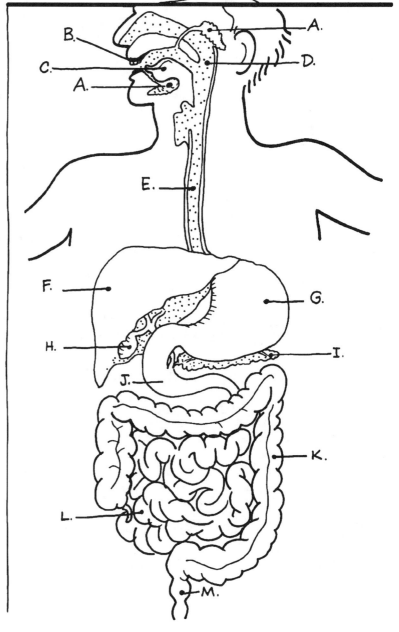

Label these structures:

____ pharynx	____ gallbladder
____ teeth	____ stomach
____ large intestine	____ pancreas
____ tongue	____ rectum
____ liver	____ esophagus
____ salivary glands	____ duodenum
	____ small intestine

Use with page 243.

Name

The doctors searched to see if they could find the pin stuck in any of these places. Write the name of the organ or structure (*not all of these structures are shown in the diagram on page 242*).

_____ 1. Was the pin stuck in the flap that closes when Bertha swallows to block off her trachea so food does not go down toward her lungs?

_____ 2. Did the pin lodge itself between the structures that break up food into small parts and mix it with saliva for easier swallowing?

_____ 3. Could the pin still be in the muscular tube that squeezes food along toward the stomach by peristalsis?

_____ 4. The doctors wondered if the pin was hiding underneath the organ whose muscles move food to force it back into the pharynx.

_____ 5. Could the pin be stuck in the organ that makes bile to help break up fats?

_____ 6. Is it somewhere in that amazingly long, winding organ where food is in a form so that it can pass through the walls of the organ into the blood?

_____ 7. Might the pin have gone no further than the opening at the back of the throat?

_____ 8. Did the pin perhaps lodge itself in one of the organs that make juices to aid in the initial mixing with food and breaking it down into particles?

_____ 9. Maybe the pin is somehow caught in the organ that stores bile until it is needed for digestion.

_____ 10. Could the pin be hiding among the millions of tiny finger-like projections where nutrients pass through the membranes to enter the blood or lymph vessels?

_____ 11. Hopefully the pin did not puncture the organ that makes insulin and other enzymes to help break up food in the small intestine!

_____ 12. Is it perhaps stuck in the wall of the organ that takes most of the water out of the food that cannot be digested?

_____ 13. Was the pin, perhaps, lodged inside the organ where food is churned around, and where hydrochloric acid digests proteins and kills bacteria?

_____ 14. Could the pin have made it all the way to the end of the large intestine to the place where solid wastes pass out of the body?

_____ 15. They've spotted it! It has worked its way into the first part of the small intestine where bile and other enzymes mix with the food as it comes out of the stomach.

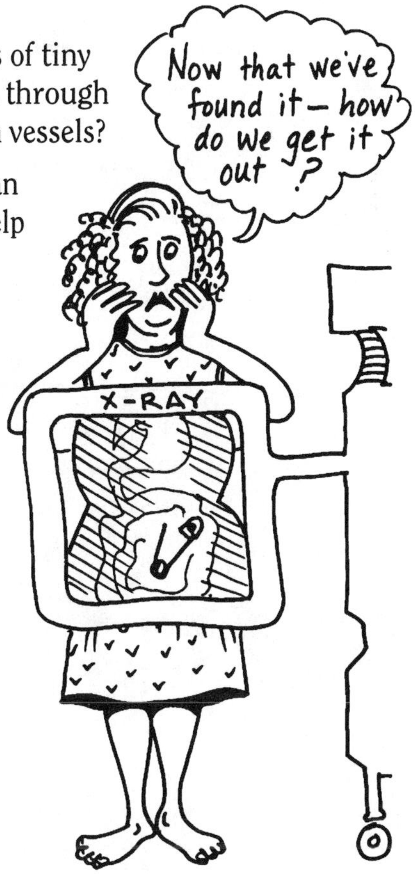

Now that we've found it — how do we get it out ?

X-RAY

Use with page 242.

Name

GLAND ALERT

In the Endocrinology Lab, lab technician G.G. Land is keeping a record of the patients and their ailments. Her notebook describes difficulties or symptoms that have brought each patient's file to the lab. Read each description in the notebook. Write the name of the gland that is likely to be involved with the problem. Answers may be used more than once.

Patient	Symptoms	Gland
1. J. Slow	trouble with control of all other glands	
2. R. Pitt	immune system not rejecting germs	
3. C. Brayne	problem with control of sugar metabolism	
4. B. Legg	body temperature, hunger, and thirst out of control	
5. M. Groe	problem with the kidneys' production of urine	
6. J. Foote	rate at which food is turned into energy is too high	

Patient	Symptoms	Gland
7. B. Nee	problem with rate of bone growth	
8. L. Bow	amount of calcium in blood and bones out of control	
9. N. Trist	adrenalin levels stay very high even when not frightened or angry	
10. T. Shugg	problem with production of eggs	
11. K. Bone	trouble with salt and water balance	
12. B. Blance	problem with production of sperm cells	

Name _____

WHAT A WASTE!

The garbage collectors spend most of the night carrying away the waste of the medical center; some of the waste is quite interesting. Tonight they have found a discarded study sheet about waste.

The student who wrote the notes apparently was doing research or studying for a test. How much of the information has this student recorded correctly?

Look for any errors in the student's notes.
Cross out or add any organs to the sheet to make it correct.

WASTE SYSTEMS
The Body's Excretory Organs

Waste-Removal Function	Names of organs that perform the function
1. Remove water from the body	*kidneys, bladder, ureter*
2. Remove carbon dioxide from the body	*lungs, liver*
3. Remove body heat	*lungs*
4. Filter toxic substances out of the blood	*gall bladder*
5. Remove salt from the body	*skin*
6. Carry urine to bladder	*small intestine*
7. Carry urine out of bladder	*Eustachian tube*
8. Store urine before it is passed out of the body	*pancreas*
9. Remove chemical wastes from the blood	*kidneys, liver*

10. How does the skin function as a waste-removal organ?

_____

_____

_____

Name _____

IT TAKES TWO

It takes two human reproductive cells joining together for human reproduction to take place. Nervously waiting in the lounge outside the hospital delivery room, Charlie pages through a book about the reproductive system. Some parts of the text are missing from the book. Supply the missing information.

Write the missing labels onto each diagram. Then write the missing description of the process of fertilization.

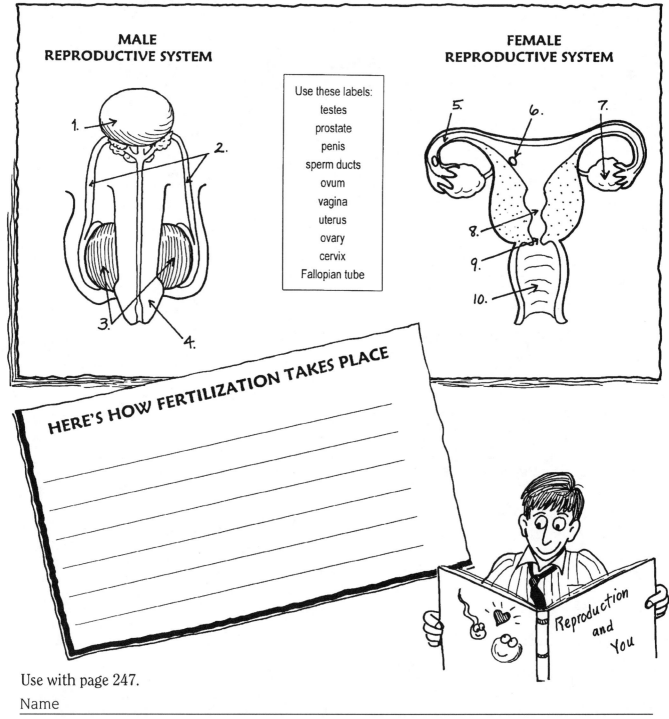

MALE REPRODUCTIVE SYSTEM

1.
2.
3.
4.

Use these labels:

testes
prostate
penis
sperm ducts
ovum
vagina
uterus
ovary
cervix
Fallopian tube

FEMALE REPRODUCTIVE SYSTEM

5.
6.
7.
8.
9.
10.

HERE'S HOW FERTILIZATION TAKES PLACE

Reproduction and You

Use with page 247.

Name

The BASIC/Not Boring Middle Grades Science Book   Copyright ©2002 by Incentive Publications, Inc., Nashville, TN.

There is more information missing about the reproductive system and process. Complete these sentences.

1. The eggs (ova) are stored in the _____.

2. The process in which an ovum is released is _____.

3. After an egg is released, it is drawn into one of the _____.

4. The egg passes into the _____, a hollow organ with muscular walls.

5. Sperm are made in _____.

6. Sperm swims in a fluid called _____.

7. Sperm travels from its origin to the penis through tubes called_____.

8. The function of sperm is _____.

9. Fertilization of eggs by sperm takes place in the _____.

10. If an egg is fertilized, it may implant itself in _____.

11. If an egg is not fertilized, it _____.

12. The uterus gets ready to nurture a fertilized egg by_____.

13. A fertilized egg begins to _____ and grows into an embryo.

14. The embryo grows into a fetus, and the fetus develops. This takes place in the _____.

15. The function of the placenta in fetal development is_____.

16. The function of the umbilical cord is_____.

17. It takes about_____(time) for the fetus to develop.

18. The process of preventing fertilization of eggs is called _____.

This is all about me!

Use with page 246.

Name _____

DESIGNER GENES

Why do the babies in the nursery look the way they do? Why are they each different from one another? The answer has to do with their designer genes! Each of them has a unique set of genes that determine the many characteristics that make the baby an individual person, unlike others.

Track down the answers to questions about genetics and heredity to finish the Genetics Review below.

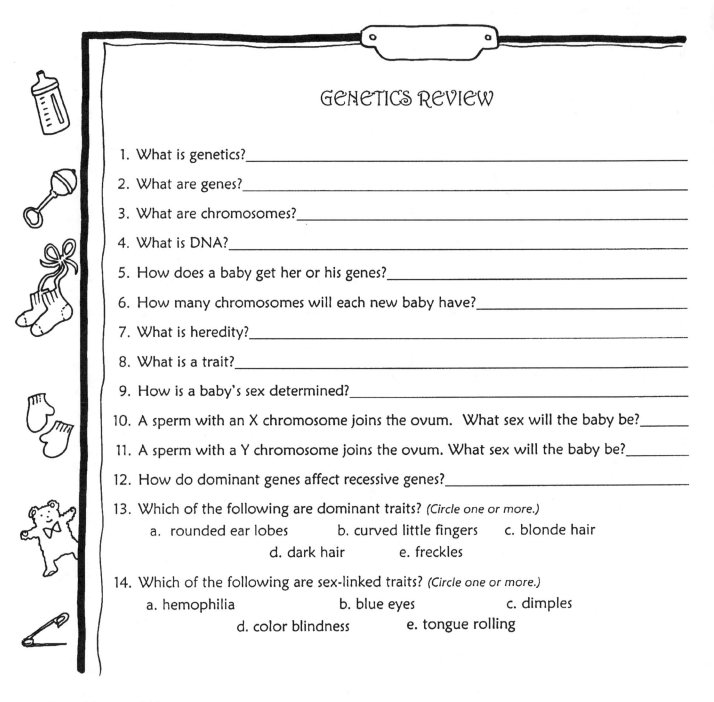

GENETICS REVIEW

1. What is genetics?_____

2. What are genes?_____

3. What are chromosomes?_____

4. What is DNA?_____

5. How does a baby get her or his genes?_____

6. How many chromosomes will each new baby have?_____

7. What is heredity?_____

8. What is a trait?_____

9. How is a baby's sex determined?_____

10. A sperm with an X chromosome joins the ovum. What sex will the baby be?_____

11. A sperm with a Y chromosome joins the ovum. What sex will the baby be?_____

12. How do dominant genes affect recessive genes?_____

13. Which of the following are dominant traits? *(Circle one or more.)*
    a. rounded ear lobes   b. curved little fingers   c. blonde hair
                d. dark hair   e. freckles

14. Which of the following are sex-linked traits? *(Circle one or more.)*
    a. hemophilia   b. blue eyes   c. dimples
            d. color blindness   e. tongue rolling

Use with page 249.

Name

While admiring the babies in the nursery, the visitors ponder some heredity questions. Write the answer to each question.

A. Cici has a colorblind father. Her mother is not colorblind and does not carry a gene for colorblindness. What are the chances that she will be colorblind?

_____

F. Tad's dad has blonde hair and dimples. His mom has dark hair and no dimples. Which traits are the most likely for Tad? *(Circle one.)*

    a. blonde hair and dimples

    b. dark hair and dimples

    c. dark hair and no dimples

    d. blonde hair and no dimples

B. Casey's dad has free earlobes. His dad has attached lobes. Is Casey more likely to have free earlobes or attached lobes?

_____

G. Ramon's mother is a carrier for hemophilia. Are the chances 50% or higher that Ramon will be a hemophiliac?

_____

C. Both of Janie's parents have dark hair. How likely is Janie to have blonde hair? *(Write a fraction for the answer.)*

_____

D. William has brown eyes. Is it likely that both of his parents have blue eyes?

_____

H. Lana's mom has freckles. Her dad does not. Are the chances 50% or higher that Lana will have freckles?

_____

E. Angie's mom can roll her tongue. Will Angie be more likely to have that ability or more likely NOT to have that ability?

_____

I. Michael's parents both have long eyelashes. His dad has a turned-up nose; his mother does not. Is Michael likely to have long eyelashes and a turned-up nose?

_____

Use with page 248.

Name _____

DOCTOR, DOCTOR, I FEEL SICK

The emergency room is packed tonight! There is a long line of patients needing care. Read the description each patient gives of his or her ailments. Write the number of the description beside the name of the possible ailment. Use the descriptions and ailments from both pages (250–251).

1. I have an infection of my stomach and intestines.

2. Hurry, doctor! I'm suffering from an infection of my liver.

3. I have lost my voice! I have an inflammation of my voice box.

4. There is a rash breaking out all over my body. It is caused by an infectious viral disease.

5. My feet itch from a fungal infection.

6. All of my body's defenses against disease are permanently weakened.

7. There is an abnormal division of some cells and they are invading the surrounding tissues.

8. My leg is broken!

9. My muscles are so sore after I lifted a piano.

10. There is a hole in my tooth caused by decay.

11. This is a terrible disease I have. It causes lesions on my lungs.

12. My lungs are infected.

13. My gums are inflamed!

14. My trachea and bronchi are infected with bacteria, and I have this terrible, chronic cough.

15. I have a cut. It is an emergency because my blood will not clot.

16. Could this be a serious viral infection of my spinal nerve cells?

____ influenza   ____ polio   ____ strep throat   ____ athlete's foot   ____ measles   ____ mumps

____ stroke   ____ acne   ____ scarlet fever   ____ hemophilia   ____ rabies   ____ cancer

____ malaria   ____ AIDS   ____ gastroenteritis   ____ whooping cough   ____ arthritis   ____ botulism

Use with page 251.

Name

17. After a mosquito bit me, I got this infectious disease with terrible chills and fever.

18. I got really sick after I ate some food with a toxic germ in it.

19. My appendix is so inflamed and infected that I think it's about to burst!

20. Can you give me some medicine for all these blackheads and pimples on my skin?

21. My body is unusually sensitive to pollen. I sneeze all the time!

22. I twisted my ankle joint too far.

23. I have a bacteria-infected wound. I'm afraid I may have nerve paralysis caused by a toxin in those bacteria.

24. My parotid glands are infected.

25. A germ caused this skin infection in an oil gland.

26. The walls of my bronchi are infected.

27. I have an infected eyelid.

28. An injury to my muscle caused blood vessels to be broken.

29. My joints are swollen and sore all the time.

30. My body temperature is too high.

31. I've got this contagious skin disease spreading everywhere.

32. A dog bit me. I'm afraid I have a deadly viral disease.

Me, too!

OW OW OW

EMERGENCY ROOM

Admittance Desk

____ bruise	____ fever	____ pneumonia	____ tetanus	____ cavity	____ tuberculosis	____ earache
____ hepatitis	____ boil	____ bronchitis	____ fracture	____ allergy	____ appendicitis	____ pyorrhea
____ pinkeye	____ strain	____ cold sore	____ typhoid	____ sprain	____ impetigo	____ laryngitis

Use with page 250.

Name

DISEASE-FIGHTERS

An ambulance rushes Omar to the hospital after he took a frightful fall from his trapeze. He's covered with scrapes and bruises. Some bones may be broken. There may be internal injuries.

Fortunately for Omar, his body has some natural defenses that will help prevent some further problems, and some defenses that will help him heal.

Describe the job that each of these body parts or processes does in helping the body defend against disease or heal from ailments.

> **Describe the natural reaction to a germ that enters the body.**

1. white blood cells _____

_____

2. lymph cells _____

_____

3. antibodies _____

_____

4. bone cells in the periosteum _____

_____

5. platelets in blood _____

_____

6. mucus in the nose and throat _____

_____

7. acid in the stomach _____

_____

8. clean, unbroken skin _____

_____

9. passive immunity _____

_____

10. active immunity _____

_____

Use with page 253.

Name

Although the body's defense system is amazing, it sometimes needs some help from outside. The patients picked up by the ambulance crew might get some help from other defense practices in the hospital. Or, they might avoid the trip to the hospital altogether, with the help of some of these practices.

Briefly describe a way that each of these practices helps to defend against disease or the spread of disease.

11. disinfectants	15. sunshine	19. antiseptics
12. quarantine	16. exercise	20. good dental care
13. food inspection	17. healthy eating	21. good hygiene
14. water treatment	18. surgery	22. hazard avoidance

Use with page 252.

Name

SMART EXERCISING

Mario M. Ussle runs the Fitness Center near the hospital. He sees to it that the visitors to the center get the three different kinds of exercise needed by their bodies. He knows that exercise helps all the parts of the body work more efficiently.

Describe the three kinds of exercise needed.

AEROBIC EXERCISE

What is it?

How does it benefit the body?

What kinds of activities give this kind of exercise?

STRENGTHENING EXERCISE

What is it?

How does it benefit the body?

What kinds of activities give this kind of exercise?

FLEXIBILITY EXERCISE

What is it?

How does it benefit the body?

What kinds of activities give this kind of exercise?

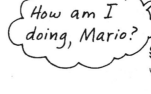

How am I doing, Mario?

Use with page 255.

Name

Mario's clients are constantly asking him questions.
What answers do you think he will give to these questions?

1) **Lester Legg:** What will happen to my muscles if I don't exercise much?

2) **Al Violli:** What happens to my heart when I exercise?

3) **Alvin Slump:** How will bad posture affect my health?

4) **Paula Presser:** What is isometric exercise?

5) **Ms. A. Orta:** How does lack of exercise contribute to heart disease?

6) **Andy McClactic:** If I exercise vigorously and stop suddenly, what will happen to my body?

7) **Mr. N. Hale:** What happens to my lungs when I exercise?

8) **Lou A. Chou:** How can regular exercise help me if I get pneumonia?

1)_____

_____

2)_____

_____

3)_____

_____

4)_____

_____

5)_____

_____

6)_____

_____

7)_____

_____

8)_____

_____

*Mario's Motto:
If you have your health — you have everything!*

Mario

Use with page 254.

Name

The BASIC/Not Boring Middle Grades Science Book   Copyright ©2002 by Incentive Publications, Inc., Nashville, TN.

SMART EATING

Leonard Tillis is the hospital's dietician. Today he has written a menu of foods and dishes for the cooks to prepare in the hospital kitchen. Use the foods on the menu to help you answer the questions.

Name one or more menu items that . . .

1. . . . are high in protein. (Name 3 choices.)
   _____

2. . . . are good sources of Vitamin C.
   _____

3. . . . are sources of calcium.
   _____

4. . . . supply the body with carbohydrates.
   _____

5. . . . might be high in fat. (Name 3.)
   _____

6. . . . are high in fiber. (Name 3.)
   _____

7. . . . would be good for providing energy.
   _____

8. . . . are a source of iron.
   _____

9. . . . would help a body repair damaged tissue.
   _____

10. . . . will help a patient's eyesight.
    _____

11. . . . contain both protein and carbohydrates.
    _____

12. . . . contain a lot of sugar.
    _____

Bon apetit!

Saturday's Menu

lean roast beef
fresh steamed cod
grilled chicken breasts
mixed nuts
lentil soup
bean burritos
corned beef sandwich
wild rice
granola
grapefruits & pineapples
spinach
green peppers
broccoli
apples
yellow squash
carrots
skimmed milk
cheddar cheese soup
whole wheat pancakes
tomato-onion omelet
sausage pizza
chocolate cake
cherry cola soda
cottage cheese
berry yogurt
home-made pie
white rolls & butter
French fries
butterscotch pudding
coffee & tea
banana milkshake
orange juice & prune juice
lime meringue cookies

Use with page 257.

Name

Sometimes Leonard wants to leave personal suggestions to patients about how they can maintain or improve their nutritional health after they leave the hospital. Today he has dictated these notes for his assistant, Casey Crunch. Casey has made some mistakes, and the notes give some advice that is NOT what Leonard intended to give.

Use with page 256.

Name

SMART CHOICES

Everyone who graduates from the fitness course at the hospital's Fitness Center leaves with a certificate and a personal checklist of smart health choices. This checklist reminds them of smart ways to take care of their health and fitness.

Check up on your choices. How many of these smart choices do you make on a regular basis?

✓	Which SMART CHOICES do YOU make?
	Get regular aerobic exercise for 40 minutes or more 3 or more times a week.
	Warm up your muscles before exercising. Cool your body down gently after exercise.
	Regularly do activities to keep your muscles strong.
	Keep your joints and muscles flexible with regular stretching.
	Exercise wisely and carefully to minimize the risk of injuries.
	Eat a balanced diet that includes lean protein sources, unsaturated fats, fiber, and healthful carbohydrates.
	Eat a diet with a variety of fresh foods to get enough vitamins and minerals.
	Drink several glasses of water a day.
	Include sweets, caffeine, food additives, salt, and animal fats in small amounts in your diet.
	Keep your skin, hair, and teeth clean.
	Get dental and eye checkups regularly.
	Pay attention to your posture when standing and sitting. Keep that backbone in correct alignment!
	Lift heavy things by bending your legs. Don't put unnecessary strain on your back.
	Get plenty of rest—8 hours a night.
	Pay attention to the stressors in your life. Find ways to avoid them when possible.
	Learn to relax.
	Avoid alcohol, drugs, and tobacco products.
	Avoid prolonged exposure to the sun without sunscreen protection

Name

     Copyright ©2002 by Incentive Publications, Inc., Nashville, TN.

HUMAN BODY & HEALTH
ASSESSMENT AND ANSWER KEYS

HUMAN BODY & HEALTH SKILLS TEST

Each correct answer is worth 1 point. Total possible points = 75

1–12: Which body part performs these functions?
Write a letter from the list for each part.

Some Body Parts

A. alveoli
B. aorta
C. bronchi
D. cerebrum
E. cornea
F. diaphragm
G. duodenum
H. epidermis
I. larynx
J. lymph cells
K. pancreas
L. periosteum
M. pituitary
N. plasma
O. retina
P. tendon
Q. trachea
R. urethra
S. vena cava

_____ 1. repairs broken bones

_____ 2. carries blood to the heart

_____ 3. controls thinking and awareness

_____ 4. carries nutrients, oxygen, and minerals in the blood

_____ 5. protects the eye

_____ 6. regulates 11 glands in the body

_____ 7. carries urine away from the bladder out of the body

_____ 8. makes antibodies

_____ 9. exchange oxygen and carbon dioxide in and out of the blood

_____ 10. helps increase the size of the chest cavity when inhaling

_____ 11. attaches muscles to bones

_____ 12. produces insulin to regulate sugar levels in the body

13–23: Write an answer for each question or item.

13. What purpose do ligaments have in the body? _____

_____

14. What is the purpose of cartilage? _____

_____

15. What kind of muscle tissue lines blood vessels? _____

16. What kind of muscle tissue is found in the heart? _____

17. What happens when muscles contract? _____

_____

18. Give an example of a sliding joint. _____

19. What kind of joint is shown here? _____

20. Name two joints of this kind: (1)_____ (2)_____

21. Which brain part controls swallowing? _____

22. Which neurons carry impulses away from the central nervous system to muscles? _____

23. Which brain part controls balance, coordination, and muscle activity? _____

Name _____

Copyright ©2002 by Incentive Publications, Inc., Nashville, TN.

24–29: For each organ or body part pictured, write the name of the structure, the body system in which it functions, and a brief description of its function.

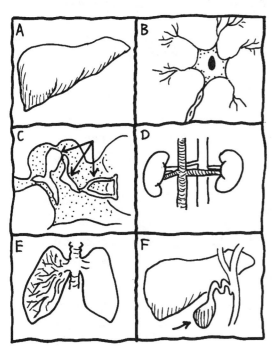

24. **A** name _____ system _____

function _____

25. **B** name _____ system _____

function _____

26. **C** name _____ system _____

function _____

27. **D** name _____ system _____

function _____

28. **E** name _____ system _____

function _____

29. **F** name _____ system _____

function _____

30–39: Write an answer for each question or item.

30. How is a tissue different from an organ? _____

31. What body system produces hormones and chemicals to control functions? _____

32. What system removes toxic substances from the blood? _____

33. What determines a baby's sex? _____

34. Which organs of the body are parts of the central nervous system? _____

35. What space must impulses cross when they travel between neurons? _____

36. Which side of Max's brain is most in use when he imagines wild monsters? _____

37. How do taste buds make it possible to taste food? _____

38. How are characteristics (traits) passed from parents to offspring? _____

39.
> Both Jordan's parents have long eyelashes. His mom has blonde hair. His dad has dark brown hair. His dad can curl his tongue. His mom carries the gene for color blindness.

Which of the traits of Jordan's parents are dominant and likely to be passed on to Jordan? *(Circle one or more.)*

blonde hair   brown hair

long eyelashes   tongue curling   color blindness

Name _____

The BASIC/Not Boring Middle Grades Science Book   Copyright ©2002 by Incentive Publications, Inc., Nashville, TN.

40–49: Circle one or more answers for each.

40. Nerve impulses are produced in response to sound waves within the ear structure called
    a. the eardrum.   b. the cochlea.   c. the semicircular canals.   d. the auditory canals.

41. Nerve endings in the skin that sense heat, cold, pressure, and pain are located in
    a. the epidermis.   b. the dermis.   c. the oil glands.   d. the fat cells.

42. Which kind of tissue would be found in the lining of the blood vessels?
    a. connective   b. epithelial   c. muscle   d. nerve

43. Freddy broke two bones in his leg. Which of these could NOT be the bones he broke?
    a. scapula   b. femur   c. tibia   d. radius   e. humerus   f. fibula   g. clavicle

44. Todd's tongue tastes bitter black tea
    a. on the front.   b. on the sides and front.   c. on the sides.   d. on the back.

45. When skin becomes sunburned, its exposure to the sun's ultraviolet rays has exceeded the protection available from the
    a. epidermis.   b. melanin.   c. sweat glands.   d. pigment.

46. A person with Type O blood can donate blood to which other blood types?
    a. none   b. A   c. B   d. AB   e. O

47. Blood flowing away from the heart is red because of the oxygen-carrying
    a. hemoglobin.   b. pigment.   c. vessels.   d. epidermis.

48. Food is absorbed into the body through the walls of the
    a. esophagus.   b. rectum.   c. stomach.   d. large intestine.   e. small intestine.

49. When Lottie bends her knee to climb a step, which will happen?
    a. The quadriceps will contract.   c. The hamstrings will relax.
    b. The hamstrings will contract.   d. The quadriceps will relax.

50–57: Write a letter to show which disease or ailment matches the description.

_____ 50. an infection of the lungs

_____ 51. results from abnormal insulin production

_____ 52. chronic inflammation of joints

_____ 53. a serious infection of the liver

_____ 54. inflammation of the gums

_____ 55. an environmental disease

_____ 56. a mental disease

_____ 57. abnormal division of cells that invade surrounding tissues

BODY AILMENTS

A. arthritis	J. hemophilia	S. pneumonia
B. asthma	K. hepatitis	T. psoriasis
C. bruise	L. impetigo	U. pyorrhea
D. bronchitis	M. lead poisoning	V. rabies
E. cancer	N. laryngitis	W. schizophrenia
F. typhoid	O. malaria	X. small pox
G. diabetes	P. measles	Y. strep throat
H. encephalitis	Q. pinkeye	Z. tetanus
I. fracture	R. poison ivy	

Name _____

58. Describe the difference between active and passive immunity. _____

_____

59. Describe the body's reaction to germs entering the body. _____

_____

60–65: Circle one or more answers for each.

60. Which of these would be good activities for increasing muscle flexibility?
a. isometric exercises   d. jogging   g. rowing
b. cross-country skiing   e. stretching   h. yoga
c. brisk walking   f. jumping rope   i. tennis

61. Which of these activities would increase aerobic fitness?
a. isometric exercises   d. jogging   g. rowing
b. cross-country skiing   e. stretching   h. yoga
c. brisk walking   f. jumping rope   i. tennis

62. To build essential amino acids needed for growth and repair of body tissue, it is important to eat
a. fats   c. minerals.   e. carbohydrates.
b. vitamins.   d. proteins.   f. fiber

63. In order to be used by the body as an energy source, food needs to be broken down into
a. glucose   d. carbohydrates
b. protein.   e. water.
c. fats.

64. For which first aid emergency should you keep the victim's affected area below the heart level?
a. stroke   c. snake bite   e. fainting
b. hypothermia   d. fall

65. For which first aid emergency should you keep the victim lying still with feet slightly elevated?
a. burns   c. fracture   e. frostbite
b. bee sting   d. shock

66–75: Write a letter from at least one of the foods pictured to match each description.

_____ 66. high in protein
_____ 67. good source of Vitamin C
_____ 68. source of calcium
_____ 69. good source of fiber
_____ 70. source of carbohydrates
_____ 71. high in sugar
_____ 72. will help eyesight
_____ 73. helps repair body tissue
_____ 74. good source of iron
_____ 75. source of Vitamin D

SCORE: Total Points _____ out of a possible 75 points

Name _____

The BASIC/Not Boring Middle Grades Science Book   263   Copyright ©2002 by Incentive Publications, Inc., Nashville, TN.

HUMAN BODY & HEALTH
SKILLS TEST ANSWER KEY

1. L
2. S
3. D
4. N
5. E
6. M
7. R
8. J
9. A
10. F
11. P
12. K
13. help body bend and stretch; connect bones
14. cushion places where bones meet each other
15. smooth muscle
16. cardiac muscle
17. they thicken, tighten, do work
18. spine (Accept other examples of a sliding joint.)
19. ball & socket
20. shoulder, hip
21. medulla
22. motor neurons
23. cerebellum
24. liver; digestive; makes bile
25. nerve cell or neuron; nervous; carries impulses
26. hammer, anvil, & stirrup; sensory system or nervous system or ear; vibrate and pass vibrations along
27. kidneys; digestive or excretory; remove wastes from the body or produce urine
28. lungs; respiratory; get oxygen into body and expel carbon dioxide
29. gallbladder; digestive; store bile
30. tissue is made of specialized cells; organ is made of tissues
31. endocrine
32. digestive or excretory
33. a sperm that fertilizes the egg has either an X or Y chromosome
34. brain and spinal cord
35. synapse
36. right
37. they have receptor cells which receive stimuli from chemicals in saliva

38. chromosomes are passed to offspring from parents (carrying genes)
39. brown hair, long eyelashes, tongue curling, color blindness
40. b
41. b
42. b
43. a, d, e, g
44. d
45. b
46. b, c, d, e
47. a
48. e
49. b, d
50. S
51. G
52. A
53. K
54. U
55. M
56. W
57. E
58. Active: body makes its own antibodies to protect against disease; passive: body gets antibodies from outside source.
59. White blood cells surround and destroy germs. Lymph cells make antibodies to kill toxins from germs.
60. e, h
61. b, c, d, f, g, i
62. d
63. a
64. a
65. d
66. A, B, E, I, or L
67. C, F, G, or K
68. F of L
69. C, D, G, H, K, or N
70. C, D, G, H, K, M, N
71. K, O
72. D
73. A, B, E, F, I, L
74. A
75. B, F, L

The BASIC/Not Boring Middle Grades Science Book
Copyright ©2002 by Incentive Publications, Inc., Nashville, TN.

ANSWERS

Pages 220–221
1. peristalsis
2. bile
3. teeth
4. impulses, signals, or messages
5. blood
6. insulin
7. fats
8. oxygen
9. vomiting
10. pivot joint
11. cochlea; the ear
12. bile and pancreatic juices
13. the eye
14. ova or eggs
15. mucus
16. a tooth
17. water
18. digested food and waste products
19. fingernails or toenails
20. the closing of the heart valves
21. adrenalin
22. platelets

Pages 222–223
1. arteries or aorta
2. kidneys
3. periosteum
4. larynx
5. trachea
6. Eustachian tubes
7. quadriceps or muscles or ligaments
8. triceps or biceps
9. myelin
10. pancreas
11. ureters
12. cerebellum
13. diaphragm
14. parathyroid gland
15. white blood cells
16. villi
17. cartilage
18. tongue
19. retina
20. thymus
21. tendon
22. liver
23. pituitary gland
24. medulla
25. coccyx
26. epiglottis
27. marrow
28. molars or teeth
29. ovaries
30. alveoli

Page 224
1. cell membrane
2. nucleus
3. mitochondria
4. cytoplasm
5. ribosomes
6. Golgi complex
7. ER (endoplasmic reticulum)

Page 225
1. muscle
2. sperm
3. bone
4. blood
5. nerve

6–9. 4 kinds of tissue: connective tissue, epithelial tissue, muscle tissue, nerve tissue

10–19. Answers will vary. Check to see that student has named 10 different organs.

20–24. Answers will vary. Check to see that student has named 5 different body systems.

Page 226

A. 8	G. 1
B. 7	H. 9
C. 4 or 8	I. 10
D. 2 or 3	J. 6
E. 2 or 3	K. 9 or 10
F. 5	L. 2 or 3

Page 227

1. c	7. a	13. a
2. d	8. a	14. c
3. c	9. d	15. d
4. d	10. b	16. b
5. b	11. b	17. d
6. a	12. c	

Pages 228–229
1. Spongy bone is spongy because its cells form a network with spaces between areas of bone. This makes the bone strong, but light.
2. The periosteum is a layer of bones that has the ability to multiply and grow to repair a break.
3. Blood cells are made in the marrow of the long bones in the body.
4. calcium and phosphorus
   A. humerus—4
   B. phalanges—12
   C. radius—3
   D. patella—16
   E. femur—14
   F. pelvis—11
   G. cranium—1
   H. fibula—17
   I. ribs—9
   J. scapula—7
   K. coccyx—13
   L. ulna—2
   M. clavicle—6
   N. tibia—15
   O. sternum—8
   P. vertebrae—10
   Q. mandible—5

Page 230
1. joints or ligaments
2. ligaments
3. cartilage
4. hinge
5. pivot
6. ball & socket
7. sliding
8. sprain
9. sliding
10. hinge
11. ball & socket
12. fixed
13. pivot

Page 231
1. d
2. a
3. b
4. b
5. b
6. contracting
7. tendons
8. Smooth
9. Cardiac
10. Skeletal or Striated

Pages 232–233
Across 2. peripheral
4. axon
5. synapse
7. dendrite
10. cerebellum
12. cerebrum
13. sensory
14. motor
16. ganglia
18. autonomic
Down 1. spinal cord
3. interneurons
6. reflex
8. impulse
9. neuron
11. medulla
12. central
14. myelin
15. right
17. left

The sting of the bee stimulates the nerve endings in the arm. The nerve endings send a message along the nerve paths to the brain, and the brain sends a message back to the hand to brush away the bee.

OR

The brushing away of the bee is a reflex action. In this case, the sting excites the nerves and sends an impulse (message) that causes the hand to jerk toward the arm. This response does not involve the brain.

Page 234

1. conjunctiva	8. retina
2. cornea	9. optic nerve
3. sclera	10. eyelids
4. pupil	11. tears
5. iris	12. eyelashes
6. lens	13. muscles
7. humors	14. choroid

Page 235
1. eardrum—B
2. cochlea—D
3. auditory nerve—E
4. outer ear—A
5. Eustachian tube—F
6. semicircular canals—C
7. auditory canal—H
8. hammer, anvil, stirrup—G

Page 236
Note: Answers for 6, 7, 8, 9 may vary from the answers below.
1–4. Already answered
5. olfactory cells or receptor cells
6. They are stimulated by vapors released from the food. The vapors dissolve in the mucus held by the hairs on the cells. This causes nerve impulses to be sent to the brain.
7. The taste buds are stimulated by chemicals in dissolved food. The taste buds contain receptor cells that send nerve impulses to the brain.
8. 8000–10,000
9. The saliva dissolves the food and allows chemicals to be released. The taste buds are sensitive to these chemicals.
10. front
11. front sides
12. back

The BASIC/Not Boring Middle Grades Science Book   Copyright ©2002 by Incentive Publications, Inc., Nashville, TN.

13. sides
14. olfactory area

Page 237

1. epidermis, germs (or dirt), infection
2. receptors, dermis
3. pain, pressure, heat, cold
4. dirt (or germs), sweat glands
5. sense
6. vitamin D
7. melanin

Page 238

Corrected answers may vary.
1. Change *AB* to *O*.
2. correct
3. correct
4. Change *AB* to *O*.
5. correct
6. Change *veins* to *arteries*.
7. Change *white* to *red* and *red* to *white*.
8. correct
9. Change *arteries* to *veins*.
10. Change *arteries* to *veins*.
11. Change *veins* to *arteries* and *arteries* to *veins*.
12. correct
13. correct
14. correct
15. correct
16. change *carotid artery* to *aorta*.
17. correct
18. Change *liver* to *bone marrow*.
19. correct
20. Change *aorta* to *carotid artery*.

Page 239

1. the force (pressure) of the blood pushing through the arteries with each heartbeat
2. the number of times the heart beats per minute
3. the heart valves slamming shut
4. Answers will vary. See that student has written a clear, general explanation of heart function, something like this:

The superior vena cava brings low-oxygen blood (or blood full of carbon dioxide) from the body into the right atrium. (B)

The right atrium contracts and forces blood through the valve into the right ventricle. (D)

The right ventricle contracts, forcing blood through the pulmonary arteries toward the lungs. (C)

In the lungs, carbon dioxide is removed from the blood, and oxygen is put into the blood. The oxygen-rich blood flows back from the lungs through the pulmonary veins into the left atrium. (F)

The left atrium contracts, forcing the blood through the valve into the into the left ventricle. (E)

The heart muscle pumps the blood out of the left ventricle through the aorta to the body. (A)

Page 240

1. nasal cavity
2. nose
3. pharynx
4. mouth
5. epiglottis
6. larynx
7. trachea
8. lung
9. bronchi
10. bronchioles
11. alveoli
12. diaphragm

Page 241

1. catch dirt and germs to keep them from passing into the lungs
2. through the throat, down into the trachea, into the bronchi and bronchioles to the alveoli
3. They expand or move outward.
4. It contracts (or flattens).
5. It increases.
6. It passes through the walls (membranes) of the alveoli.
7. It closes.
8. It passes through the walls (membranes) of the alveoli.
9. from the alveoli into the bronchioles, to the bronchi, trachea, and out through the mouth or nose
10. They move inward.
11. It relaxes.
12. It increases.

Page 242

A. salivary gland
B. teeth
C. tongue
D. pharynx or throat
E. esophagus
F. liver
G. stomach
H. gallbladder
I. pancreas
J. duodenum
K. large intestine
L. small intestine
M. rectum

Page 243

1. epiglottis
2. teeth
3. esophagus
4. tongue
5. liver
6. small intestine
7. pharynx
8. salivary glands
9. gallbladder
10. villi
11. pancreas
12. large intestine
13. stomach
14. rectum or anus
15. duodenum

Page 244

1. pituitary
2. thymus
3. pancreas
4. hypothalamus or thyroid
5. pituitary
6. thyroid
7. pituitary
8. parathyroids
9. adrenals
10. ovaries
11. adrenals
12. testes

Page 245

Answers may vary.

Organs to cross out:
1. none
2. liver
3. none
4. gallbladder
5. none
6. small intestine
7. Eustachian tube
8. pancreas
9. none

Correct organs (student should have some of these listed for each):
1. kidneys, bladder, ureter, urethra, lungs, bladder
2. lungs
3. skin, lungs
4. kidneys
5. kidneys, skin
6. ureter
7. urethra
8. bladder
9. kidneys, liver, skin
10. Perspiration removes salt and other waste products.

Page 246

1. prostate
2. sperm ducts
3. testes
4. penis
5. Fallopian tube
6. ovum
7. ovary
8. uterus
9. cervix
10. vagina

How Fertilization Takes Place: Explanations will vary somewhat. The general process is this: Sperm produced in the male testes travel out through the sperm ducts and out of the penis into the vagina of the female. The sperm swim up into the Fallopian tubes where they may meet an ovum. If a sperm penetrates (joins with) the ovum, fertilization will take place.

Page 247

1. ovaries
2. ovulation
3. Fallopian tubes
4. uterus
5. the testes
6. semen
7. sperm ducts
8. to fertilize the eggs
9. Fallopian tube
10. the uterine lining
11. passes out of the vagina along with the uterine lining (menstruation)
12. thickening its lining
13. divide
14. uterus
15. protect the growing fetus
16. supply nutrients and oxygen to the fetus; carry away wastes
17. nine months
18. contraception

How Fertilization Takes Place (Answers will vary.)
An egg is released from an ovary and travels down the fallopian tube. Sperm are released from the testes, down the sperm ducts and out through the penis. They travel into the vagina and swim

up into the fallopian tubes. When one of the sperm joins with the egg, fertilization occurs.

Page 248

Answers may vary somewhat.
1. the study of heredity
2. the unit of inheritance that carries coded instructions for traits
3. threadlike structures in the nucleus of cells that carry genes
4. genetic material in the nucleus of every cell that makes up genes and chromosomes
5. from his/her parents
6. 23 from each parent; total 46
7. the passing of traits from parents to offspring
8. a characteristic
9. by the kind of sex chromosome carried by the sperm that fertilizes the egg
10. a girl
11. a boy
12. they overrule the recessive genes
13. a, d, e
14. a, d

Page 249

A. none
B. free
C. 1/4
D. no
E. more likely TO HAVE the ability
F. b
G. yes
H. yes
I. yes

Pages 250–251

1. gastroenteritis
2. hepatitis
3. laryngitis
4. measles
5. athlete's foot
6. AIDS
7. cancer
8. fracture
9. strain
10. cavity
11. tuberculosis
12. pneumonia
13. pyorrhea
14. whooping cough
15. hemophilia
16. polio
17. malaria
18. botulism
19. appendicitis
20. acne
21. allergy
22. sprain
23. tetanus
24. mumps
25. boil
26. bronchitis
27. pinkeye
28. hepatitis
29. arthritis
30. fever
31. impetigo
32. rabies

Pages 252–253

Answers will vary somewhat.
1. surround and digest germs
2. make antibodies to kill germs
3. kill germs
4. multiply and grow to heal breaks in bone
5. form clots to stop bleeding
6. trap germs and dust to keep them from going into lungs
7. kills germs
8. keeps dirt and germs from getting into the body
9. babies have natural passive immunity passed by their mothers—this lasts a few months
10. the body makes its own antibodies in response to a disease; when the person is exposed a second time to the disease, the body forms the same antibodies and the person does not get sick

The box on page 252: White blood cells surround and digest the germs. Lymph cells make antibodies to kill the germ.

11–22. Answers will vary. Make sure student's answer is sensible and accurate.

Page 254

Answers will vary.
Aerobic Exercise:
What is it?
Aerobic exercise is exercise in which the heart works harder or beats faster for a sustained period of time.

How does it benefit the body?
It builds strength and stamina in the heart, and improves lung function.

What kinds of activities give this kind of exercise?
Many—jogging, walking, running, skipping rope, swimming, cycling, stair-stepping, cross country skiing

Strengthening Exercise:
What is it?
Strengthening exercise is exercise that works muscles.

How does it benefit the body?
It increases muscle strength and endurance.

What kinds of activities give this kind of exercise?
Weightlifting, rowing, canoeing, isometrics, any work or exercise that uses upper body or lower body muscle strength

Flexibility Exercise:
What is it?
Flexibility exercise is exercise that allows muscles to stretch and relax.

How does it benefit the body?
It enables the body to stretch and bend easily without injury or stiffness.

What kinds of activities give this kind of exercise?
Stretches

Page 255

Answers will vary.
1. They become weak and flabby.
2. Your heart works harder. It beats faster and gradually the heart muscle gets stronger.
3. It weakens some muscles and keeps others too tight. You can get problems with your back and joints.
4. Exercise that works muscles by pressing against immovable objects.
5. Fatty deposits build up in the arteries bringing blood to the heart. The heart muscle gets weaker.
6. Waste products will stay in your muscles, and your muscles will get stiff.
7. It strengthens chest muscles and increases the amount of air your lungs can hold.
8. Pneumonia puts more strain on a weak heart than on a stronger heart.

Page 256

Answers will vary. Check to see that students have at least 1 of the following (except for 3 required in #1, #5, and #6):
1. roast beef, cod, chicken, nuts, lentil soup, bean burrito, sandwich, cheese soup, pizza
2. grapefruit, pineapple, orange juice, broccoli
3. milk, yogurt, cottage cheese, cheese soup, milkshake, pudding
4. rice, granola, any of the fruits or vegetables, pancakes, rolls, pizza, French fries, pudding, milkshake, orange juice, prune juice, sandwich, burrito
5. pudding, cheese soup, butter, cake, fries, milkshake, sandwich
6. rice, granola, pancakes, any fruit or vegetables
7. any of the carbohydrate items listed in # 4
8. prune juice, beef, corned beef sandwich
9. any of the proteins in # 1
10. carrots, squash, spinach, broccoli
11. sandwich, pizza, burrito, cheese soup
12. chocolate cake, soda, pudding, milkshake, lime meringue cookies

Page 257

Answers will vary.
1. Replace *fewer* with *more.*
2. Replace *high in vitamins* with *low in salt.*
3. Replace *protein* with *sugar.*
4. Replace *unsaturated* with *saturated.*
5. Replace *yogurt* with *sweets.*
6. Replace *complex* with *simple.*
7. Replace *Simple* with *Complex.*
8. Replace *best* with *worst* or replace *animal* with *vegetable.*
9. Replace *very small* with *good* or *large.*
10. Replace *saturated* with *unsaturated.*

Page 258

Answers will vary.

SCIENCE INVESTIGATIONS

Skills Exercises

SKILLS CHECKLIST FOR SCIENCE INVESTIGATIONS

✔	SKILL	PAGE(S)
	Research to find answers to questions and solutions to problems	270–310
	Show understanding of the system of classification of life	274, 275
	Identify some features of plants and plant behavior	276, 277
	Identify some features of animals and animal behavior	278, 279
	Identify the functions of human body parts	280, 281
	Explain some human body processes	282, 283
	Identify treatments for some body disorders and diseases	284, 285
	Show understanding of some of Earth's internal processes	286, 287
	Show understanding of some of the processes that change Earth's surface	288, 289
	Use physical characteristics to identify some common minerals	290, 291
	Show understanding of the ocean processes related to waves, currents, and tides	292, 293
	Identify different kinds of storms and other weather patterns	294, 295
	Identify some features of space	296, 297
	Recognize features of the different planets	298, 299
	Identify common chemical compounds and their formulas	300, 301
	Show understanding of concepts of force, motion, energy, and matter	302, 303
	Identify physics concepts at work in the real world	302–305
	Show understanding of how sound is produced and how it travels	306, 307
	Identify common elements and their symbols	308–310
	Show understanding of the Periodic Table	308–310

Investigation # 1: Unraveling
TRICKY SCIENCE MYSTERIES

It will take sharp detecting to solve these science mysteries; solve them with the help of the Internet. Find the solution to each mystery. Then write the address of the website that helped you with the answer. (Use your favorite search engine to find websites, or use some of the sites listed on page 273.)

4. How can you tell an acid from a base?

Answer _____

_____

_____

Web Address _____

1. Do spiders have good eyesight?

Answer _____

_____

Web Address _____

2. Why is the sky blue?

Answer _____

_____

_____

_____

Web Address _____

5. What good is a vacuole?

Answer _____

_____

Web Address _____

6. What does an epidemiologist study?

Answer _____

_____

Web Address _____

3. What comet is currently visible from some spot on earth?

Answer _____

_____

Web Address _____

7. Can you get pfiesteria from eating shellfish?

Answer _____

Web Address _____

Use with pages 271, 272, and 273.

Name _____

     Copyright ©2002 by Incentive Publications, Inc., Nashville, TN.

8. Why do cats cough up hairballs?

Answer _____

_____

Web Address _____

13. Could California fall into the Pacific Ocean during a bad earthquake?

Answer _____

Web Address _____

9. Of what material are fingernails made?

Answer _____

Web Address _____

14. Who are the llama's closest relatives?

Answer _____

_____

Web Address _____

10. How old are the oldest coral reefs?

Answer _____

_____

Web Address _____

15. Why don't satellites fall from the sky?

Answer _____

_____

_____

Web Address _____

11. What should you do if you get caught in quicksand?

Answer _____

_____

_____

Web Address _____

12. How many times does a heart beat in an average lifetime?

Answer _____

Web Address _____

16. Where would you find a quark?

Answer _____

_____

Web Address _____

Use with pages 270, 272, and 273.

Name _____

     Copyright ©2002 by Incentive Publications, Inc., Nashville, TN.

17. Why is it easier to float in saltwater than in fresh water?

Answer _____

_____

_____

_____

Web Address _____

18. What is the Coriolis effect?

Answer _____

_____

_____

Web Address _____

19. How is an aurora borealis different from an aurora australis?

Answer _____

_____

_____

Web Address _____

20. Where, in the U.S., could you find a black swallowtail butterfly?

Answer _____

_____

Web Address _____

21. What is the difference between fission and fusion?

Answer _____

_____

_____

_____

Web Address _____

22. Why do bubbles burst so easily?

Answer _____

_____

_____

Web Address _____

23. How much water is on Earth?

Answer _____

_____

Web Address _____

24. What is granite good for?

Answer _____

_____

_____

Web Address _____

Use with pages 270, 271, and 273.

Name _____

These websites can help you find solutions to the science mysteries on pages 270–272.

Aquatic Network – Aquatic World — http://www.aquanet.com

Ask an Expert — http://www.cln.org/int_expert.html

Ask Dr. Universe — http://www.wsu.edu/DrUniverse

The Aurora Page — http://www.geo.mtu.edu/weather/aurora

Biology Learning Center – Marine Biology — http://www.marinebiology.org/science.htm

Butterflies.com — http://www.butterflies.com

Cool Science for Curious Kids — http://www.hhmi.org/coolscience

Discovery Channel On-Line — www.discovery.com

Earth Kids – Earth Science for Kids/NASA — http://kids.earth.nasa.gov

The Exploratorium — http://www.exploratorium.edu

Fear of Physics — http://www.fearofphysics.com

The Franklin Institute Science Museum — http://sln.fi.edu

The Heart Online — www.sln.fi.edu/biosci/biosci.html

National Institute of Environmental Health Services — http://www.niehs.nih.gov/kids/home.htm

National Science & Technology Week for Kids — http://www.nsf.gov/od/lpa/nstw/kids/start.htm

Oceanlink — http://www.oceanlink.island.net

Rader's Chem4Kids — http://www.chem4kids.com

Rader's Kapili.com — http://www.kapili.com/topiclist.html

Rader's Geography for Kids — http://www.geography4kids.com

Reeko's Mad Science Lab — http://www.spartechsoftware.com/reeko

Science Made Simple — http://www.sciencemadesimple.com

Sea & Sky — http://www.seasky.org/mainmenu.html

Smithsonian Museums — http://www.si.edu

Space Kids – Space Science for Kids/NASA — http://spacekids.hq.nasa.gov

U.S. Geological Survey – California Earthquakes — http://quake.wr.usgs.gov

U.S. Geological Survey Water Science for Schools — http://ga.water.usgs.gov/edu

Whale Songs — http://www.whalesongs.org

Yucky Kids — http://yucky.kids.discovery.com

NOTE: The Internet changes daily. Websites on this page have been chosen carefully; however, a teacher or parent should review sites before directing students to the site.

Use with pages 270, 271, and 272.

273

Copyright ©2002 by Incentive Publications, Inc., Nashville, TN.

Investigation #2: Getting to Know
WHO'S WHO IN THE KINGDOMS

A one-celled organism appears in your microscope. Could it belong to the plant kingdom? Another organism, with a two-chambered heart, appears in your kitchen. Could it belong to the monerans kingdom? Use your knowledge of life classification and good investigative tools to make some identifications for these:

Organism #1
lives on the land and produces seeds and flowers. Could it be an angiosperm? _____

Name its kingdom.

_____

Organism #4
is a bacteria—a one-celled organism with no nucleus. It has a cell wall and a flagellum for movement.

Name its kingdom.

_____

Organism #7
has a body divided into two main regions. It has a hard exoskeleton, jointed legs, and two pairs of antennae. Could it be a crustacean? _____

Name its phylum.

_____

Name its kingdom.

_____

Organism #2
is a horsetail. It makes its own food, and reproduces with spores found in structures that look like pine cones. Is it an algae? _____

Name its kingdom.

_____

Organism #5
has a tube-shaped body divided into segments. Its many bristles help its movement. Could it belong to the phylum Annelida? _____

Name its kingdom.

_____

Organism #8
also has a segmented body and a hard exoskeleton. But it has three divisions, one pair of antennae, three pairs of jointed legs, and wings. Could it be an insect? _____

Name its phylum.

_____

Name its kingdom.

_____

Organism #3
has the name haliclona. It has no symmetry and no tissues. Cells form inner and outer layers around a central cavity. Name its phylum.

_____

Name its kingdom.

_____

Organism #6
All of these organisms except one belong to the same phylum.
jellyfish   anemone
hydra   fluke
            coral
Name the phylum.

_____

Name the kingdom.

_____

Use with page 275.

Name

Ah ha!

Organism #9

is a euglenoid—a one-celled organism that can make its own food. It lives in fresh water and moves with the help of a flagella.

Name its kingdom.

_____

Organism #14

is an Adder's-tongue. It is one of a group of many-celled, vascular organisms. It has fronds, which hold the spore cases that help the plant reproduce.

Name its phylum.

_____

Name its kingdom.

_____

Organism #12

All of these organisms except one belong to the same phylum.

sea urchin   sea cucumber
starfish   clam

Name the phylum. _____

Name the kingdom. _____
Which organism does
not belong?

_____

Organism #10

is a fuzzy creature with eight legs, a body with two segments, an exoskeleton, and no antennae. It shares a class with mites and ticks.

Name its class. _____

Name its phylum. _____

Name its kingdom.

_____

Organism #15

is called a Death Cap. It cannot make its own food. It reproduces by forming spores in a club-shaped sac. While some organisms in this group are helpful or edible, this organism is deadly.

Name its kingdom.

_____

Organism #13

has the scientific name *Vulpez zerda*. (This names its genus and species.) Dogs and wolves belong to the same family, Canidae.

Name its order. _____

Name its class. _____

Name its phylum. _____

Name its kingdom.

_____

Organism #11

is a hookworm, a parasite that infects humans by living in the intestine.

Name its phylum.

_____

Name its kingdom.

_____

Organism #16

is an octopus, the most intelligent member of its phylum. Which other organisms belong to the same phylum? *(Circle them.)*

snail   slug   jellyfish
squid   oyster   clam

Name its phylum. _____

Name its kingdom.

_____

Use with page 274.

Name

Investigation #3: Tracking Down
WILD & WACKY PLANTS

Find out about the weird behaviors and odd characteristics of some of the strangest plants on the earth! Read about each plant. Then track down the missing information.

1. The largest known flower in the world has an odd name. It is called the **corpse flower**. Maybe this name comes from the terrible smell of rotten fish. Another strange thing about this flower is the blooming schedule. Find out how often it blooms.

    _____

2. The **horsetail** has been around since the time of dinosaurs. It is a strange-looking plant because it has no branches, leaves, or flowers. It is just a tall stalk with a cone-shaped structure on top. Early Americans used horsetails to scour their pots and pans or to polish wood. Find out what the horsetail contains that makes the plant a good, scratchy (abrasive) tool.

    _____

3. The **Venus Fly Trap** is the most famous of the weird plants. It is known for its carnivorous behavior. Find out how the plant traps flies.

    _____

4. The **Tropical Pitcher Plant** has a shape like a pitcher. This helps the plant gobble up bugs for dinner. Find out how the bugs are lured into the plant.

    _____

5. A tiny, tiny plant called **Wolffia** has the tiniest flower and tiniest fruit in the world. The fruit weighs about the same as a grain of salt. It takes about 20–30 of the plants to fill a square inch. The plant has flat, oval-shaped leaves, and grows without real roots. Find out the common name for this plant. Where is it found?

    _____

6. There is something very unusual about the **Coco De Mer**, an endangered palm tree. It is not the tree itself that is unusual. It is not the flower. It is something about the seed. What can you find out about the seed of this plant? (Its botanical name is *Lodoicea maldivica*.)

    _____

Use with page 277.

Name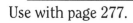

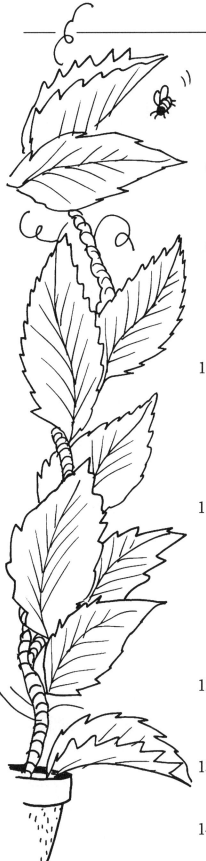

7. **Indian Pipes** look like ghosts, because they are completely white. These plants have no chlorophyll, so they cannot make their own food. Find out how Indian Pipes find food.

_____

8. The **African Witch Weed** has a big problem. It can live on its own for only about a week. Find out what it does to stay alive.

_____

9. The **Traveler's Palm** looks like a palm tree, but it is actually a member of the banana family. It is called the Traveler's Palm because it can offer water to quench the thirst of travelers. Find out how this tree holds water.

_____

10. A **Carrion Flower** has a very strange characteristic. It looks like a balloon before it opens. Then, when it opens, it looks like a starfish. But this is not the strange thing. The most "outstanding" characteristic of the Carrion Flower is its terrible smell of rotting meat. Find out what this horrible smell accomplishes for the flower.

_____

11. The **Coryanthes orchid** has a very unusual shape. A certain kind of wasp sometimes falls into this strange shape and gets drenched with the liquid it holds. The wet wasp cannot fly out of the plant; to exit, it must crawl through a narrow tunnel. This very odd plant has an "arm" that holds the wasp while it deposits pollen on the creature. Then the wasp is allowed to crawl out and fly away, loaded with pollen! Describe the flower's unusual shape.

_____

12. **Strangler Figs** are plants with a nasty habit. Find out why these are called "stranglers".

_____

13. The **Compass plant** has an unusual talent. What is this talent?

_____

14. The **rose of Jericho** practices an odd behavior. It dries up, curling its stems into a tight ball. Then it rolls around in the wind, dropping its seeds across the land. The rose of Jericho is also known as a resurrection plant. Explain what this means.

_____

Use with page 276.

Name _____

Investigation #3: Stalking
MONSTERS OF THE DEEP

Search out information to learn about these scary-looking deep sea creatures. Find out which creatures match the descriptions below. Write one or more letters for each answer.

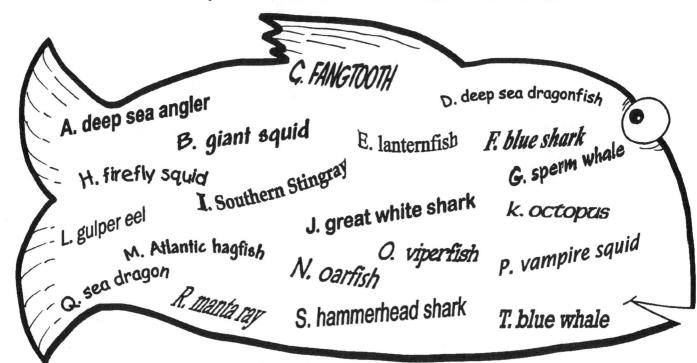

A. deep sea angler
B. giant squid
C. FANGTOOTH
D. deep sea dragonfish
E. lanternfish
F. blue shark
G. sperm whale
H. firefly squid
I. Southern Stingray
J. great white shark
k. octopus
L. gulper eel
M. Atlantic hagfish
N. oarfish
O. viperfish
P. vampire squid
Q. sea dragon
R. manta ray
S. hammerhead shark
T. blue whale

_____ 1. 4 or more creatures that spend time 1000 feet or deeper beneath the surface

_____ 2. a creature that produces huge amounts of slime to protect itself

_____ 3. creatures that use light-producing features to lure prey

_____ 4. a powerful, sharp-beaked, tentacled creature not generally found alive in the wild

_____ 5. the largest animal on earth

_____ 6. the longest bony fish in the ocean, also known as a ribbonfish

_____ 7. a graceful animal with a 15–20 ft. wingspan; scary, but harmless to people

_____ 8. a creature with an enormous mouth and long sharp teeth, who lives at 16,000 feet depths

_____ 9. a creature with a bizarre, pelican-like mouth and a tail like a whip

_____ 10. a creature that holds its breath to dive to depths of up to 10,000 feet for food

_____ 11. the fastest shark in the ocean

_____ 12. a creature that looks like seaweed and has a scary name, but is not fierce

Use with page 279.

Name _____

The BASIC/Not Boring Middle Grades Science Book Copyright ©2002 by Incentive Publications, Inc., Nashville, TN.

Which statements about "monsters of the deep" are true? Circle their numbers.
Then, investigate and answer questions A and B.

1. Sharks are mammals.

2. Sharks have no bones.

3. All sharks are predators.

4. Sharkskin is soft and smooth.

5. Only some sharks are carnivores.

6. All sharks are dangerous to humans.

7. Sharks have a keen sense of smell.

8. Sharks are closely related to rays.

9. A ray is actually a flattened shark.

10. Octopuses and squids have red blood.

11. A Southern Stingray is harmless to humans.

12. The Great White Shark can be as long as 25 feet.

13. Sharks are constantly losing and renewing teeth.

14. Squids live in dens near the floor of the ocean.

15. Rays and sharks both belong to the bony fish class.

16. Most adult octopuses and squids die after reproducing.

17. Octopuses and squids move by a system of jet propulsion.

18. Sharks are found only in the Atlantic and Pacific Oceans.

19. A shark gets some of its buoyancy from a large, oily liver.

20. The most important sense a shark uses to detect its prey is sight.

21. All sharks spend most of their time very deep in the ocean
    (below 1500 feet).

22. A hammerhead shark is one of the aggressive species known
    to attack humans.

23. A Lesser Electric Ray can deliver a powerful electric shock as high as 30 volts.

24. Octopuses and squids can protect themselves by squirting a stream of dark ink
    at a predator.

A.
What is dangerous about the *lionfish?*

_____

_____

_____

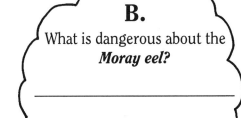

B.
What is dangerous about the
Moray eel?

_____

_____

_____

_____

_____

Use with page 278.

Name

Investigation #5: Scrutinizing
WEIRD & WONDERFUL BODY PARTS

Five doctors are taking part in some research. Their names are: Dr. B. J. Renal, Dr. L. Bowe, Dr. S. Turnam, Dr. G. Larynx; and Dr. A. Orta. Each has each been asked to scrutinize five different body parts or substances. (These are not necessarily the areas that each doctor would ordinarily study in his or her field.) The pictures are labeled with the doctors' blood types.

Read the clues on the next page. Use them to help discover which doctor is which, and what each is studying. Write their names in the correct places. Also write the names of the body parts or substances being studied by each doctor. (See the five lines in each box.)

1.
a. _____
b. _____
c. _____
d. _____
e. _____
Dr._____   blood type **O+**
Endocrinologist

2.
a. _____
b. _____
c. _____
d. _____
e. _____
Dr._____   blood type **B+**
Oncologist

3.
a. _____
b. _____
c. _____
d. _____
e. _____
Dr._____   blood type **A**
Hematologist

4.
a. _____
b. _____
c. _____
d. _____
e. _____
Dr._____   blood type **B-**
Podiatrist

5.
a. _____
b. _____
c. _____
d. _____
e. _____
Dr._____   blood type **AB+**
Cytologist

Use with page 281.

Name _____

Clues

1. Dr. S. Turnam's parents both have Rh-negative blood.

2. Dr. G. Larynx has a blood type known as the universal donor.

3. Dr. L. Bowe's lifelong work involves studying cancer.

4. Dr. B. J. Renal can receive blood from any other blood type donor.

5. The doctor who specializes in cell study has been asked to investigate an organ behind the stomach that filters blood and stores extra blood for emergencies. He also is looking at the long branches of nerve cells.

6. The doctor who studies feet is now looking at the eye muscle that regulates pupil size. This doctor also will look at the five long bones in the foot.

7. Dr. Bowe is examining a hard layer of the tooth that protects the tooth's center, and a gland that secretes a substance to regulate glucose.

8. The doctor who can receive only type O blood investigates an organ that stores bile, and a nerve that carries sound signals to the brain.

9. The doctor who is studying the large muscles at the sides and front of the abdomen can donate blood only to persons with type AB or type B blood.

10. Dr. Renal is studying the largest salivary gland.

11. The doctor who can receive blood only from type O or A studies the large veins on either side of the neck that bring carbon dioxide-laden blood from the head to the heart. This doctor also studies the structures in blood that form blood clots.

12. The doctor who studies feet is examining the part of the brain that regulates heartbeat. This doctor also looks at the substance that gives skin its color.

13. The doctor whose field is the study of blood now examines the calf muscle.

14. Dr. Larynx examines an iron-containing red pigment in red blood cells and the large nerves that run down the legs. (These nerves sometimes get pinched when the back is injured.)

15. Dr. Renal studies the lower chambers of the heart, and a substance released by the liver that breaks up fats.

16. Dr. Turnam is studying the shoulder muscle.

17. The doctor who ordinarily studies tumors is now examining the gland in the upper chest which functions to fight infection.

18. The doctor who specializes in hormones is now studying a gland in the neck. This gland regulates the rate at which the body produces energy for food.

19. The hematologist is studying tubes that carry ovum from the ovaries to the uterus. She also investigates the two tubes carrying oxygen from the trachea into the lungs.

20. Dr. Bowe is studying the large, wide, flat bone of the pelvis.

Use with page 280.

Name

   Copyright ©2002 by Incentive Publications, Inc., Nashville, TN.

Investigation #6: Explaining
STRANGE BODY EPISODES

Strange things are happening around Dr. Wilma Wiggle's body. These are body processes that just happen-sometimes she cannot even control them. Tell what is happening in each "incident."

1. While Wilma Wiggle was sleeping, oil, tears, and sweat were dripping down from tubes in her eyes. This stuff collected near her carnucles. What has happened?

   _____

2. Wilma is giving a speech at an important meeting, when a nerve that controls her diaphragm suddenly stimulates it, and her diaphragm contracts without warning. This keeps happening over and over, and she keeps sucking in air quickly, which causes her epiglottis to snap shut suddenly. She cannot stop this from happening. Wilma gets terribly embarrassed about the repeated noises and interruptions in her speech. Finally, she has to leave the meeting. What is happening?

   _____

3. Wilma has been swallowing gases (mostly air). Suddenly, some of the gas escapes quickly from her stomach and travels up through her esophagus and out through her mouth. She is embarrassed by the sound. What is happening?

   _____

4. Something has irritated the lining of Wilma's sinus passages. She tries to ignore it, but her body can't. Without her permission, nerve endings are stimulated and she suddenly expels air quickly from her nose and mouth. A lot of other stuff, like moisture and mucus, is also expelled. So, she's embarrassed again. What's happened?

   _____

5. Thousands of dead skin cells have gotten mixed with the oozing oil from Wilma's hair follicles. These dead skin cells and dirt from the air have combined into a messy gunk. The flakes of this gunk are breaking off and falling onto her shoulders. What is happening?

   _____

6. It has been a long meeting, and the air is stuffy. Dr. Wiggly has fallen asleep. Somehow the flow of air through the passages at the back of her mouth and nose got obstructed. Structures in the back of her throat strike each other and vibrate when she breathes. This makes another embarrassing sound. But, since she is asleep, she doesn't hear it! What is happening?

   _____

Use with page 283.

Name _____

Conduct more investigations to see if you can explain other strange body happenings. For each of these "episodes," describe what the body is actually doing.

A. skin wrinkling in the bathtub

B. a funny "funny bone" feeling

C. a yawn

D. bad breath

E. ears popping on an airplane

F. a shiver

G. earwax

Use with page 282.

Name

     Copyright ©2002 by Incentive Publications, Inc., Nashville, TN.

Investigation #7: Delving Into
DISTURBING DISORDERS

Dr. Cam B. Kurred sees a seemingly endless line of patients with disturbing disorders and diseases. He has to make judgments every day about treatments for the patients.

Survey the list of diseases and disorders on this page and the next page. Do some investigating to learn about treatments for these ailments. Choose 15 ailments. For each one, suggest one or two possible options for treatment. If you suggest medicines or drugs, try to describe specific kinds of drugs that could be used.

═══ AILMENTS ═══

acne	asthma		fainting	
AIDS	athlete's foot	chicken pox	fever	hepatitis
allergies	botulism	dehydration	fracture	hypothermia
anthrax	broken bones	depression	fungus	impetigo
anxiety	bronchitis	diabetes	gastroenteritis	influenza
appendicitis	cancer	earache	heart disease	insect stings
arthritis	cavity	exhaustion	heat stroke	

1. Disease/disorder _____
   Treatment(s) _____
   _____

2. Disease/disorder _____
   Treatment(s) _____
   _____

3. Disease/disorder _____
   Treatment(s) _____
   _____

4. Disease/disorder _____
   Treatment(s) _____
   _____

5. Disease/disorder _____
   Treatment(s) _____
   _____

Some Treatment Ideas
decongestants
liquids
vaccine
radiation
surgery
casting
antibiotics
immobilization
aspirin
antiseptics
rest
antihistamines
a cool bath
transplant
inhaler

Use with page 285.

Name

AILMENTS

kidney disease

laryngitis

lead poisoning

malaria

measles

meningitis

mumps

pneumonia

poison ivy

pyorrhea

rabies

roseola

scarlet fever

schizophrenia

shock

smallpox

snake bite

sprain

strep throat

stroke

tetanus

torn ligaments

tuberculosis

typhoid

6. Disease/disorder _____

   Treatment(s) _____

   _____

7. Disease/disorder _____

   Treatment(s) _____

   _____

8. Disease/disorder _____

   Treatment(s) _____

   _____

9. Disease/disorder _____

   Treatment(s) _____

   _____

10. Disease/disorder _____

    Treatment(s) _____

    _____

11. Disease/disorder _____

    Treatment(s) _____

    _____

12. Disease/disorder _____

    Treatment(s) _____

    _____

13. Disease/disorder _____

    Treatment(s) _____

    _____

14. Disease/disorder _____

    Treatment(s) _____

    _____

15. Disease/disorder _____

    Treatment(s) _____

    _____

More Treatment Ideas to Use for Both Pages

chemotherapy
blood thinning drugs
dialysis
physical therapy
medicine
cleaning wounds
exercise
change in diet
physical therapy
change of residence
removal of irritant
steroids
desensitization
quarantine

Use with page 284.

Name

Investigation #8: Exploring
EARTH'S RUMBLES, RATTLES, & ROLLS

Follow that scientist! Geologist Sylvester S. Izmic spends his life figuring out the bubblings and groanings, eruptions, quivers, and quakes of the earth. Look at his list of earth "antics" to investigate. Keep your own log book, with a brief explanation for each Earth event or feature. *What makes it happen?*

1. seismic waves

2. a strato-volcano

3. a caldera

4. a fault

5. a dome volcano

6. hot springs

7. folding in rocks

8. a shield volcano

Is the ground moving?

9. a geyser

Use with page 287.

Name

     Copyright ©2002 by Incentive Publications, Inc., Nashville, TN.

Use your good investigative skills to learn about some of history's major earthquakes. Then finish the log that Dr. Izmic began.

Some Deadly Earthquakes of the Twentieth Century

	Date	Location	Estimate of Deaths	Magnitude of Quake
1	Apr 18–19, 1906	San Francisco, CA, USA		
2	Dec 28, 1908	Messina, Italy		
3	Dec 16, 1920			
4	Sept 1, 1923	Yokohama, Japan		
5	May 22, 1927	Nan-Shan, China		
6	Dec 25, 1932			
7	May 30, 1935			
8	Oct 5, 1948	Turkmenistan, USSR		
9	Mar 27, 1964	Alaska, USA		
10	May 31, 1970	Yungay, Peru		
11	Feb 4, 1976	Guatemala		
12	Jul 28, 1976			
13	Dec 7, 1988	Armenia		
14	Oct 17, 1989			
15	Jun 21, 1990	Iran		
16	Jan 17, 1994	Northridge, CA, USA		
17	Jan 16, 1995			
18	May 30, 1998	Northeast Afghanistan		
19	Aug 17, 1999	Turkey		
20	Jan 26, 2001	Gujarat, India		

21. What, exactly, is an earthquake?

_____

_____

_____

_____

_____

_____ .

Use with page 286.

Name _____

Copyright ©2002 by Incentive Publications, Inc., Nashville, TN.

Investigation #9: Looking For
CHANGES—SWIFT & SLOW

Earth is always changing. If you blink your eyes, you might miss a quick change. If you stare all day, some changes might be happening right before your eyes—too slow for you to see.

Four things change Earth's surface: the wind, moving water, gravity, and ice. They are each very powerful. Do you know what they can do to the Earth?

What can wind do?

1. Wind can pick up loose material from the ground surface and move it. This process is called _____ .

2. Wind can carry particles along and "sandblast" rock surfaces, polishing or pitting them. This process is called

   _____ .

3. Wind can pick up material from one spot and deposit it somewhere else. The deposited material is called _____ .

4. _____ , the most common wind deposits, are formed when wind full of blowing sand drops the sand as it blows across an obstacle.

What can gravity do?

5. Gravity pulls loose material down slopes. Material that collects at the foot of a steep slope or cliff is called

   _____ .

6. In a _____ , large amounts of rock loosen and fall.

7. _____ are caused when large amounts of material slide quickly down slopes.

8. Soil and other material from weathering mixed with rain can move rapidly down a slope, causing a

   _____ .

9. Sometimes materials move so slowly that the movement cannot be seen. This is called _____ .

Use with page 289.

Name _____

 Copyright ©2002 by Incentive Publications, Inc., Nashville, TN.

What can moving water do?

10. Moving water running off soil and slopes, carries dirt and debris, and leaves it in apron-shaped deposits called _____ .

11. Moving water in a river or stream can pick up sediment and carry it along in a _____ load, or drag heavy material along, scraping the river bottom. This load is a _____ load.

12. During a flood, a river carries large amounts of sediment. When it spills over its banks, the river drops the heaviest sediment along the edge, forming a ridge called a _____ . Fine sediment is carried farther from the river channel and dropped to form a _____ .

13. A river usually deposits sediment at its mouth in the shape of a fan. This deposit is called a _____ .

14. Groundwater seeping into limestone regions can dissolve the stone. This can create openings in the bedrock, called _____ . If a "roof" is left when an area is dissolved, a _____ bridge might remain. Funnel-shaped depressions beneath the surface, left when the rock dissolves, become dangerous _____ .

What can ice do?

15. In a process called _____ , a glacier (moving ice) scours the bedrock as it moves. It leaves long scratches, or _____ , on the rock.

16. In another process, called _____ , the moving glacier picks up debris and moves it along to other places.

17. When the glacier melts or recedes, it drops this debris (called _____) into piles around the edges. These piles are _____ .

Use with page 288.

Name

Investigation #10: Confirming
MISSING IDENTITIES

This adventuresome scientist has located several interesting mineral specimens. She knows all about the characteristics of the minerals, because she has been examining them closely. Now she needs to know their names. Find the missing identities. Write the name of each mineral on its label. (See list of minerals on the next page.)

Rocks are so exciting!

Specimen #1

color: white
crystals: cubic
luster: nonmetallic
hardness: fingernail can scratch
it; it cannot scratch
a penny
streak: colorless
other: salty

Specimen #2

color: red
crystals: dodecahedron
luster: nonmetallic
hardness: can scratch glass
but not topaz
streak: colorless

Specimen #3

color: brassy yellow
crystals: cubic
luster: metallic
hardness: 6.5
streak: greenish-black

Specimen #4

color: colorless or white
crystals: hexagonal
luster: nonmetallic
hardness: can be scratched
by a fingernail
streak: colorless or white

Specimen #5

color: white
crystals: monoclinic
luster: nonmetallic
hardness: 2
streak: white

Specimen #6

color: colorless
crystals: hexagonal
luster: nonmetallic
hardness: can scratch feldspar;
can be scratched
by garnet
streak: colorless

Specimen #7

color: silver grey
crystals: cubic
luster: metallic
hardness: can be scratched
by a penny, but
not by a fingernail
streak: grey

Specimen #8

color: yellow
crystals: prismatic
luster: nonmetallic
hardness: scratches garnet
streak: colorless
other: very dense

Use with page 291.

Name

_____

silver   garnet
gold   graphite   galea
sulfur   copper
corundum
topaz   quartz   magnetite   calcite
diamond   halite   pyrite
talc   bauxite
gypsum

Specimen #11

_____

color: copper red
crystals: cubic
luster: metallic
hardness: 3
streak: copper red

Specimen #14

_____

color: greenish-white
crystals: monoclinic
luster: nonmetallic
hardness: 1
streak: white
other: soapy feel

Specimen #9

_____

color: blue
crystals: hexagonal
luster: nonmetallic
hardness: scratches topaz
streak: white

Specimen #12

_____

color: yellow
crystals: orthorhombic
luster: nonmetallic
hardness: can scratch glass
        but not topaz
streak: colorless
other: strong odor when
        wet

Specimen #15

_____

color: colorless
crystals: isometric
luster: nonmetallic
hardness: can scratch all
        other minerals
streak: white
other: brilliant luster

Specimen #10

_____

color: black
crystals: hexagonal
luster: metallic
hardness: can be scratched
        by a fingernail
streak: black
other: flaky, leaves fingers
        black

Specimen #13

_____

color: black
crystals: cubic
luster: metallic
hardness: 6
streak: black

Specimen #16

_____

color: silver
crystals: cubic
luster: metallic
hardness: cannot scratch
        a penny
streak: silvery grey

Use with page 290.

Name

Investigation #11: Untangling
SECRETS OF MOVING WATERS

What secrets lie tossed about in the waves or rising and falling with the tides? Do you know them?

The water of the ocean is constantly in motion. What makes it move? Search for the information that will untangle the mysteries of moving waters. When you find it, write the answers that tell the secrets.

1. **The secret of surface currents:** *What causes them?*

2. **The secret of density currents:** *What causes them?*

3. **The secret of waves:** *What causes them?*

4. **The circle secret:** *How do water particles move in a wave?*

5. **The secret of waves:** *How is a deep-water wave different from a shallow-water wave?*

6. **The secret of breaking waves:** *What causes a wave to break?*

7. **The secret of surf:** *What causes it?*

8. **The secret of surfing:** *How can a surfer ride a wave?*

Use with page 293.

Name _____

292   Copyright ©2002 by Incentive Publications, Inc., Nashville, TN.

9. **The secret of tides:** *What causes the tides?*

Label each of the diagrams below as ***spring tide*** or ***neap tide***.
Explain what the tides in each diagram would be like.

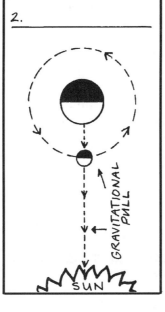
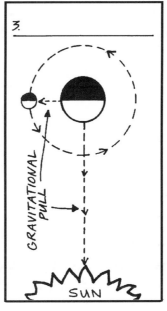
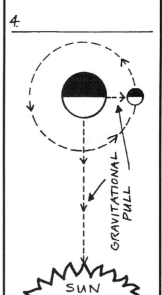

_____

_____

_____

_____

_____

Use with page 292.

Name _____

The BASIC/Not Boring Middle Grades Science Book   Copyright ©2002 by Incentive Publications, Inc., Nashville, TN.

Investigation #12: Chasing Down
WILD WEATHER & SPECTACULAR STORMS

Meteorologist Dr. Gail Storm is always caught up in some wild weather. She just can't keep away from any storm or other form of inclement weather!

Here are some of her diary entries from the past few months. For each weather predicament she names, write the details to show that you, too, are savvy about storms and wild weather. (Briefly describe what conditions would be present in that weather situation.)

	Date	Weather
1	Jan 14	**wind chill factor** today is –30° F
2	Feb 1	terrible **blizzard** today in Minneapolis
3	Mar 27	flew over **flood** areas today
4	Apr 12	**sleet** continued all day
5	Apr 28	stranded for two days by a huge **sandstorm**
6	May 13	**typhoon** hit further south than expected
7	Jun 20	**monsoon** season in full force here
8	Jul 15	**rainstorms** off and on all day
9	Jul 23	**hail** the size of golf balls this afternoon
10	Jul 31	my first view of a **waterspout**

Use with page 295.

Name

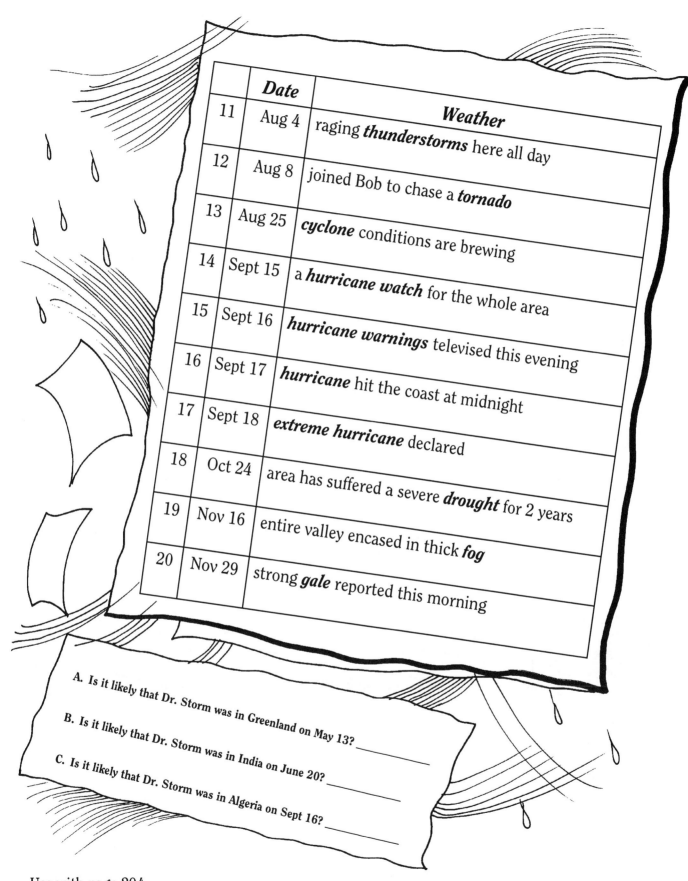

	Date	Weather
11	Aug 4	raging **thunderstorms** here all day
12	Aug 8	joined Bob to chase a **tornado**
13	Aug 25	**cyclone** conditions are brewing
14	Sept 15	a **hurricane watch** for the whole area
15	Sept 16	**hurricane warnings** televised this evening
16	Sept 17	**hurricane** hit the coast at midnight
17	Sept 18	**extreme hurricane** declared
18	Oct 24	area has suffered a severe **drought** for 2 years
19	Nov 16	entire valley encased in thick **fog**
20	Nov 29	strong **gale** reported this morning

A. Is it likely that Dr. Storm was in Greenland on May 13? _____

B. Is it likely that Dr. Storm was in India on June 20? _____

C. Is it likely that Dr. Storm was in Algeria on Sept 16? _____

Use with page 294.

Name

The BASIC/Not Boring Middle Grades Science Book   295   Copyright ©2002 by Incentive Publications, Inc., Nashville, TN.

Investigation #13: Probing Into
MARVELS OF THE UNIVERSE

What's behind these awesome, wonderful, and mysterious features of the universe?
Do some probing to find out. Then write a brief description or explanation for each one.

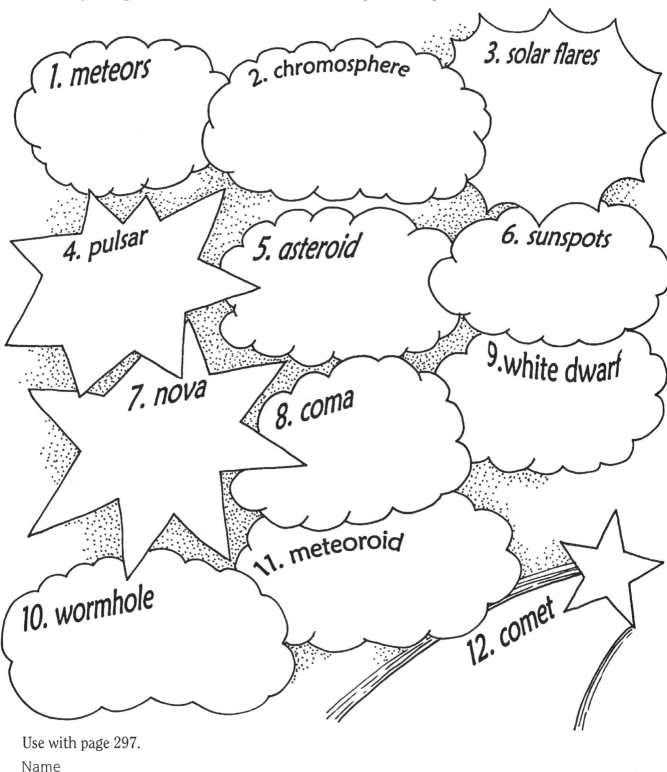

1. meteors

2. chromosphere

3. solar flares

4. pulsar

5. asteroid

6. sunspots

9. white dwarf

7. nova

8. coma

11. meteoroid

10. wormhole

12. comet

Use with page 297.

Name

     Copyright ©2002 by Incentive Publications, Inc., Nashville, TN.

13. binary stars

15. nebulae

14. black hole

17. meteorite

16. shooting star

The Life Story of a Star

18. Write a brief explanation of the birth, life, and death of a star.

Use with page 296.

Name

Copyright ©2002 by Incentive Publications, Inc., Nashville, TN.

Investigation #14: Pursuing
PLANETARY PECULIARITIES

Each planet has its own unique features and oddities. No two are alike.

Use good references about space (and all you know about the solar system) as you pursue the peculiarities of the nine *known* planets. Write the name of one or more planets to match each feature described. Use the abbreviations for the planets listed here.

E	Earth
J	Jupiter
M	Mars
MR	Mercury
P	Pluto
N	Neptune
S	Saturn
U	Uranus
V	Venus

_____ 1. These planets have rings.

_____ 2. Its atmosphere is mostly nitrogen and oxygen.

_____ 3. There are ice caps at both poles.

_____ 4. It's the most brilliant body in the sky.

_____ 5. This sphere is drastically tilted— at 82.1° on its axis.

_____ 6. One of its moons, Europa, was named by Galileo.

_____ 7. It has the most moons.

_____ 8. It's a planet of rocks and ice.

_____ 9. These two planets are the closest to Earth.

_____ 10. Twenty-nine years is the time it takes to orbit the sun.

_____ 11. The planet is often covered by huge dust storms.

_____ 12. It's a blue-green planet.

_____ 13. It is the furthest known planet from the sun.

_____ 14. It takes 88 days to circle the sun.

_____ 15. This is a pale blue planet.

_____ 16. It is 5900 million miles from the sun.

_____ 17. The force of gravity here has less than half the pull exerted by gravity on Earth.

_____ 18. It's called the red planet because the rocks are covered with rusty dust.

_____ 19. Its orbital speed is about 30 kilometers per second.

_____ 20. It has two moons.

_____ 21. This is the fastest rotating body in the solar system.

Where am I ?

Use with page 299.

Name

    Copyright ©2002 by Incentive Publications, Inc., Nashville, TN.

_____ 22. It takes 29 Earth years to travel around the sun one time.

_____ 23. These planets have no moons.

_____ 24. It's the smallest planet known.

_____ 25. Titan is one of its moons.

_____ 26. This planet rotates more slowly than any other.

_____ 27. These planets are mostly "balls of gas".

_____ 28. The length of its day is close to the length of Earth's day.

_____ 29. Rotation takes 10 hours.

_____ 30. It's a colorful, banded planet.

_____ 31. It circles the sun faster than any other planet.

_____ 32. This is closest in size to Earth.

_____ 33. It's the third planet from the sun.

_____ 34. It's called the giant planet.

_____ 35. It is the seventh planet from the sun.

_____ 36. It's the closest planet to the sun.

_____ 37. It is famous for its elaborate system of rings.

_____ 38. It takes 165 years to travel around the sun.

_____ 39. This planet is about half the size of Earth.

_____ 40. It's about 149.6 million miles from the sun.

_____ 41. It takes 59 days to rotate.

_____ 42. The length of a day (daytime and night) is 9 hours.

_____ 43. It has more moons than Jupiter

_____ 44. It moves around the sun at the slowest speed of any planet.

_____ 45. The trip around the sun takes 84 Earth years.

_____ 46. A thick atmosphere of deadly gasses surround this planet.

_____ 47. An asteroid belt is found between the orbits of these two planets.

_____ 48. Only one moon orbits this planet.

Use with page 298.

Name _____

Investigation #15: Inquiring Into
CURIOUS COMBINATIONS

Follow Cathy Lyst around as she investigates some chemical combinations around her house. These are some compounds that make up common substances she uses in her everyday life.

Read the description of each substance. Then do your own investigations to find the chemical formula and the common name for each. Write the missing names and formulas.

1. Cathy washes the hard, calcium carbonate surface of her counters.

2. She adds a cup of sodium hypochlorite to her laundry to whiten and remove stains.

3. While cooking dinner, Cathy adds sodium chloride to her stew to bring out the flavors.

4. She makes fluffy biscuits with the help of sodium hydrogen carbonate.

5. When it's time to eat, she enjoys a nice atmosphere caused by the burning of sticks made of a carbon and hydrogen compound.

6. After dinner, she sweetens her coffee with a compound made of carbon, hydrogen, and oxygen.

7. A compound of carbon and hydrogen burns in her gas heater, keeping the apartment warm.

8. Cathy uses another form of calcium carbonate to write notes to her children on a board in the kitchen.

9. Cathy uses window-cleaning liquid that is a solution of a gas dissolved in water.

Common Name

1. _____
2. _____
3. _____
4. _____
5. _____
6. _____
7. _____
8. _____
9. _____

Formula

1. [ ]
2. [ ]
3. [ ]
4. [ ]
5. [ ]
6. [ ]
7. [ ]
8. [ ]
9. [ ]

Use with page 301.

Name

     Copyright ©2002 by Incentive Publications, Inc., Nashville, TN.

I could do with a few _less_ chemicals in my life right now.

Common Name

Formula

10. Cathy's children love to play outside in the box of silicon dioxide.

11. Cathy is happy when her car has a full supply of this compound of carbon and hydrogen.

12. When she scrapes her arm on the garbage can, Cathy washes the wound thoroughly with a liquid from a brown bottle. It is a compound of hydrogen and oxygen.

13. She soaks a sore ankle in a solution of water and magnesium sulfate hepta-hydrate.

14. Cathy's family members regularly breathe a carbon-oxygen compound into the air in the house.

15. Cathy feeds a spoonful of magnesium hydroxide to her daughter, who has an upset stomach.

16. At the beginning of the summer, Cathy makes sure her car has a good supply of dichlorodifluoromethane.

17. Cathy and her family have a lot of this substance around the house. It is a thick, transparent liquid compound that is used in soap, cosmetics, and inks.

18. Cathy put this compound of calcium oxide on her lawn to help with the growth of new grass seed by reducing the high acidity in the soil.

10. _____   10. [   ]

11. _____   11. [   ]

12. _____   12. [   ]

13. _____   13. [$MgSO_4 7H_2O$]

14. _____   14. [   ]

15. _____   15. [   ]

16. _____   16. [   ]

17. _____   17. [$C_3H_8O_3$]

18. _____   18. [   ]

Use with page 300.

Name _____

Copyright ©2002 by Incentive Publications, Inc., Nashville, TN.

Investigation #16: Hunting For
PHYSICS IN THE NEIGHBORHOOD

Whether you know it or not, physics is lurking all around your neighborhood. Sharpen your physics skills and use them to answer these questions.

1. Why don't people fall out of rollercoasters at the amusement park?

2. Why does water run down a bathtub drain in a swirl?

3. Why do you weigh more at home than you would on the moon?

4. Why is soda pop fizzy?

5. Why does a teakettle sing?

6. Why is salt added to ice when you're making homemade ice cream in an ice cream freezer?

Use with page 303.

Name

Copyright ©2002 by Incentive Publications, Inc., Nashville, TN.

7. Why does a suction cup stay on a window?

11. Why do you get an electric shock if you touch a doorknob after walking across a carpet?

8. Why can you slide faster down a slide when you sit on a plastic or fiberglass mat?

12. What makes your milkshake go up your straw?

9. How does a sand sculpture keep from falling apart?

13. When you row a boat on the pond, why does the boat go forward when you are pulling the oars back toward you?

10. Why do you keep moving forward when you slam on the brakes on your bicycle?

Use with page 302.

Name

The BASIC/Not Boring Middle Grades Science Book

Copyright ©2002 by Incentive Publications, Inc., Nashville, TN.

Investigation #17: Discovering
THE SCIENCE BEHIND THE SPORT

Science hangs around every place where sports are happening, whether it's indoors, outdoors, in the air, or underground.

Investigate the science in sports. Choose 3 of the extreme sports listed, and briefly describe a way that science makes the sport possible. Think about the sport's purpose, skills, and equipment.

Lucy runs down a track with a tall, flexible pole until she approaches a sandpile in front of a high bar suspended between two poles. She plants her pole in the sandpile and gives herself a hard push off the ground. The kinetic energy from the running and pushing bends the poles. The kinetic energy is converted for a time into potential energy in the pole. Lucy holds onto the pole while the pole springs back to its original straight shape. As this happens, the potential energy converts into kinetic energy again. This boosts Lucy, clinging to the pole, up into the air. She lets go of the pole, and the inertia keeps her body moving, up and over the bar. Eventually, gravity pulls her downward and she falls to the ground. Thankfully, she lands on a thick, padded mat.

Draw Lucy's Sport

surfing

ski jumping

scuba diving

rafting

snorkeling

windsurfing

snowshoeing

The Sport: _____

The Science: _____

_____

_____

_____

_____

_____

_____

Use with page 305.

Name

   Copyright ©2002 by Incentive Publications, Inc., Nashville, TN.

hot air ballooning

mountain bike racing

bungee jumping

snowboarding

cross-country skiing

bobsled racing

spelunking (caving)

wakeboarding

water skiing

rock climbing

inline skating

ultimate Frisbee

The Sport: _____

The Science: _____

_____
_____
_____
_____
_____
_____
_____
_____
_____
_____

The Sport: _____

The Science: _____

_____
_____
_____
_____
_____
_____
_____
_____
_____
_____

Use with page 304.

Name _____

Investigation #18: Uncovering
MUSICAL MYSTERIES

Fans of the Splitting Atoms rock band are wild about their music. When the group puts on a concert, how are the musical sounds made? And how do the sounds travel to the fans' ears? Investigate the science of sound to find out.

1. What causes the sounds that come from the drums?_____
   _____
   _____

2. What causes the sounds that come from the voices? _____
   _____
   _____

3. What causes the sounds that come from the guitars and piano?_____
   _____
   _____

4. What causes the sounds that come from the trumpet and the saxophone? _____
   _____

5. How does the sound travel from the band to the fans? _____
   _____

6. Describe a compressional wave. _____
   _____
   _____

7. Define the amplitude of a sound wave. _____
   _____
   _____

8. Define the frequency of sound waves. _____
   _____
   _____

9. What amplitudes of sound waves can be heard by humans? _____
   _____

10. Which sounds from the bands will have the lowest frequencies—
    high-pitched or low-pitched? _____

Use with page 307.

Name _____

     Copyright ©2002 by Incentive Publications, Inc., Nashville, TN.

The band is very loud tonight.

11. Do the sound waves probably have small or large amplitudes?

12. Which would be the most likely measurement of the band's loudness?
    (Circle one.)
    3dB   15dB   60dB   115dB

Tonight the band is playing outdoors.

13. It is a cool night. Would the sound travel faster or slower if the temperature were much warmer? _____

14. Is the music likely to sound louder or softer than when the band plays indoors? _____

15. Give an explanation for your answer. _____
    _____
    _____
    _____

During the concert, a jet plane flies over the outdoor stadium.

16. Describe how the Doppler Effect will determine the way the sound of the jet is heard by the fans as it approaches and passes by the stadium.
    _____
    _____
    _____
    _____
    _____

Use with page 306.

Name _____

Investigation #19: Snooping for
ELUSIVE ELEMENTS

Follow the trail to find the missing elements. Use the Periodic Table (page 310), your knowledge about atomic structure, and your investigative skills to figure out which missing element will fit each clue. Write each element AND its symbol.

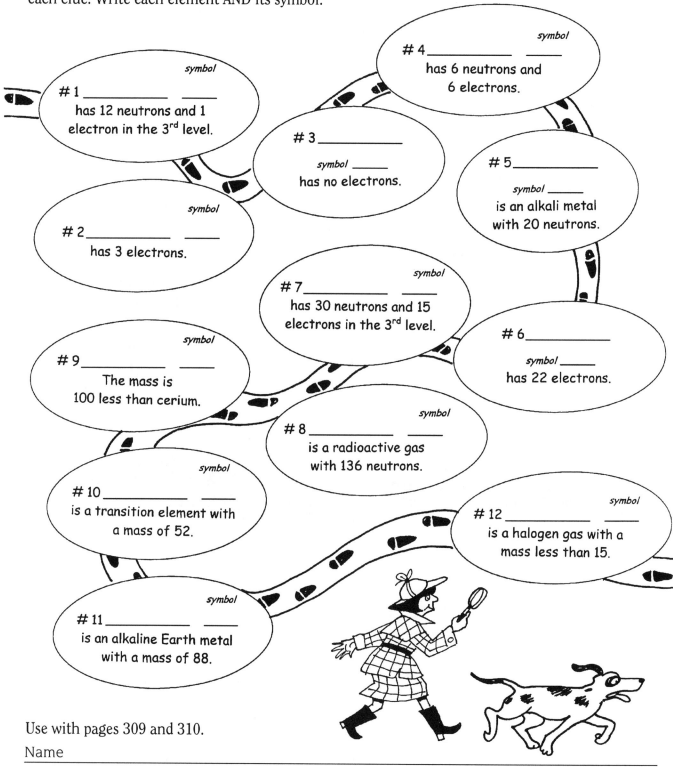

1 _____ _____ symbol
has 12 neutrons and 1 electron in the 3rd level.

4 _____ _____ symbol
has 6 neutrons and 6 electrons.

3 _____
symbol _____
has no electrons.

5 _____
symbol _____
is an alkali metal with 20 neutrons.

2 _____ _____ symbol
has 3 electrons.

7 _____ _____ symbol
has 30 neutrons and 15 electrons in the 3rd level.

6 _____
symbol _____
has 22 electrons.

9 _____ _____ symbol
The mass is 100 less than cerium.

8 _____ _____ symbol
is a radioactive gas with 136 neutrons.

10 _____ _____ symbol
is a transition element with a mass of 52.

12 _____ _____ symbol
is a halogen gas with a mass less than 15.

11 _____ _____ symbol
is an alkaline Earth metal with a mass of 88.

Use with pages 309 and 310.

Name

Copyright ©2002 by Incentive Publications, Inc., Nashville, TN.

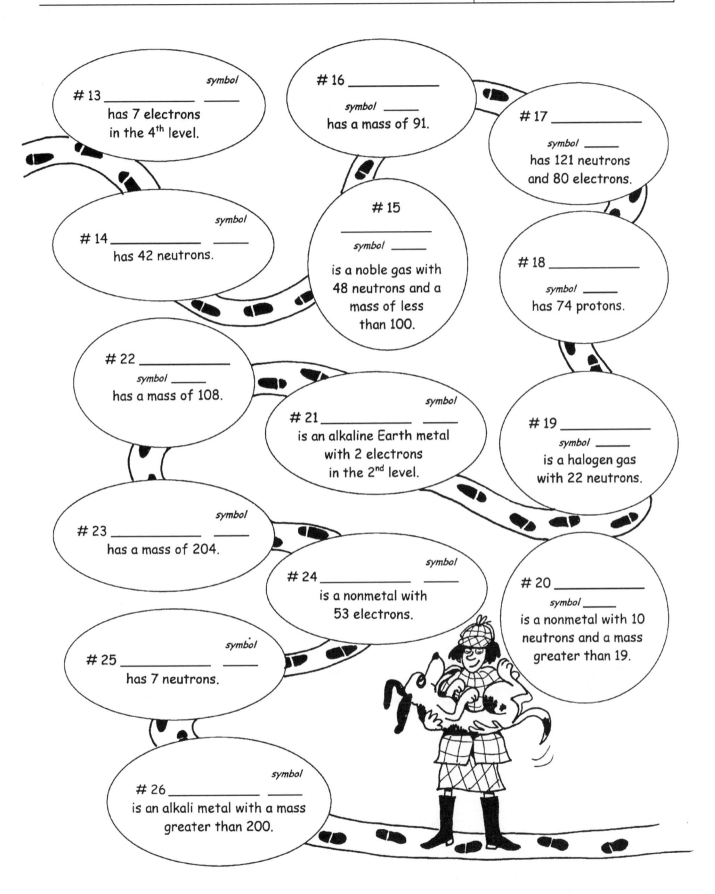

13 _____ ____ *symbol*
has 7 electrons
in the 4th level.

16 _____
symbol ____
has a mass of 91.

17 _____
symbol ____
has 121 neutrons
and 80 electrons.

14 _____ ____ *symbol*
has 42 neutrons.

15
_____
symbol ____
is a noble gas with
48 neutrons and a
mass of less
than 100.

18 _____
symbol ____
has 74 protons.

22 _____
symbol ____
has a mass of 108.

21 _____ ____ *symbol*
is an alkaline Earth metal
with 2 electrons
in the 2nd level.

19 _____
symbol ____
is a halogen gas
with 22 neutrons.

23 _____ ____ *symbol*
has a mass of 204.

24 _____ ____ *symbol*
is a nonmetal with
53 electrons.

20 _____
symbol ____
is a nonmetal with 10
neutrons and a mass
greater than 19.

25 _____ ____ *symbol*
has 7 neutrons.

26 _____ ____ *symbol*
is an alkali metal with a mass
greater than 200.

Use with pages 308 and 310.

Name

The BASIC/Not Boring Middle Grades Science Book   Copyright ©2002 by Incentive Publications, Inc., Nashville, TN.

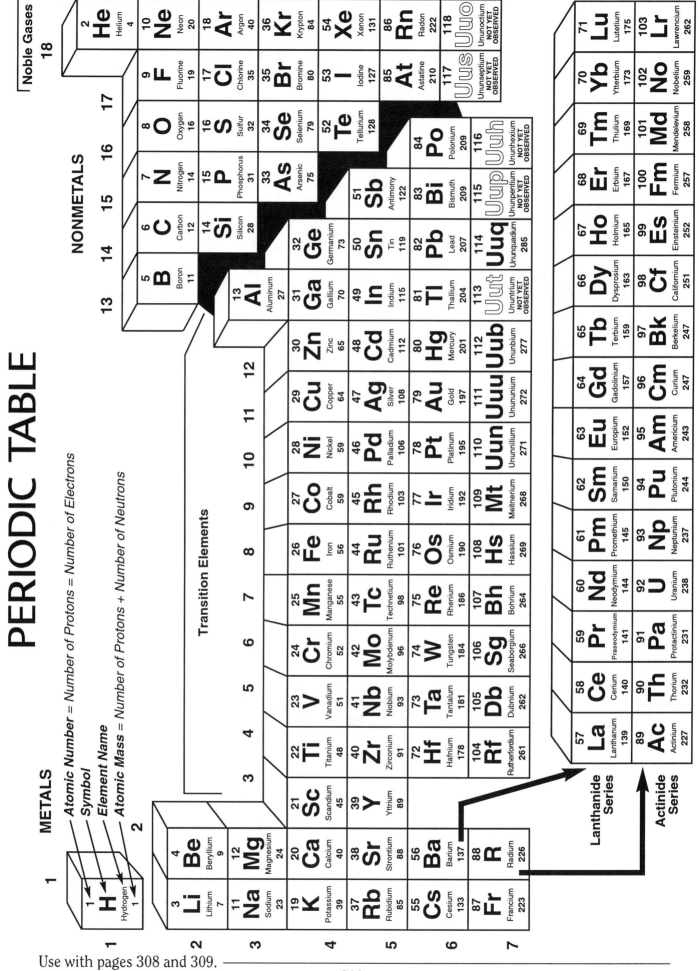

PERIODIC TABLE

Atomic Number = Number of Protons = Number of Electrons
Symbol
Element Name
Atomic Mass = Number of Protons + Number of Neutrons

METALS

NONMETALS

| Noble Gases 18 |

Transition Elements

Lanthanide Series

Actinide Series

Use with pages 308 and 309.

The BASIC/Not Boring Middle Grades Science Book

310

Copyright ©2002 by Incentive Publications, Inc., Nashville, TN.

SCIENCE INVESTIGATIONS
ASSESSMENT AND ANSWER KEYS

SCIENCE INVESTIGATIONS TEST

Each answer is worth one point. Total possible points = 70

1–8: Write T for each true statement and F for each false statement.

_____ 1. A substance that has excess OH^+ ions will turn blue litmus paper red.

_____ 2. A quark is a subatomic particle.

_____ 3. You could see an aurora borealis in Argentina or Borneo.

_____ 4. In the light spectrum, the red waves are shorter than the blue waves.

_____ 5. Fresh water has greater density than saltwater.

_____ 6. About 50% of Earth's surface is water.

_____ 7. Vacuoles are structures for storing food and water in living cells.

_____ 8. Sharks and squids squirt a dark ink to protect themselves from predators.

9–20: Write an answer to each question. (Not all answers are found on the signs.)

_____ 9. This is the phylum of a zebra.

_____ 10. Bacteria belong to this kingdom.

_____ 11. This is the phylum of sponges.

_____ 12. A mouse belongs to this class.

_____ 13. This is the kingdom of a euglenoid.

_____ 14. Roundworms belong to this phylum.

_____ 15. A tarantula, lobster, and ladybug share this phylum.

_____ 16. Daddy Longlegs, ticks, and mites belong to this class.

_____ 17. Starfish, sea cucumbers, and sea urchins share this phylum.

_____ 18. A snail, slug, squid, octopus, and oyster share this phylum.

_____ 19. A jellyfish, sea anemone, hydra, and coral share this phylum.

_____ 20. Algae, horsetails, and liverworts belong to this kingdom.

Kingdoms
Protist
Moneran
Fungus
Plant
Animal

Animal Phyla
Porifera
Coelenteratata
Platyhelminthes
Nematoda
Annelida
Mollusca
Arthropoda
Echinodermata
Chordata

Name _____

Copyright ©2002 by Incentive Publications, Inc., Nashville, TN.

21–23: Write each answer in the box containing each question.

21. What causes a shiver?

22. Why does water swirl
    down a bathtub drain?

23. Why don't people fall
    out of a rollercoaster?

24–33. Circle one or more correct answers for each question.

24. Which of these ailments is NOT likely to be treated with antibiotics?
    a. pneumonia   c. diabetes   e. shock
    b. hypothermia   d. anthrax   f. ankle sprain

25. Which is true of sharks?
    a. They are predators.   c. They have smooth skin.
    b. They have bones.   d. They are carnivores.

26. Which is a large salivary gland?
    a. parotid   b. thymus   c. thyroid   d. pituitary   e. hypothalamus

27. Which organ stores bile in the human body?
    a. the spleen   b. the liver   c. the gallbladder   d. the stomach

28. What regulates the human heartbeat?
    a. the medulla   b. the cerebrum   c. the spinal cord   d. the cerebellum

29. What secretes a substance that regulates glucose in the human body?
    a. the sciatic nerve   b. the dendrites   c. the adrenal glands   d. the pancreas

30. What weather condition is characterized by a warm, moist air mass behind held close to the
    ground by a heavier, colder air mass above it?
    a. sleet   b. fog   c. hail   d. a cyclone   e. a strong gale

31. What is the amplitude of sound waves that can be heard by humans?
    a. 20–20,000 Mz   b. 200–200,000 Mz   c. 20–2000 Mz

32. A collapsed star from which no light can escape is a
    a. black hole.   c. pulsar.   e. red giant.
    b. wormhole.   d. white dwarf.   f. nova.

33. While Mrs. Laze lounges, sunbathing in her yard, the neighbor mows his lawn. Which is true
    about the sound Mrs. Laze as the mower approaches her chair?
    a. The waves compress together.   d. The waves have a higher frequency.
    b. The waves get farther apart.   e. The pitch gets higher.
    c. The waves have a lower frequency.   f. The pitch gets lower.

Name _____

34–37: Write the answer.

34. What blood types can donate to AB negative? _____

35. To which blood types can an A type donate? _____

36. Does sound travel faster through cold air or warm air?_____

37. Of what materials is a comet composed? _____

38–45: Write the letter that shows the correct chemical formula for each compound.

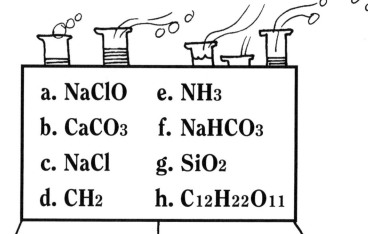

_____ 38. baking soda

_____ 39. candle wax

_____ 40. sugar

_____ 41. ammonia

_____ 42. bleach

_____ 43. sand

_____ 44. salt

_____ 45. chalk

a. NaClO   e. NH_3

b. $CaCO_3$ f. $NaHCO_3$

c. NaCl   g. SiO_2

d. CH_2 h. $C_{12}H_{22}O_{11}$

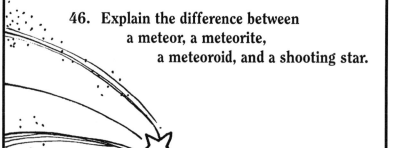

46. **Explain the difference between a meteor, a meteorite, a meteoroid, and a shooting star.**

47–51. Circle the numbers of the statements that are true.

47. Saturn, Uranus, and Jupiter have rings.

48. Mars is the only planet with polar ice caps.

49. Mars and Venus are the closest planets to Earth.

50. Jupiter is the fastest rotating planet.

51. Mercury is the closest planet to the sun.

Name _____

    Copyright ©2002 by Incentive Publications, Inc., Nashville, TN.

52–58: Name the earth surface feature or process that matches each description.

_____ 52. Slow-flowing basalt erupts from vents in the Earth's surface to form this volcano.

_____ 53. Movement takes place along a fracture in Earth's surface.

_____ 54. Material pulled downward by gravity collects at the foot of a steep slope.

_____ 55. A flooding river deposits fine sediment outside of the river channel.

_____ 56. A moving glacier picks up debris and moves it to other places.

_____ 57. Steam pressure forces water through an opening in the crust at regular intervals.

_____ 58. Wind picks up loose material from the surface and moves it around.

---

59. This rock hound has found a chunk of a mineral.
It is white, non-metallic, and can be scratched by a fingernail.
Which of these could it be? *(Circle one or more.)*

   talc   **halite**   **calcite**

   quartz   **gypsum**   **galena**   **diamond**

---

60. Which statements about ocean water are true? *(Circle one or more answers.)*
   a. Cold water is more dense than warm water.
   b. Increased salinity decreases density.
   c. Water moves from an area of greater density to lesser density.

61. Which statements are true of a spring tide? *(Circle one or more answers.)*
   a. Gravitational pull of the Earth, moon, and sun are lined up.
   b. High tides are at their highest and low tides are at their lowest.
   c. There is a smaller tidal range than during neap tides.

62–66: Name the element indicated
   by each symbol below.

_____ 62. He

_____ 63. Mn

_____ 64. Ag

_____ 65. Hg

_____ 66. Na

13
Al
27

_____ 67. What is this element?

_____ 68. What is the mass?

_____ 69. What is the atomic number?

_____ 70. How many electrons are in the 3rd level?

SCORE: Total Points _____ out of a possible 70 points

Name _____

SCIENCE INVESTIGATIONS
SKILLS TEST ANSWER KEY

1. F
2. T
3. F
4. F
5. F
6. F
7. T
8. F
9. chordata
10. moneran
11. porifera
12. mammal
13. protist
14. nematoda
15. arthropoda
16. arachnid
17. echinodermata
18. mollusca
19. coelenterata
20. plant
21. Muscles contract involuntarily to release chemicals that produce heat and keep the body warm.
22. Earth's rotation causes the swirling.
23. Inertia and centripetal forces keep people pushed back in their seats.
24. b, c, e, f
25. a, d
26. a
27. c
28. a
29. d
30. b
31. a
32. a
33. a, d, e
34. A negative, B negative, AB negative, and O negative

35. A and AB
36. warm
37. ice, dust, dirt
38. f
39. d
40. h
41. e
42. a
43. g
44. c
45. b
46. Meteoroid: .... small fragment of matter moving in space (or small pieces of asteroids)

    Meteor: .... meteoroid that burns up in Earth's atmosphere

    Meteorite: .... meteor that strikes Earth

    Shooting Star: ..... briefly visible meteor

47–51: Numbers 49, 50, and 51 should be circled.
52. shield volcano
53. fault
54. talus
55. flood plain
56. plucking or till
57. geyser
58. loess or deflation
59. talc, halite, calcite, gypsum
60. a, c
61. a, b
62. helium
63. manganese
64. silver
65. mercury
66. sodium
67. aluminum
68. 27
69. 13
70. 17

        Copyright ©2002 by Incentive Publications, Inc., Nashville, TN.

ANSWERS

Pages 270–273

Answers will vary. Those shown here offer basic guidelines against which to check answers. Web addresses will vary.

1. no
2. Most of the wavelengths from light pass through the air. The short, blue waves get scattered around the sky so it is the blue color that reaches the eyes.
3. visible comets depend on year and season (answers will vary)
4. acid has excess H+ ions and turns blue litmus red; base has excess OH+ ions and turns red litmus blue
5. vacuoles store food or water in the cells
6. epidemics
7. no
8. Cats ingest hair from cleaning their fur. Fur cannot be digested, so they cough it up.
9. a protein called keratin
10. 25 million years (approximately)
11. Do not struggle. Use slow swimming movements, float on top and roll to solid ground.
12. 2½ billion times (approximately)
13. no
14. camels (also: alpaca, guanaco, vicuña)
15. they are in an orbit—a combination of speed and altitude that keeps them circling instead of being pulled down by Earth's gravity
16. in an atom
17. salt water is heavier (more dense) than fresh water
18. the force that affects anything moving through air and makes it turn slightly—because the Earth is rotating
19. borealis is seen in northern hemisphere; australis is seen in southern hemisphere
20. New England, Midwest, southwest deserts, or southeast

21. fission splits atoms apart; fusion joins atoms
22. forces between the water molecules pull them apart
23. 326 million cubic miles–70% of Earth's surface
24. good, hard material for building; many monuments are made of granite

Pages 274–275

1. yes; plant
2. no; plant
3. porifera; animal
4. moneran
5. yes; animal
6. coelenterata; animal
7. yes; arthropoda; animal
8. yes; arthropoda; animal
9. protist
10. arachnid; arthropoda; animal
11. nematoda (roundworms); animal
12. echinodermata; animal; clam
13. carnivore; mammal; chordata; animal
14. fern; plant
15. fungus or fungi
16. snail, oyster, slug, squid, and clam; mollusca; animal

Pages 276–277

Answers may vary somewhat.

1. every 12–37 years
2. silica (sand)
3. Little hairs are triggered by the fly, making the plant spring shut.
4. sweet nectar near the top, slippery sides
5. duckweed; on ponds
6. seeds are huge-weighing up to 50 pounds
7. They attach their roots to fungi that are already attached to tree roots.
8. It attaches itself to the roots of other plants.
9. The bottom of each frond holds up to a quart of water.
10. The smell attracts flies to pollinate the plant.
11. shape of a bucket
12. they surround a tree and acquire nutrients from it, in the process they grow so fast that they suffocate or strangle the tree.
13. Its leaves line up in a north-south direction.

14. The plant dries out but turns green again when water is available.

Page 278

1. 4 of the following: A, B, C, D, E, G, H, L, M, N, O, P
2. M
3. A, D, E, H, O, P
4. B
5. T
6. N
7. S
8. C
9. L
10. G
11. F
12. Q

Page 279

1–24. The following numbers should be circled to show true statements: 2, 3, 7, 8, 9, 12, 13, 16, 17, 19, 22, 23, 24
A. sharp spines with poisonous venom
B. They have razor-sharp teeth.

Pages 280–281

1. Dr. G Larynx
   auditory nerve; gallbladder; hemoglobin; thyroid; sciatic nerves
2. Dr. L. Bowe
   dentine; pancreas; thymus; iliac; external obliques
3. Dr. A. Orta
   platelets; gastrocnemius; bronchi; Fallopian tubes; jugular veins
4. Dr. S. Turnam
   iris; metatarsals; medulla; melanin; deltoid
5. Dr. B. J. Renal
   spleen; dendrites; ventricles; bile; parotid

Pages 282–283

1. She has sleep residue in the corners of her eyes.
2. She has hiccups.
3. She is burping.
4. She sneezed.
5. She has dandruff.
6. She is snoring.

A–G. Answers may vary.
A. The protective, waterproof layer on the skin (keratin) absorbs water and stretches out to form wrinkles.

(particularly on hands and feet where the keratin layer is thickest)
B. The ulnar nerve runs from the shoulder to the hand, passing over the elbow. When it is pinched between the bone and a hard surface, the nerve sends a signal of pain to the brain.
C. When the brain or body needs more oxygen, a reflex action causes an inhalation of air that forces oxygen into the lungs.
D. Odor caused from chemicals in foods or from bacteria in the mouth
E. Air pressure changes when a plane ascends or descends. Eardrums bulge or sink because the pressure in the inner ear is different from that outside. The Eustachian tubes eventually open up and allow air in or out to equalize the pressure. This returns the eardrum to its normal position with a "pop."
F. Muscles involuntarily contract to release chemicals which produce heat and warm the body. This is a reflex response to cold.
G. It is cerumen that coats the ear canal, produced by glands in the ear canal to catch dust and debris and protect the ears against germs.

Pages 284–285

Answers will vary according to diseases chosen. Review student responses to see that they are sensible.

Page 286

1. seismic waves—vibrations set up by sudden movement of Earth surface rocks (earthquakes)
2. strato-volcano—flows of lava, ash, cinders and rock fragments erupting through a vent in Earth's surface
3. caldera—valley at the top of a volcanic peak caused when the volcano becomes hollow and collapses, or when the top is blown during an eruption

The BASIC/Not Boring Middle Grades Science Book   Copyright ©2002 by Incentive Publications, Inc., Nashville, TN.

4. fault—movement that takes place along fractures in Earth's surface

5. dome volcano—slow-flowing rhyolite erupts from a crack or vent in Earth's surface

6. hot springs—water, heated by intrusive igneous rock or magma beneath the surface, bubbles unrestricted to the surface

7. folding—compressional forces move rock layers from horizontal position to bends

8. shield volcano—slow-flowing basalt erupts from vents in Earth's surface

9. geyser—hot springs with a small surface opening, through which the heated water is forced upward at regular intervals by steam pressure beneath the surface

Page 287

Answers will vary depending upon the source of information.
1. 700; 8.3
2. 160,000; 7.5
3. Kansu, China; 200,000; 8.6
4. 143,000; 8.3
5. 200,000; 8.3
6. Kansu, China; 70,000; 7.6
7. Quetta, India; 50,000; 7.5
8. 110,000; 7.3
9. 131; 9.2
10. 66,000; 7.8
11. 23,000; 7.5
12. Tang-Shan, China; 225,000; 8.0
13. 55,000; 7.0
14. San Francisco, CA; 62; 7.1
15. 40,000; 7.7
16. 61; 6.8
17. Kobe, Japan; 5502; 7.2
18. 4700; 7.9
19. 30,000; 7.4
20. 20,000; 7.7
21. An earthquake consists of vibrations caused by sudden movement in surface rocks.

Pages 288–289

1. deflation
2. abrasion
3. loess
4. Dunes
5. talus
6. rock fall
7. Landslides
8. mudslides or mudflows
9. creep
10. alluvial fans
11. suspended; bed
12. levee; floodplain
13. delta
14. caves or caverns; natural; sinkholes
15. abrading; striations
16. plucking
17. till; moraines

Pages 290–291

1. halite
2. garnet
3. pyrite
4. calcite
5. gypsum
6. quartz
7. galena
8. topaz
9. corundum
10. graphite
11. copper
12. sulfur
13. magnetite
14. talc
15. diamond
16. silver

Pages 292–293

Explanations may differ somewhat.

1. winds

2. differences in water density due to differences in temperature and salinity of water

3. winds, tides, and earthquakes

4. Each water particle moves in a circle within the wave.

5. In a deep-water wave the water is deeper than $\frac{1}{2}$ the wavelength; in a shallow-water wave, the water is shallower than $\frac{1}{2}$ the wavelength.

6. The top of a wave moves faster than the bottom of the wave, so the wave gets lopsided and collapses.

7. breaking waves

8. The surfer must paddle to move as fast as a coming wave. When the wave picks up the board, the surfer must guide the board to stay ahead of the crest of the wave.

9. The gravitational attraction among Earth, moon and sun. The forces pulling cause a bulge in the ocean water on the side of Earth facing the moon. The rotational force of the Earth and moon cause another bulge to form on the side of the Earth opposite the moon.

Diagrams on page 293:

1. spring tide; high tides are highest and low tides are lowest—with greatest tidal range (Moon's, sun's, and Earth's gravitational pull are all lined up.)

2. spring tide; high tides are highest and low tides are lowest—with greatest tidal range (Moon's, sun's, and Earth's gravitational pull are all lined up.)

3. neap tide; tides are minimal—with lesser tidal range (Moon's, sun's, and Earth's gravitational pull are not lined up, but pulling in different directions.)

4. neap tide; tides are minimal—with lesser tidal range (Moon's, sun's, and Earth's gravitational pull are not lined up, but pulling in different directions.)

Pages 294–295

1. cooling effect of wind takes the heat from the body, making the temperature feel colder than it is

2. snowstorms with high winds

3. overflowing of water onto land that is normally dry

4. raindrops falling through a layer of air colder than –3° C, causing raindrops to freeze

5. strong wind carrying clouds of sand through the air

6. name given to hurricanes in the southwest Pacific Ocean and the South China Sea

7. heavy rainy season in areas of India, South Asia, West Africa, and Northern Australia

8. heavy rains and high winds

9. ice crystals are tossed up and down in the cloud, water freezes in crystals in layers

10. tornado formed over the sea

11. intense heating of air caused it to rise and form large cumulonimbus clouds with heavy rain, lightning, and thunder

12. funnel-shaped storm; strong rotating column of air reaching from a cumulonimbus cloud to the ground

13. warm low pressure weather system surrounded by cooler air

14. hurricane conditions are possible in a specified area within the next 36 hours

15. hurricane conditions are expected in specified area within 24 hours

16. tropical cyclone—storm with great energy and winds over 75 mph

17. hurricane with winds between 130–155 mph

18. long period without precipitation

19. warm, moist air mass near the ground covered and held down by heavier mass of cold air

20. wind of between 47 and 54 mph

A. no

B. yes

C. no

Pages 296–297

1. meteoroids that have reached Earth's atmosphere

2. bright red layer of sun's surface, which contains hydrogen gas

3. sudden increases in brightness of the sun's chromosphere

4. rapidly rotating neutron star gives out a beam of radiation that looks like a pulse

5. fragments of matter orbiting the sun, similar material to material in planets

6. dark spots on the sun where temperatures are colder

7. a star suddenly exploding with increased brightness

8. large halo of dust and gas formed around the nucleus of a comet

9. star that has collapsed after using all its fuel

10. theoretical tunnels that link one part of space-time with another

11. small piece of asteroid material flying in space

12. balls of soot, dust, and ice that orbit the sun; as they get close to the sun, they turn to steam, showing a long tail

13. two stars orbiting a common center of gravity

14. a collapsed star from which no light can escape

15. clouds of dust and gas where stars are born

16. briefly visible meteor

17. meteor that strikes Earth's surface

18. (Explanations may vary somewhat.) A star is born inside a cloud of gas and dust. Gravity condenses some of the cloud into a red protostar. Spinning flattens this into a disk. The contractions heat the core and set off nuclear reactions that make the star shine. The star shines for millions of years until the fuel is sued up. Then the core contracts, and the outer layers swell to a red giant. Eventually outer layers expand into space, leaving a white dwarf. Then it cools and leaves a cinder, called a black dwarf.

Pages 298–299

1. S, U	25. S
2. E	26. V
3. M	27. J, U, N, S
4. J	28. M
5. U	29. S
6. J	30. J
7. S	31. MR
8. P	32. V
9. M, V	33. E
10. S	34. J
11. M	35. U
12. U (N optional)	36. MR
13. P	37. S
14. MR	38. N
15. N	39. M
16. P	40. E
17. MR	41. MR
18. M	42. J
19. E	43. S
20. M	44. P
21. J	45. U
22. S	46. V
23. V, M	47. M, J
24. P	48. P, E

Pages 300–301

1. marble; $CaCo_3$
2. bleach; $NaClO$
3. salt; $NaCl$
4. baking soda; $NaHCo_3$
5. candle wax; CH_2
6. sugar; $C_{12}H_{22}O_{11}$
7. natural gas or methane; $CH4$
8. chalk; $CaCo_3$
9. ammonia; NH_3
10. sand; SiO_2
11. gasoline; C_8H_{18}
12. hydrogen peroxide; H_2O_2
13. Epsom's salt
14. carbon dioxide; CO_2
15. milk of magnesia; $Mg(OH)_2$
16. Freon; CF_2Cl_2
17. glycerin
18. lime; CaO

Pages 302–303

1. The inertia and centripetal force keeps everyone pushed back into their seats.

2. because of the spinning of the Earth

3. Gravity pulls down on a person with more force on Earth than on the moon.

4. As water heats, small particles turn to bubbles of steam. The bubbles float up and hit colder water. The bubbles collapse or pop with a noise. Hundreds of popping bubbles causes a noise that sounds like singing.

5. It is a solution of liquid and a gas, CO_2. The gas causes the fizz.

6. The salt lowers the freezing temperature of the water (or ice), making the temperature cold enough to be able to freeze the cream.

7. When the suction cup is squeezed, some of the air is removed. When the cup is placed against the window, the air pressure outside the cup is greater than inside the cup. This pressure holds the cup against the window.

8. The mat reduces the friction that slows down movement.

9. Sand sculptures are made with wet sand. The water

added to sand makes the molecules adhere to each other. The force of cohesion also causes molecules of the sand to stick together.

10. The first law of motion—inertia keeps a body moving in the same direction and at the same rate; *or* an object resists a change in velocity

11. Static electricity has built up in your body from the rubbing against the carpet.

12. When you suck on the straw, you reduce the air pressure in the straw. Then, the pressure above the liquid is greater than the pressure inside the straw, so the liquid is pressed up into the straw.

13. The third law of motion: for every force there is an equal and opposite force; OR action-reaction causes the boat to move in the opposite direction from the force of the pull.

Pages 304–305

Lucy's sport is pole vaulting. Student should draw this sport. Other answers will vary depending on the sports chosen. Check to see that student answers are accurate and reasonable.

Pages 306–307

1. vibrations of drum surfaces setting up sound waves

2. vibrations of vocal cords setting up sound waves

3. vibrations of the strings in the instruments

4. vibrations of columns of air in the instruments

5. through the air in waves

6. a wave in which the matter vibrates in the same direction that the wave moves

7. the greatest distance wave particles travel in rising or falling from their resting position

8. number of waves that pass a point in a given amount of time

9. Answer may vary slightly

depending on the source: 20–20,000 HZ (megahertz)

10. low pitched

11. large

12. 115dB

13. faster

14. softer

15. Indoors there are surfaces that bounce sound waves back to the ear.

16. As the jet approaches, the sound waves compress together more tightly, so waves have a higher frequency and a higher pitched sound. As the jet passes, sound waves get farther apart, so the waves have lower frequency and the sound has a lower pitch.

Pages 308–309

1. sodium; Na
2. lithium, Li
3. hydrogen; H
4. carbon; C
5. potassium; K
6. titanium; Ti
7. manganese, Mn
8. radon; Rn
9. calcium, Ca
10. chromium; Ca
11. strontium; Sr
12. helium; He
13. bromine; Br
14. arsenic; As
15. krypton; Kr
16. zirconium; Zr
17. mercury, Hg
18. tungsten; W
19. argon; Ar
20. neon; Ne
21. beryllium; Be
22. silver; Ag
23. thallium; Tl
24. iodine; I
25. nitrogen; N
26. francium; Fr